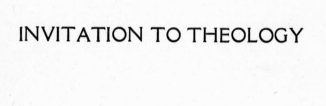

INVITATION TO THEOLOGY

ALLEN O. MILLER

Invitation to Theology

Resources for Christian Nurture and Discipline

The Christian Education Press

Philadelphia   Pennsylvania

230
M612

149563

Library of Congress Catalog Card No. 58-11704

Dedicated

to my parents

ELBERT A. and ALICE OTT MILLER

who brought me up
in the nurture and admonition of the Lord

and to my wife

DOROTHY EYER MILLER

whose steadfast love
has been a bulwark
in the nurturing and disciplining of
Richard, Carol, June, and David

CONTENTS

PART TWO

A Covenant Theology

The Story of Our Life in Encounter with the Living God

PART THREE

Christian Nurture and Discipline

Reclaiming Our Covenant Heritage in Christian Education

INDEXES

ACKNOWLEDGMENTS

ONE is never able to acknowledge adequately all the evidences of divine providence that are mediated through the life and work of those people whom God chooses as his servants and our benefactors. Nonetheless, it is important that we should attempt to do so.

First of all, as I look back upon the many blessings of my childhood and youth, I am grateful for the influence of my parents, and of my teachers and pastors, notably Dr. John O. Reagle, in Christ Church (Stone Church), Pennsylvania. Together they have left an indelible mark upon my thinking. Through them I came to the deeply entrenched awareness that "the Bible is the story of our life in covenant with the living God." The divine authority of the Scriptures, the reality of the divine presence when they are read, their relevance for the guidance of our lives, their belonging to today as well as to the ages—all of these are part of my heritage of church and home.

Second, much of the language that is used to express my understanding of the Christian faith comes from the work of contemporary biblical and theological scholars. Many teachers have contributed to my tools and the skill which is involved in their use.

For the functional understanding of revelation as "God himself confronting us" in a "personal encounter," I am deeply grateful to Professor H. Richard Niebuhr at the Yale Divinity School, and for his book, *The Meaning of Revelation*, as well as Dr. Emil Brunner's book, *The Divine-Human Encounter*. For the idea of *The Unfolding Drama of the Bible*, I am indebted to Professor Bernhard W. Anderson and his excellent study booklet by that title. For the inspiration to put these together in the context of the biblical covenant as the basis for Christian communication between the generations, I acknowledge the influence of Professor Eugene Rosenstock-Huessy, whose lectures at Eden Seminary Convocation in 1952 were entitled provocatively "Liturgical

Thinking vs. Theology." The way in which the plot of the covenant drama[1] develops within the Bible story and as the story of
our lives has been hammered out in the give-and-take of class-
room discussion with my students in systematic theology at Eden
Theological Seminary.

The philosophical tools for understanding the divine confrontation of our human situation as a process of diagnosis, prescription, and therapy are drawn from the contemporary schools of
existential philosophy and depth psychology. Here my mentors
have been another one of my Yale professors, Dr. Robert L. Cal-
houn, and Dr. Paul Tillich, formerly of Union Seminary, now at
Harvard University.

Finally, for the inspiration, the encouragement, and the critical
participation of my colleagues and many generations of students
at Heidelberg College and at Eden Seminary I am immeasurably
grateful, especially to Professors Lionel A. Whiston in biblical
studies, Elmer J. Arndt in theology, and Harold A. Pflug in
Christian education; and to my former students, Alexander
Campbell, Ernest A. Rueter, and Charles T. Hein, for reading
and discussing various chapters with me while they were being
formulated. Mr. Rueter has also constructed the index. Dr.
Samuel D. Press, our beloved patriarch and president emeritus
of Eden Seminary, and Mr. Arthur O. Leutheusser, neighbor,
scholar, and lay theologian extraordinary, have honored me in
reading and commenting upon the whole work. Dr. Louis H.
Gunnemann of the Mission House Seminary and Dr. Charles F.
Penniman of the Educational Center in the Episcopal Diocese of
Missouri, have been friendly and helpful critics of the whole
enterprise.

I am indebted to many good friends for opportunities to discuss the concerns of this book with interested groups of church
men and women: ecumenical lay leadership training schools;
parent-teacher study groups in individual congregations; synodi-
cal and diocesan retreats of ministers and teachers; an adult class

---

[1] "Covenant plot" is the term I employ to express the meaning of the technical German word used by biblical scholars, *Heilsgeschichte*, sometimes translated as salvation-history, that is, biblical history seen as the drama of man's
redemption by God.

and a summer pulpit at Pilgrim Congregational Church, St. Louis, Missouri, the Rev. Allen Hackett, pastor; the Swander Memorial Lectures at the Theological Seminary, Lancaster, Pennsylvania; and convocations of ministers at the Seminary of Dubuque University, Dubuque, Iowa, and at the Mission House Seminary, Plymouth, Wisconsin.

A sabbatical year in 1956-1957, granted by the kindness of President F. W. Schroeder and the Board of Directors of Eden Theological Seminary, the gracious and efficient work of Mrs. Lynn Stauffer in producing the various type-scripts during this year, the limitless patience and careful guidance of Dr. Fred D. Wentzel and other members of the staff of the Board of Christian Education and Publication of the Evangelical and Reformed Church, and the critical wisdom and the constant encouragement and help of my wife have conspired miraculously to bring this book into print.

Grateful acknowledgment is made to Dr. T. C. Braun of *The Messenger* for the privilege of using again material first published in its pages under the title "Our Heritage of Life-giving Faith," and to other publishers for permission to quote from their publications. The Revised Standard Version translation of the Old and New Testaments has been used throughout. We have, however, taken the liberty to extend the use of the poetic format in presenting some passages.

ALLEN O. MILLER

Eden Theological Seminary
Webster Groves, Missouri
February, 1958

FOREWORD

I AM very glad to commend Allen Miller's *Invitation to Theology* to the studious attention of pastors, church school teachers, and parents. They will find in it a fresh, original, and dramatic approach to the message of the Bible, the essentials of the Christian faith, and the task of Christian education.

The word "dramatic" is valid on three separate counts, in speaking of this book. In Part One, the Bible is treated as a great drama, with an enthralling "covenant plot" marching on from Genesis to Revelation. In Part Two, the Christian faith is treated as a drama, with three stress-filled Acts, framed in a Prologue (the creation) and an Epilogue (God's kingdom), summarized in a chart. In Part Three, Christian education is treated as a drama, in which the covenant plot of the Bible, the core of the Christian faith, is seen to be recapitulated in Christian nurture and discipline, Christian worship, the Christian year, and the Christian sacraments.

Each of these three parts involves a real revolution in customary ways of thinking. I know of no other book which correlates these three revolutions with one another and shows their oneness. To study this book might well cause a great stirring of dry bones in any parish.

WALTER MARSHALL HORTON
Oberlin Graduate School of Theology

INTRODUCTION

Church and Home: Partners in Christian Education

A VERITABLE revolution is currently taking place in Christian education. One of its symptoms is the fact that a number of the major denominations in American Protestantism are experimenting with what is commonly being called "The New Curriculum." Just as with many another revolution, however, some of the new features of the church's approach to the education of her people are no longer "brand-new." Indeed, some of the motifs of this revolution have been operating for generations.

Generally speaking, the key to the revolution is expressed in the title of the "Church and Home Series," used in the church school curriculum by the Evangelical and Reformed Church since 1950 to represent the new emphasis upon the family as the unit of Christian life. Its complement in the Congregational Christian Churches has been the "Pilgrim Series." The United Church of Christ will carry forward this emphasis upon the family in the "United Church Series." Pioneering work in the same vein is being done in the "Faith and Life Series" of the Presbyterian Church; the "Christian Growth Series" of the Lutheran churches (United, American, and Augustana); and in the "Seabury Series" of the Episcopal Church.

The common concern running through each of these new efforts is this: *Christian education involves the communication of the Christian gospel to and through two generations at one and the same time.* The normative setting for the Christian life is the home. In the family one finds all the cross-currents of personal relationships that make life both a continuing struggle and an unparalleled joy. Indeed, not only little children, but children of all ages *and* their parents, are continuously being involved in the life of this little community in which the love and righteousness of God are being experienced, no matter how eagerly or reluctantly we may respond.

xvii

Religious education and Christian theology have not always been on friendly terms. When I was at the seminary, students in religious education and budding theologians "wouldn't have been seen dead together." This, of course, was largely because of the chasm which always separates the practical from the theoretical disciplines, the professional technicians from the philosophers.

In more recent times, however, another kind of conflict has arisen. The last generation has experienced a change in theological climate regarding the estimate of man and the extent to which education can be said to make a man a Christian. On this issue, theologians and educators are split, not so much into professional as into ideological camps. What has happened is that there are now two opposing theologies of education with which to reckon. The one is aligned with the Renaissance brand of liberal theology of the last generation, whose textbook was Horace Bushnell's *Christian Nurture*, and whose educational psychology has been deeply influenced by the pragmatic philosophy of John Dewey. The other is more sensitive to the neo-orthodox, biblically oriented Reformation theology taught by Karl Barth, Emil Brunner, the Niebuhr brothers, and others, and is heavily indebted to the "existential" philosophy of Sören Kierkegaard and Paul Tillich and to the insights of contemporary "depth" psychology.

Although my sympathies lie with this second type of theological approach, I have deliberately chosen to include the term "nurture" in the subtitle of this book, *Invitation to Theology: Resources for Christian Nurture and Discipline*.

In the first instance, it must be said that the term "Christian nurture" did not originate with the discourses bearing that title which Horace Bushnell published in 1847. Rather, it is derived from a New Testament injunction in Ephesians 6: 4, in which fathers are directed to bring up their children "in the nurture and admonition of the Lord." Nonetheless, Bushnell must be credited with one great achievement. He has made it quite clear that *Christian education belongs to the family*. Family relationships of parents and children, and of children with each other, are "the church" within the church, and the center of Christian nurturing. In this he is to be revered as one of the strongest advocates in recent times of the view that *church and home, teachers and parents, are partners in the Christian education enterprise.* At this point we heartily agree with Bushnell. Indeed, our Christian education is keeping faith with the best in our biblical tradition when we deal with ourselves and our relationships in personal, everyday family terms.

Moreover, it is important to remember, with appreciation, that a century ago Horace Bushnell was struggling against a sterile theological dogmatism and an extreme form of revivalism in the New England churches. His recovery of the family as the basic unit of life in the Christian church and of infant baptism as a sign of God's gracious election of each new generation of his people has put the churches of our day deeply in his debt. He has set the Christian education movement firmly against the tendency to make American "religion" as atomistic in its emphasis upon the individual as the *laissez-faire* philosophy has made our public life.

Nonetheless, we can see from our perspective in time that the theology of the pioneer of modern Christian education lacked a profound understanding of the radical nature of sin that our biblical heritage mirrors for us. Bushnell assumed that the Christian life can be the product of good family upbringing and training without benefit of spiritual conversion, declaring "that the child is to grow up a Christian, and never know himself as being otherwise." The truth of the matter seems rather to be that the nurture of Christian families does not actually make conversion unnecessary. On the contrary, Christian nurture is important just because it will help to make conversion possible!

A. Christian Nurture and Discipline

The term "nurture" expresses only one aspect of our Christian heritage of love and righteousness as it is being communicated from one generation to another. At the heart of our Order for Baptism of Infants, in which the full teaching of Ephesians 6: 4

is enshrined, parents are directed to bring up their children "in the nurture and admonition of the Lord." Nurture and admonition, that is, nurture and discipline,[1] I believe, when taken together, define the Christian education enterprise in its broadest scope. A discussion of the major channels through which the church carries on such a broad-gauged Christian education program is the subject matter of Part Three in this book.

We have been coming through a period in the life of the church in which Christian education has been subject to conflicting influences, ranging from old-fashioned authoritarianism to new-fangled permissivism. The one emphasizes, as of primary importance, the teaching of the traditional dogmas of the faith, the other the uninhibited psychological and social adjustment of the child.

Under the influence of progressive education, many of us have been emancipated from the older pattern of teaching in which, every Sunday morning, we were regularly hit over the head with ideas from the Bible and expected to memorize quantities of Scripture. To be sure, ideas and information about God and Christ may be "learned" in this fashion under the pressure of an authoritative teacher, but they will have no meaningful effect upon the learner's character and personal relationships unless his life is involved in the learning process. Just as "one plus one is two" is a mere abstraction until we know how to encounter apples and pennies, so also God is only an abstraction until he is known in an encounter as real as the meeting of two friends or the news of the death of a loved one.

---

[1] The original Greek text of Ephesians 6:4 *ektrephete auta en paideia kai nouthesia kuriou,* has been subjected to a variety of interpretations in English translations. The familiar King James reading, "Bring them up in the nurture and admonition of the Lord," has been replaced in the Revised Standard Version by "Bring them up in the discipline and instruction of the Lord." Probably the most literal English reading would be, "Nurture them in the discipline and on the admonitions of the Lord." (Cf. Moffatt.)

The verb *ektrephete* means "to nourish" or to bring up. *Paideia* also means "child-rearing" literally, but has the connotation of education or discipline. *Nouthesia* means, literally, "bringing to mind," i.e., instruction or admonition. The sense of the entire injunction is to hold two distinctive emphases in bipolar interrelationship: *nurture* and *discipline.*

On the other hand, some of us are tempted to go so far toward the side of psychological integration as "to throw out the baby with the bath." It is easy to become so obsessed with the growth and development of personalities that we forget both the radical demands and the glorious promises which are inherent in the gospel of Jesus Christ. Psychological integration, peace of mind, and positive thinking too easily become a cheap substitute for "the peace of God, which passes all understanding." Such peace comes only on the far side of a cross on which our sick and disordered selves have submitted to radical surgery and re-creation.

Actually, there is much more occasion for authority and discipline in Christian education than is recognized by the devotees of the progressive education movement. At the same time, there can be no minimizing of the need for the tender care and nurture which go with helping a person to grow up. The task of Christian education involves both aspects of personality development: *the need to be significant in a responsible way, and the need to have the security of belonging and being loved.*

A word of caution is clearly in order, however. Very practical questions arise and deserve consideration. How do you know when to discipline and when to nurture? How do you maintain the right balance between righteousness and love? Perhaps this is raising the question in the wrong way. It might be more correct to ask: "How can we exercise discipline in love and for love?" and "How can we nurture righteousness and responsibility?" These are concerns with which we shall be struggling in Part Three. It is enough here to acknowledge the fact that this is the most difficult and persistent of all of the problems of Christian education, and to admit that there is no simple rule of thumb.

Although we cannot pretend to know the formula, it appears that the unity for which the purpose of God has created human personality is significantly like a chemical mixture. In both instances the elements retain their fundamental identity while at the same time they lose themselves in the compound. There is a mysterious fusion in the divine order whereby, in the mighty acts of God, both aspects of our twofold human need are met at once. The living God revealed himself to us in Jesus Christ as at once "righteous Lord" and "merciful Father." He brought the children of Israel to judgment, for they were weak and supine, rebellious and irresponsible; but he did so because he loved them. In order that his people might share with him in the kingdom of love, he sought to bring out in them the powers of courage and responsible decision with which he had endowed them.

"Christian nurture *and* discipline" is obviously much more than a human enterprise. Its character is fundamentally rooted in divine-human encounter. That is to say:

(1) Christian education is the task of *nurturing* each new generation *in the discipline of the Lord*. We bequeath to our children what we ourselves have received—the gracious renewal of our being in the gospel of Jesus Christ our Lord.

(2) God himself is the main actor in all Christian nurture and discipline. It is his love and righteousness which he is entrusting to us to transmit from generation to generation. Since it is God himself who begets faith in each member of the ongoing faith-confessing community, Christian education is the labor and travail of the church by which God's act becomes embodied in human lives. Thus we are all children conceived of God and born of the church.

B. Theological Instruction for Lay Theologians

The intention of this book begins, now, to come into focus. It is designed as a course of theological instruction for all parents, teachers, and pastors who are engaged in the task of Christian education, whether it be in church or home.

(1) Our first purpose is *to help Christian parents and teachers to understand the church's teaching about God and man, and the meaning of our existence as members of the church of Jesus Christ.*

Part One, "The Living Word of God," is an attempt to help the

reader to understand the Bible as the record of God's revelation
of himself in the history of his chosen people. The most important term for understanding those mighty acts of God in human
history is "the covenant." Covenant is the word which the Bible
uses to explain the unique relationship of love and righteousness
which God establishes and maintains with his people. The prophets of Israel and the apostles of Jesus Christ both define the
covenant in terms of God's announcement: "You shall be my
people, and I will be your God." The Old Testament records the
events which lead up to and flow from "the old covenant" with
Moses; the New Testament proclaims "the new covenant" in our
Lord Jesus Christ.

Part Two, "A Covenant Theology," is a brief account of what
is usually called systematic theology—an orderly presentation of
the whole divine-human covenant drama, from the creation of
the world to the coming of the kingdom of God. Within these
limits we read "the story of our lives in covenant encounter with
the living God."

Part Three, "Christian Nurture and Discipline," examines the
church's means of grace, her teaching, preaching, liturgy (worship), and sacraments, as media for communicating God's love
and righteousness. They are the channels through which the
church recapitulates for her people, day after day, week after
week, year after year, and in every generation, the vital truth of
the renewal, growth, and fulfillment of our beings in Jesus Christ.

Theology is a demanding intellectual discipline, and anyone
who pretends to write a theological do-it-yourself book is fooling
no one but himself. Theological seminaries spend at least three
years in training a minister to pursue theological studies fruit-
fully. It is too much to expect untrained men and women to do
it alone and "on the side." For a book on theology to contribute
most effectively to the understanding of the reader, therefore, it
must be taught. Furthermore, I believe that it is one of the most
solemn duties of the Christian minister to be a teacher of parents
and of teachers, helping them to interpret the meaning of the
church's faith to successive generations of God's people. *This*

book is meant, therefore, to be a study guide for use in the teaching ministry of the church. It should be most useful when the minister and his colleagues in church and home study it together, either in special leadership training schools or in regular parent-teacher training classes.

(2) Our second purpose is *to invite parents and teachers to accept the role of lay theologian.*

Contrary to popular usage, where the word "layman" means nonprofessional and tends to be a term of depreciation, the original biblical word *laos* means "the people," that is, "the covenant people of God." Moreover, the leader of the people is not understood to be standing over against them in another class. He is one of them, called to be their servant in the fulfillment of a particular function within the life of the group, such as prophet, priest, or judge, but he is still one of "the people," and they share with him in his responsibility.

The recovery of this biblical point of view, called "the universal priesthood of believers," was one of the major concerns of the sixteenth-century Protestant Reformation and is an important factor in the present-day twentieth-century ecumenical Reformation.

To be a theologian is a high responsibility in the life of the Christian church, but it is by no means as specialized a function as it is sometimes imagined. By the same token that all theologians are teachers, every teacher of the Christian faith is cast in the role of theologian. Mothers and fathers who attempt to answer the little child's "Why, Daddy?" or "Why, Mommie?" are their children's first theologians. Whenever one talks reasonably about God and his relationship to man and his creation, one is being a theologian. This is the role in which, willingly or unwillingly, our lives are being cast, both in church and in home.

Whether you are a parent, a church school teacher, a preacher, or any combination of these three, you may be the theologian destined to be the most influential teacher in someone's life. God is placing a tremendous responsibility upon each one of us in asking us to interpret to our children and to one another the meaning of his covenant of love and righteousness. The most serious aspect of our human situation is that whatever we do or do not do, whatever we say or do not say, has theological significance. Our whole lives are a mirror in which younger people see themselves, either as responsible servants of God or as irresponsible servants of self. Since we shall aways be carrying the "heavenly treasure" of God's love and righteousness in the "earthen vessels" of our human person-to-person relationships, does it not behoove us all to learn to walk, and to help each other to walk, without stumbling?

Perhaps it is because we are living in an age which is so unsympathetic to God's righteousness, and so unaware of his love, that I am struck by the awesomeness of the responsibility that has been given to us, as parents and teachers, to bequeath this heritage to our children unbroken.

> "This is my covenant with [you],"
>   says the Lord:
> "My spirit which is upon you,
>   and my words which I have put in your mouth,
>   shall not depart out of your mouth,
>   or out of the mouth of your children,
>   or out of the mouth of your children's children, . . .
>   from this time forth and for evermore."

(Isaiah 59: 21)

INVITATION TO THEOLOGY

PART ONE

The Living Word of God
Our Biblical Heritage of Life-giving Faith

Our heritage of life-giving faith
   is the story of the sovereign love of God,
   and of his everlasting covenant with humankind;
It is recorded in the Holy Scriptures,
   and relived, in each new generation,
   by the community of the faithful
Who acknowledge that Jesus Christ is Lord.

And God said to Moses,
"I am the Lord,
   and I have remembered my covenant.
I will take you for my people,
   and I will be your God."

             (Exodus 6: 2, 5, 7)

The Lord is gracious and merciful,
   slow to anger and abounding in steadfast love.
The Lord is good to all,
   and his compassion is over all that he has made.
One generation shall laud thy works to another,
   and shall declare thy mighty acts.
They shall pour forth the fame of thy abundant goodness,
   and shall sing aloud of thy righteousness.

           (Psalm 145: 8-9, 4, 7)

At that time Jesus declared,
"Come to me, all who labor and are heavy-laden,
   and I will give you rest.
Take my yoke upon you, . . . for my yoke is easy,
   and my burden is light."

           (Matthew 11: 25, 28-30)

ONE

THE MYSTERY OF GOD AND MAN

HUMAN beings are the only creatures on the face of the earth who are able to ask questions. Most of the time we ask for information: What is it? Where did it come from? How does it work? What is it good for? But in our deeper, more reflective moments we ask questions concerning the meaning of our existence: Who am I? Where did I come from? Where am I going? What does life mean? How may I become what I am meant to be? Why is it so?

Pastors will recognize these latter questions as the kind often asked in times of crisis by troubled parishioners standing upon the threshold of decision. Teachers will identify them as the kind asked in utter innocence, but in profound sincerity, by even the youngest children in the Sunday church school.

A. Theology Begins in Wonder

For young or old these questions properly lie in the realm of wonder. Wonder is akin to curiosity, but it is the farthest extreme from the disinterested curiosity of the scientist, as well as from mere inquisitiveness. There is plenty of curiosity in wonder, but it is always motivated by a deep concern and a sense of personal involvement. To encourage serious-minded wondering about the meaning of our existence, therefore, is an "invitation to theology." Moreover, when Christian faith, that is, our personal response of confidence to the grace of God in Jesus Christ, sets about to deal with these questions concerning the meaning of our life, the discipline called Christian theology is born. This is the task to which the Lord himself invites us. Theology is loving God "with our whole mind."

Our biblical heritage assures us that God is involved in everything that happens, from our most joyous occasions to our most bewildering concerns. Moreover, life confronts us with the fact that the most satisfying answers to our queries are found when we acknowledge his involvement and accept his purpose as final. *Christian theology, therefore, is fundamentally a confession of what God has done, of what he is doing, and of what he promises yet to do.* It stems from his initiative and is bounded by the limits of his self-revelation. Although theology means literally "a discourse about God," its content is more like a prayer of praise and thanksgiving than a scientific description of a matter of fact.

The theologian is correspondingly humbled by his limitations and heartened in his expectations. He knows that he is in no position to make new discoveries that would revolutionize human knowledge through his carefully planned experimentation. Rather, like a news reporter, he is "given a scoop" on what is actually an open secret, that "God loves humankind." On top of that, God has called the theologian to the glorious task of helping each new generation, and, in particular, individuals day by day, to acknowledge the truth "God loves me too!"

There is, however, a powerful temptation which confronts theological thinking. It is the perennial lure to sell our birthright of wonder for a mess of information. We are prone to forget that our knowledge of God, like all communication with other persons, is fundamentally different from the spectator's knowledge about things.

Where the natural universe is concerned, knowledge means diligent attention to a specialized area, steady improvement in the techniques of investigation, and a growing body of verifiable facts.

God, however, is unlike the universe around us because of his unique status in relation to everything else and because he confronts us primarily in personal relationships. On the one hand, God is for Christian faith the fundamental and ultimate reality, by virtue of whose activity we account for both the world we know and our human capacity to know it and each other. On the other hand, God is not an object to be known. He is a mysterious Presence to be acknowledged. We know him as he works through us from the center of our being. We know him because he subjects himself to a personal life the like of which we know very well from being persons ourselves. Indeed, God and man are so inextricably bound together that it is next to impossible to conceive of one without the other. Christian theology, however, is not a statement about "my" feelings or of "my" beliefs about God. It is, rather, a confession of what God is and does "for me," and "in and through me."

Anyone who has been or is in love will have appreciation for the mysterious quality of all personal involvement.

The unique individuality of each person you meet, the unfathomable depth of creativity that is revealed in every intimate personal encounter, become an ever recurring occasion for surprise and wonder. The more intimate the acquaintance the more speechless we are to define what it is that draws us to another person, and the more deeply we become involved ourselves in the mystery. In similar fashion, the human response which the mystery of God evokes is primarily appreciation and commitment rather than understanding or intellectual satisfaction. The divine mystery is an everlasting foe of the commonplace and the complacent. Our hearts are overwhelmed with awe and fascination. Moreover, just as we make a distinction in the English language between second and third personal pronouns for direct personal communication as against the transmission of information, we reserve a special form of personal pronoun for addressing God. The overawing mystery of his Being calls forth the words "thee," "thou," and "thy" upon our lips.

Furthermore, we must never mistake the word "mystery" as a synonym for human ignorance, that is, for that aspect of our environment which is still unknown to us. Mystery does not belong at all to the impersonal universe of the unknown and the known. In the proper meaning of the word, mystery belongs to that dimension of personal life which involves "the hidden and the revealed." The truth is that the mystery of a personal relationship is never so mysterious as when the hidden is revealed (John 21: 4-14)!

In this matter, God is the perfect example. Revelation is always "self-revelation," and God's self-revelation in Christ is the most miraculous event in all history. The mystery of the revealed and the hidden is the glory of the gospel (Eph. 3: 1-13) and the reason for the central significance of the sacraments (*mysteria*) in the life of the Christian church. How true the maxim that "Christian theology begins in wonder, and when theological thought has done its best, the wonder still remains."[1]

Thus we are continually being assured of the intimate relevance of Christ's gospel as well as of its eternal significance. We know the gospel's relevance by its power to evoke our wonder, and its eternal significance because the mystery is never dissipated.

Theology begins in wonder: first of all, because of the concerned curiosity that human beings have regarding their origin and destiny, and second because awe, or reverence, is the normal human response to the marvelous and the unexpected. Theology begins in wonder, but not all wonder is theological. Wonder, without faith and hope, is either sterile or pernicious. For example, wonder is pernicious when it arises in a human mind that is distorted by the use of narcotics, and sterile when it is elicited by the mushroom cloud that hung over the Japanese city of Hiroshima in midsummer of 1945. This is to say that not all that is wonderful ushers us into the mystery of divine self-disclosure. What is more important is that personal self-disclosure does not, indeed cannot, take place in a vacuum. Communication requires the responsive, personal involvement of another person.

---

[1] This is a paraphrase of a statement made by Professor Alfred North Whitehead regarding philosophy in its relation to scientific thought, in *Nature and Life*, University of Chicago Press, 1934.

B. God's Revelation and Our Response of Faith

We may assume, as an axiom of biblical understanding, that revelation always occurs in a personal encounter, as a direct disclosure of one person to another. *God's purpose, whenever he reveals himself, is to elicit our response of faith.*

"Faith" is a term with several levels of meaning. The Christian faith, the faith of our fathers, usually comes down to us as a body of "beliefs." When it is received on this level, the question that people ask is: "What must I believe to be a Christian?" The answer, on the same level, is: "The Articles of our Creed—believe in God, believe in Jesus Christ, believe in the Holy Spirit, the one holy universal Church, the life everlasting."

Now, indeed, these are the articles which express "what Christians believe" (cf. the Apostles' Creed). Taken alone, however, they throw only a faint light upon the question that really has to be answered first: "How am I to become a Christian?" One does not become a Christian by accepting or rejecting beliefs; one becomes a Christian by "a hearty trust" in God's gracious love. (Cf. Heidelberg Catechism, Q. and A. 21.) *The truth is that in Christ, God reveals himself and not doctrines about himself.* Therefore, faith as trust always runs one whole level of experience deeper than belief. Belief is a matter of the acceptance of ideas, to which the mind gives assent; and doubt is the corresponding rejection. Faith, on the other hand, is a question of life or death. *The question, with which our very existence is confronted, is always this: "Do you accept or reject the love of God?"* (Cf. Matt. 16: 13-26; John 21: 15-19.)

Christianity, however, is a complex affair, concerned with personal relationships on several dimensions at once. The gospel incorporates, at one and the same time, a religion, a theology, and a morality.

It would be simple and neat to say that religion and theology are distinguished from each other as faith and belief, respectively, and that morality is different from both in that it involves action. Such a caricature, however, is only partially true. Doctrinal beliefs are an important part of theology, but they are not the heart of it. The heart of theology is like the heart of religion and of morality, a personal relationship. Moreover, all three express action. In fact, in our Christian understanding, theology, religion, and morality are all concerned with activity—the activity of God's holy love in human affairs.

The primary category of Christian theology is the biblical revelation, God's act in making his will and character known through personal covenant encounter. By the same token faith, as a "confession of confidence," man's acknowledgment of the covenant claim of God, is the primary category of the Christian religion. Moreover, Christian morality is distinctive as a form of human existence in that its categories of personal freedom and social responsibility originate in this unique covenant relation of revelation and faith.

The trouble with limiting theology to traditional beliefs is that so often these beliefs find their only expression in a monologue, in which a man, within his own mind, sorts over his doubts and his prejudices. Theological beliefs are empty if they do not *re*present the underlying divine-human encounter of revelation and response. When, however, we face the fact that the whole of life involves our response of faith or unfaith to God's holy love and righteousness, we see clearly that *Christian theology is a recording of our Christian church's dialogue with God through Jesus Christ.* In this perspective we realize that the most important things in life, namely, God's revelation in Christ, our confession of faith, and the responsible exercise of our Christian freedom, that is, Christian morality, cannot be taught as theoretical disciplines. They need, rather, to be caught contagiously from and with others who are already participating in the divine-human covenant relationship. Hence the fellowship of the church and the home is essential to Christian nurture and discipline.

"The Mystery of God and Man" is the most thrilling story ever told. The Holy Scriptures of the Christian church have recorded and preserved the script of this story, in which the meaning of our existence may be discerned by those who are willing to join the cast and accept a role in the "Covenant of the Living God."

TWO

GOD'S HOLY COVENANT OF LOVE AND RIGHTEOUSNESS

THE biblical way of expressing the divine-human dialogue of
revelation and faith is to tell the story of God's everlasting
covenant with his people. The covenant motif is of primary importance for our understanding of the Bible as a whole. It gives
the original meaning to the terms we use for the two major historical divisions within the Bible. The Old and New Testaments
are the record of God's old and new covenants. The full title
page of the Revised Standard Version of the New Testament
helps us recover the proper perspective: *The New Covenant,
Commonly Called the New Testament of Our Lord and Savior
Jesus Christ.*

To be sure, the Bible as a written record is a collection of
testaments. The common English word, "testament," carries over
from the Latin word, *testamentum,* meaning "last will and testament," the emphasis of the root verb which means "to bear witness or testify." Here are many writers bearing witness to what
has happened to them and to their people. The prophets of the
Old Testament and the apostles of the New Testament are those
who testify concerning what God has done and what his purpose
is for human life. When we ask, "What has God done?" the
answer is that he has established an everlasting bond of love and
righteousness with his people. To understand what this relationship means we are driven back to the original Hebrew word,
berith, that is, "covenant."

In the heritage of the Bible, "covenant" is a unique kind of personal relationship whereby two parties, either individuals or groups, or an individual and a group, bind themselves to each other for their mutual well-being. Although a covenant is superficially like a contract, the two are fundamentally different and must not be confused. A covenant is by many dimensions much the deeper kind of personal relationship.

In the first place, a contract is usually a bargain between two parties involving things. A man contracts to build you a house; you contract to pay him a reasonable fee. A covenant, on the other hand, is an agreement between persons about themselves. Marriage, for example, is a covenant in which a man plights his troth to a woman, and she gives her troth to him in return. A covenant thus becomes the basis for a living dialogue.

A further difference arises out of the fact that a contract is usually put in such legal terms that, if one person fails to fulfill the bargain, the other is released. A covenant is "for better for worse, for richer for poorer, in sickness and in health, to love and to cherish, till death us do part." A living dialogue becomes the occasion for a lifetime drama of personal encounter.

The Lord said to his people, Israel:

"In that day you will call me, 'My husband,'
    and I will make for you a covenant.
I will betroth you to me forever.

I will betroth you to me in righteousness and in justice,
    in steadfast love, and in mercy.
I will betroth you to me in faithfulness,
    and you shall know the Lord."

(Hosea 2: 16, 18, 19-20. Adapted)

In our human life, the marriage covenant deteriorates all too often into a mere contract, but the divine covenant with man never does this. God is always *holy* love toward us. When our lives cease being *wholly* love, no bargaining contractually with him will fix things up! Only his healing acts of forgiveness can overcome our sickness and deliver us from the threat of death. On this assurance we live by faith and with hope for the future.

This same principle is true when the covenanting parties are both human beings. Unfortunately, however, our human wellspring of healing love is never great enough by itself to assure reconciliation and renewal. Therefore, the Christian family, like all other human covenants, must look for its sustaining power to the divine-human covenant of love and righteousness. Nonetheless, despite all our shortcomings in the marriage-covenant relationships, family life offers the best human possibility of a healthy covenant community. This becomes eminently clear when one compares covenant family life, inadequate as it may be, with other forms of interpersonal group relationships, such as occur in business or in politics, for example, where the fundamental principle of life is either outright cutthroat rivalry or at best a *quid pro quo* (tit for tat) kind of contractual relation. Indeed, the consequences of reducing the marriage covenant to a mere contract show up in sharp relief the uniqueness of the covenant form of life and make us everlastingly grateful that God is a "Covenanter" and not a "contractor."

The divine-human covenant is the silken thread which runs through the whole fabric of the Bible. Although it might appear that, in order to discover it, one should begin at the beginning of Genesis and simply read on through, there is little assurance of understanding unless there are guideposts that point to the more important passages. On the other hand, just to read a few selected verses here and a story out of context there yields simply a collection of scraps without any pattern. This is like going on a treasure hunt in which there is no continuity between the clues.

In order, therefore, to understand the central role of the covenant in the biblical revelation, we must remember that the covenant is, first of all, central to the lives of the people whose story the Bible records. Certain events in their history become important guideposts for reading the Bible, because they point beyond the human scene to the gracious activity of God in the life of his people. Although all human history moves along from past through present toward the future, its meaning rests upon the fact that some events are more important than others. To know which are the crucial and pivotal events in our Hebrew and Christian history is to begin to think from inside the Bible itself, for it is to catch the perspective of the authors themselves.

A. Two Events, One Covenant of Grace: Exodus and Calvary

There are many different incidents in the Bible that refer to God's covenant with his people. Two events, however, are singled out by the prophets of the Old Testament and the apostles of the New Testament, respectively, as central and crucial. The one is called the Mosaic Covenant, because it roots in God's miraculous "Act of Deliverance" in bringing about the exodus of the children of Israel from their bondage in Egypt.

> "You have seen what I did to the Egyptians,
>   and how I bore you on eagles' wings
>   and brought you to myself.
> Now therefore, if you will obey my voice
>   and keep my covenant,
> you shall be my own possession
>   among all peoples;
>   for all the earth is mine,
> and you shall be to me a kingdom of priests
>   and a holy nation."
>   (Exodus 19: 4-6; cf. 14: 19—15: 21)

The prophets return to this incident again and again in their preaching. Indeed, for Israel all divine-human covenants[1] are either a renewal or an anticipation of this one.

The other crucial event is the New Covenant[2] in the life, death, and resurrection of our Lord Jesus Christ.

> The Lord Jesus on the night when he was betrayed took bread,
>   and when he had given thanks, he broke it, and said,
>   "This is my body which is broken for you.
>   Do this in remembrance of me."

---

[1] Cf. Chapter 3, "The Plot of Israel's Covenant History."
[2] Cf. Chapter 4, "Promise and Fulfillment of the New Covenant."

In the same way also the cup, after supper, saying,
"This cup is the new covenant in my blood.
Do this, as often as you drink it,
in remembrance of me."

(1 Corinthians 11: 23-25; cf. Mark 14: 22-24)

And Peter opened his mouth and said:
You know the word which [God] sent to Israel:
how God anointed Jesus of Nazareth
with the Holy Spirit and with power;
how he went about doing good
and healing all that were oppressed
by the devil,
for God was with him.

They put him to death by hanging him on a tree;
but God raised him on the third day
and made him manifest;
not to all the people but to us
who were chosen by God as witnesses,
who ate and drank with him
after he rose from the dead.

And he commanded us to preach to the people,
and to testify that he is the one
ordained by God
to be judge of the living and the dead.

(Acts 10: 34, 36, 38-42; cf. Romans 10: 5-13)

In each instance a significant event in human history is singled out by God's witnesses as the time in which God acted definitively to establish a servant people, whose task is to proclaim his righteousness and to mediate his love.

These two covenants, when taken separately, however, become the confessional center for two of the three (the third being *Islam*) great religious traditions which trace their origin to the biblical revelation: *Judaism* in the covenant of Moses and *Christianity* in the covenant of Jesus Christ. The relationship between these two confessional groups has always been fraught with misunderstanding and either potential or open conflict. The issue is not so simple, as if it were a case of mutual rejection and contradiction of each other's confession. The relationships of these two with each other differ. Whereas Judaism pretty clearly rejects entirely the Christian claim to a new covenant in Jesus Christ, and thereby impairs from the Christian point of view its own Messianic hopes, Christians are not in position to reject the validity of the Mosaic covenant, either for themselves or for the Jews who claim it to be theirs alone. As Christians, we cannot reject the old covenant for ourselves, for without it the new covenant would be meaningless.[3] And, moreover, we cannot repudiate it for the Jews without denying it to ourselves. If as Christians we may say, "The church is our mother," we must also add, "and Israel is our grandmother."

It is evident that much of historic Christian interpretation of the Mosaic covenant, in so far as it has to do with our Christian faith and life, has been distorted by an effort to depreciate the claims of Judaism. To a large extent, this has roots in the New Testament itself. There is a tendency to depreciate the Law as against the Gospel in The Letter of Paul to the Galatians (3: 10-18) and in his letter to the Romans (7: 1-6), and to derogate the old as against the new covenant in The Letter to the Hebrews (8: 6-13). This reflects more accurately the first-century antipathy between Gentile "spiritualizers" and Jewish "legalizers" within the early Christian community than it gives light upon how the Mosaic covenant is properly to be understood, either by Jews or by Christians. The apostle Paul is right in affirming the grace of God in Christ alone as the source of our salvation, and therefore must deny that the Law can save us. This is quite different, however, from the conclusion that the old covenant has no proper and necessary function in the Christian life.

---

[3] "The church affirms . . . that Christ is the key to the central meaning of the Old Testament; but at the same time it must be emphasized that the Old Testament is the clue to Christ."—"The Faith of Israel" by G. Ernest Wright, *The Interpreter's Bible*, Vol. 1, page 389.

A much more helpful starting point may be found in the quotation of Jesus which stands as the lead sentence in that section of the Sermon on the Mount which has to do with the Christian life. Jesus himself says:

"Think not that I have come
to abolish the law and the prophets;
I have come not to abolish them
but to fulfil them."

(Matthew 5: 17)

The truth of the matter is that we take a wrong course entirely if, from the starting point of the controversy in the time of Paul or of the author of The Letter to the Hebrews, we proceed to equate the old covenant with the Law and call it a covenant of works, and the new covenant with the Gospel of forgiveness and call it the covenant of grace. The Mosaic covenant[4] is entirely rooted in grace, as the prophets never tire of reminding Israel, and the new covenant in the grace of our Lord Jesus Christ cannot dispense with the Law. Even the apostle Paul, usually regarded as the strongest opponent to the Law, clearly teaches its indispensability in both Romans and Galatians.

What our study leads us to say is that there is but one covenant, and that it is a covenant of grace. Its fundamental identity is clearly maintained throughout the many events in which God's holy love is encountered, both in the history of Israel and in the life of the early Christian church.

"You shall be my people,
and I will be your God,"

is the word of God from the time of the election of Israel to the age of the church of the New Jerusalem (Exod. 6: 7 to Rev. 21: 3).

---

[4] "The primary attention of the Jew is . . . given to the Law and especially to the Talmud. Christianity, on the contrary, refuses to see the Law as the center of the Old Testament. The redemptive activity of God is the primary content of the Pentateuch, not the Law, and that activity continues through the remaining historical books."—"The Faith of Israel" by G. Ernest Wright, *The Interpreter's Bible,* Vol. 1, page 389.

B. Renewed "Once for All"

The term "new," when applied to the covenant, does not indicate the substitution of a good covenant for a bad one. Rather,
it means the *re*newal, *re*storation, and fulfillment of God's original covenant with his people. Actually one cannot ignore the
fact that the covenant had to be renewed in every generation in
Israel's history (cf. Judges 2) and that each event of its renewal,
like its creation and sustaining, marks the unmerited grace of
God.

The new covenant, in Jesus Christ, moreover, could never have
been understood without the old. The Lord's Supper, which is
called by Jesus "the new covenant in my blood" (Luke 22: 20),
"which is poured out for many for the forgiveness of sins" (Matt.
26: 28), occurred at Passover time, the festival of the exodus.
Yet there are differences within the continuity between the
Mosaic covenant and the new covenant in Jesus Christ, which
make the old unsatisfactory to those who are the recipients of
the new. The old Israel rooted her faith in her deliverance from
physical bondage in Egypt. The new Israel, both in the finest
anticipation of the Old Testament and in the fulfillment of the
New Testament, recognizes her need for a deeper deliverance
from sin and the bondage to her own infidelity.

> "Behold, the days are coming, says the Lord,
>   when I will make a new covenant
>   with the house of Israel
>   and the house of Judah,
> not like the covenant which I made with their fathers
>   when I took them by the hand
>   to bring them out of the land of Egypt,
> my covenant which they broke,
>   though I was their husband, says the Lord.
>
> But this is the covenant
>   which I will make with the house of Israel
>   after those days, says the Lord:

I will put my law within them,
and I will write it upon their hearts;
and I will be their God,
and they shall be my people.

And no longer shall each man teach his neighbor
and each his brother, saying, 'Know the Lord,'
for they shall all know me,
from the least of them to the greatest, says the Lord;
for I will forgive their iniquity,
and I will remember their sin no more."

(Jeremiah 31: 31-34; cf. Hebrews 8: 8, 12)

The most significant difference, however, between the old and the new understanding of the covenant is the broadening of its scope from the Hebrew nation to include all humanity. In the whole new covenant perspective there is a heavy underscoring of the demand, spoken by the later prophets, that the covenant people be the Lord's servant in the deliverance of the nations of the world.

Thus says God the Lord,

"Behold my servant, whom I uphold,
my chosen, in whom my soul delights;
I have put my spirit upon him,
he will bring forth justice to the nations.

I have given you as a covenant to the people,
a light to the nations,
to open the eyes that are blind,
to bring out the prisoners from the dungeon,
from the prison those who sit in darkness."

(Isaiah 42: 1, 6-7; cf. 49: 6)

It is in fulfilling the "suffering servant" role which God had meant for Israel, Christians believe, that Jesus of Nazareth stands head and shoulders not only above Moses but also above those prophets whose insights gave him the pattern for understanding his mission.

Moses and the prophets are human spokesmen for God to his chosen, but Jesus is more than these; he is the Chosen One in whom the divine purpose is not only revealed but fulfilled.

> [Christ] is the mediator of a new covenant,
>> so that those who are called
>> may receive the promised eternal inheritance.
> He has appeared once for all at the end of the age
>> to put away sin by the sacrifice of himself.
>
> (Hebrews 9: 15, 26)

Upon moving into the New Testament, our first and most lasting impression is that here, in a more complete fashion than in the Old Testament, the atmosphere is permeated with joy, and the people of God are motivated by a sense of urgent mission. That the New Testament begins with a group of writings called the Gospels (good news) gives us the clue to the source of this joy. All that the Old Testament had promised in terms of the faithfulness of God and of his people's covenant hope has been brought to fulfillment in one victorious event: God's re-creation of human nature in the death and resurrection of Jesus Christ.

We conclude, therefore, that the old and new covenants are actually two historically different, but continuous, expressions of the way in which the one living God has bound his people to himself throughout their history. From beginning to end the biblical covenant defines a personal bond of love and righteousness which is established by God with his "chosen people" and is acknowledged by them as his gracious gift. The everlasting troth of fellowship and service between God and man gives us a living setting within which to observe the character and activity both of God and of man in the relationship.

THREE

THE PLOT OF ISRAEL'S COVENANT HISTORY

<hr>

THE drama of the Bible begins and ends in mystery. It begins in the mystery of God's having chosen a people (election) and points toward the consummation of his covenant troth with them in the age to come (destiny). In between these two, the Alpha and Omega of "the Mighty Acts of God," the Bible tells the story, generation after generation, of the covenant people in encounter with their Lord.

Time after time prophets and apostles tell the story:

   (1) of the people's infidelity to the covenant and their consequent estrangement from God and enslavement to evil,

   (2) of God's gracious deliverance and the people's rebirth of freedom, and

   (3) of the people being restored to responsible service as a remnant community of the faithful.

When this three-episode sequence of covenant encounter is set in the framework of the divine origin and the eternal destiny of humankind, we have incorporated the whole biblical story in the plot of the covenant drama. In each generation the plot develops as follows:

PROLOGUE—ELECTION (Covenant Troth)

ACT I—SIN (Estrangement and Enslavement)

ACT II—GRACE (Reconciliation by Redemption)

ACT III—RENEWAL (Restoration to Responsibility)

EPILOGUE—DESTINY (Covenant Fulfillment)

In this chapter and the next we shall be presenting the biblical basis for the thesis that the covenant drama is "The Story of Our Life in Encounter with the Living God" (cf. Part Two). That is to say, the relationship between God and the Hebrew people as to fellowship and service, or broken fellowship and disobedience, finds its counterpart today in the relationship between God and ourselves, both as groups and as individuals.

The reader may be struck, as we were, with the multiplicity of historical variations of the plot of the covenant drama recorded within the Bible. Even more striking is the underlying unity expressed in the variety.

The place at which we shall begin the study of the dramatic story of God's covenant with the Hebrew people is in the writings of the eighth-century prophets. This is, in effect, to start to read the story of the people of Israel in the middle. When, indeed, one recognizes the peculiar function of the Hebrew prophet, the middle is the right place to start.

The prophets of Israel were the teachers and the preachers of their time. Those who were engaged in the teaching function used the stories of former experiences in the lives of their people to remind them of God's gracious covenant election and faithful guidance and protection. They operated on the assumption that a hallowed memory of God's mighty acts in times past would motivate the people to accept his promises for and demands upon the present. Teachers had, apparently, been filling this role in Israel's life from the age of the exodus. Earliest reports of this function are found in the song of Miriam (Exod. 15: 20-21), the instruction of Moses (Deut. 6: 20-25), and the counsel of Joshua (Josh. 24: 2-28). Generation after generation was taught to repeat the story of God's glorious covenant and miraculous deliverance. Not until much later, however, did their work appear in written form. In the meantime it had been passed down from parents to their children by word of mouth.

The writings we find in the first half of our Old Testament are the work of these "teaching" prophets: (a) the Torah, commonly called the books of the Law, or the Pentateuch (Genesis, Exodus,

Leviticus, Numbers, Deuteronomy), interpreted as God's covenant revelation; (b) an account of Israel's national history
(Joshua, Judges, Ruth, 1 and 2 Samuel, 1 and 2 Kings), called
the books of the Former Prophets, interpreted as a record of how
God established and prospered, judged and saved his chosen
people.

As one can see, these books are not listed under the names of
their authors. Rather, their names are interpretative, with special
reference to events and heroes in the story. This is why it was
so easy for the later Jewish tradition to accredit the whole Torah
to their greatest hero, Moses.

The "preaching" prophets, on the other hand, have produced
the books of the latter one third of the Old Testament. These
writings are generally known by the original author's name:
Amos, Hosea, Isaiah, Micah, Jeremiah, and so on, although Bible
scholars recognize that they have often been edited and supplemented by the work of their successors. They are largely sermons preached to Israel in times of national crisis. Their thrust
is toward the future and their accent is upon decision. Contrary
to much popular thinking, however, these prophets are not primarily interested in predicting the future. To be sure they have
a very profound concern for the future, but not in the same way
as the soothsayer or the palm reader. The prophet's primary
concern is with the present state of affairs in the life of his
people. In this respect, as in all others, he is actually the mouth
of God. The word "prophet" means one who speaks in behalf of
another. Since a prophet's life is not his own but belongs to the
Lord, in whose service it is spent, the perspective for his interpretation is God's point of view. This is why we call the Bible
"the Word of God," and the prophets his "mouth" (Jer. 15: 19).

The Bible is a continuing dialogue between God, speaking
through the prophets, and the people of God, whose affairs are
so often in critical condition. In fact, the prophets were most
prominent in the nation's history in times of crisis—when life
was confused and threatened and the people needed to have a

word from God. This accounts for the preponderance of diagnosis and criticism in the sermons which the prophets preached.

If, however, interpreting the meaning of events in the present crisis is the prophet's task, it is by no means the limit of his concern. The present is limited in two directions—by the future which is to be and by the past which has already been. As between the past and future, the prophet has one eye cast in each direction. The future will soon be the present and cannot be escaped. The past has already been present and is still shaping it and is, therefore, one of the most formidable sources of understanding to which to turn.

To put it simply, the prophet speaks to the present, anticipating the future by interpreting the past. History is his main stock in trade. This is why the Jews called their history books of the Old Testament the "Former Prophets," and why historical writing constitutes a major portion of the Bible. But in his retelling of history, the prophet is not interested in a dispassionate, objective chronicle of events. In fact, such historical writing is a modern invention. Rather, he is opening up the meaning of this or that historic event for the light that it will shed upon God's purpose for his people in their own times. Indeed, this is still precisely the reason we have for studying the historic events of the Bible in our times.

The place to begin to study the plot of the biblical covenant drama, therefore, is the middle, because from this position one can soon read oneself into the prophetic literature and find one's way both backward and forward in the manner of the prophet's own approach.

For example, Israel's status as a covenant people was already over five hundred years old when Amos, Hosea, and Isaiah preached and taught (750-700 B.C.). The exodus, the event in which Moses led the enslaved children of Israel out of Egypt into their new life in covenant with the living God, occurred about 1300 B.C. Written literary records, however, of the exodus and of their early national history did not appear until about 850 B.C., scarcely one hundred years before the time of Amos and Hosea, and continued to be written during their time. From our perspective, it appears that the full dramatic import of the plot of Israel's covenant history did not begin to be fully recognized until Hosea and Isaiah began to preach.

A. The Drama of a Husband and His Prodigal Wife

A clear outline of the plot of Israel's covenant drama is to be found in the opening chapters of the book of Hosea. The bitter and disappointing experience of a broken marriage furnished Hosea with the symbols for his prophetic message to Israel. Hosea had married an attractive young woman named Gomer, with whom he settled down to establish a family. But he soon discovered that his wife was being unfaithful to him. After giving birth to three children, two of them illegitimately, to one of whom Hosea gave the name "Not my people," Gomer left his home entirely and became enslaved to her illicit lovers. The story of his own broken heart and the broken life of Gomer suggested to Hosea the parallel situation in the covenant story of God and Israel. Moreover, he says, it was the Lord who gave him this insight and who prompted him to do what no man would expect a deserted husband to do—to buy back his disgraced wife from her enslavement and restore her to his home again. By this recognition of the story of his life as the clue to the story of God's life with his people, Hosea made bold to affirm that God would surely renew the broken covenant of the people of Israel. God would betroth the nation to him again (2: 19-20).

A comparative chart of the two stories, found interwoven in chapters 1–3, will help to fasten the basic plot of the covenant drama in our minds.

HOSEA AND HIS PRODIGAL WIFE

PROLOGUE—Hosea has taken Gomer in marriage. (1: 2-3)

ACT I—Gomer is unfaithful. She is estranged from her husband. (1: 4-9)

ACT II—Gomer is redeemed by Hosea. (3: 1-2)

ACT III—She is restored to Hosea's home. (3: 3)

EPILOGUE—There is promise for the future. (3: 3)

THE LORD AND HIS PRODIGAL PEOPLE

PROLOGUE—The Lord had made a covenant with Israel when he called her out of Egypt in her youth. (2: 15)

ACT I—Israel has played the harlot with the Baals and is suffering evil consequences. (2: 1-13)

ACT II—The Lord promises to renew his covenant with Israel, in righteousness and steadfast love. (2: 16-20)

ACT III—He promises to restore Israel as a covenant community of justice and faithfulness. (2: 21-23)

EPILOGUE—There is hope for Israel in her "latter days." (3: 4-5)

Of course this story raises some questions in our minds. We would like to know whether there were no conditions that were laid upon Gomer for her redemption. If not (and apparently there were not), were there conditions for her staying free? How did she readjust to her new life?

It is important that we search for the answers to questions of this sort, but it is fruitless to expect much help from Hosea's writing. All that we have of his sermons are but brief fragments, which leave many of our questions unanswered. For us, the important thing is to recognize Hosea's great contribution to our understanding of God's ways with humankind; namely, his assurance that there are no conditions attached to God's love. God loves his people not because they are good or because they can do him some good, but solely because of his faithfulness to his covenant promises.

B. The Encounter of Isaiah with the Lord

More light is forthcoming from a prophet who lived and worked a little later, in the land of Judah. Isaiah, too, marked the covenant as being rooted in Israel's deliverance from Egypt, and proclaimed God's judgment and promise of eventual redemption and restoration (1: 1—2: 4). Moreover, he recorded autobiographically, in chapter 6, what happens to unfaithful people whom God restores to covenant fellowship.

The report of the covenant drama is actually even more personal in Isaiah than it was in Hosea. Hosea's experience of being rejected had led him to understand God's position in the covenant story. Isaiah, on the other hand, identified himself as one with the unfaithful people of God (6: 5). This is the Hosea-Gomer story from Gomer's side. In this brief chapter, Isaiah recorded the incident of his call to be a prophet as he looked back upon his youthful encounter with God. His account, like the Hosea-Gomer story, falls into a five-episode sequence of dramatic events, and is, we believe, the clearest Old Testament basis for the thesis that the covenant plot of divine-human encounter is a three-act drama, with a prologue of preparation and an epilogue of anticipation. The plot reads:

PROLOGUE—God's Covenant Affirmed by the Seraphim (Isaiah 6: 1-3)

ACT I—Isaiah's Confession of Sin (6: 5)

ACT II—The Seraphim's Healing Work (6: 6-7)

ACT III—God's Call and Isaiah's Commitment (6: 8)

EPILOGUE—God's Mysterious Promise (6: 9-13)

Although the plot is basically the same as that in the story of Gomer and Hosea, there are many obviously new factors in the drama of Isaiah and the Lord. There is still the symbolic identification of a person with the whole nation of Israel, but this person has been called to be a prophet to and for the rest of the people.

PROLOGUE—*God's Covenant Affirmed by the Seraphim*

Isaiah had, quite apparently, been brought up in the covenant faith and in effect acknowledged that it laid a claim upon his life. This is evident from the fact that he went to the temple in a time of great crisis in Judah's life—the year King Uzziah died. There Isaiah saw a vision of God's sovereignty as the Lord of Creation, and heard the seraphim, who were his faithful servants, singing the Lord's praises:

"Holy, holy, holy is the Lord of hosts;
the whole earth is full of his glory."

ACT I—*Isaiah's Confession of Sin*

The effect upon Isaiah was soul-searching and deeply disturbing. In the face of this awful vision Isaiah confessed his own and his people's woeful state of spiritual ill-health. Unlike Israel and perhaps Gomer, the memory of God's covenant faithfulness drove him to confess both his own and Israel's infidelity and estrangement.

> "Woe is me! For I am lost,
>   for I am a man of unclean lips,
>   and I dwell in the midst of a people of unclean lips."

It is here that Isaiah, unlike Hosea, placed himself on the side of Gomer, identifying himself with the sinning nation, acknowledging that at best he and God's people alike had been mouthing "empty clichés" when they ought to have been bearing a living witness to God's covenant.

ACT II—*The Seraphim's Healing Work*

Like Gomer, Isaiah was healed of his infidelity and redeemed from his estrangement. A seraph cauterized Isaiah's lips and declared:

> "Your guilt is taken away,
>   and your sin forgiven."

ACT III—*God's Call and Isaiah's Commitment*

There followed an event of tremendous import for the understanding of God's purpose in the dramatic encounter in which he engages his people. God himself spoke to Isaiah, calling him to be his servant. And, significantly, Isaiah willingly accepted the responsibility and set about to work as one divinely chosen.

> "Here am I! Send me."

EPILOGUE—*God's Mysterious Promise*

If anyone thinks that the covenant drama is a Hollywood success story, he is badly mistaken. Looking back upon his life work, Isaiah reflected somewhat wryly how God had used the prophet's own failure in his mission to point out the heartbreaking task that the Lord has, generation after generation, in seeking to beget fidelity in his people.

And [God] said, "Go, and say to this people:
  'Hear and hear, but do not understand;
  see and see, but do not perceive.'"

* * * * *

To whatever extent his own life work may have appeared to him fruitless, when he evaluated it in retrospect Isaiah, *the preacher*, was at once sharp in his denunciation of the people's infidelity and confident in the steadfast love of God. Chapters 1 and 2 in his book record sermons which develop the whole plot of the covenant story.

PROLOGUE—*Election for Freedom and Fellowship*
  "Sons have I reared and brought up."
  (Isaiah 1: 2)

ACT I—*Sin and Judgment*
  "But they have rebelled against me."
  Ah, sinful nation,
    a people laden with iniquity,
  offspring of evildoers,
    sons who deal corruptly!
  They have forsaken the Lord,
    they have despised the Holy One of Israel,
    they are utterly estranged.
  Your country lies desolate,
    and your cities are burned with fire;
  in your very presence
    aliens devour your land.
  (Isaiah 1: 2, 4, 7)

ACT II—*Redemption Through Purgation*
  "Come now, let us reason together,
    says the Lord:
  though your sins are like scarlet,
    they shall be as white as snow;
  though they are red like crimson,
    they shall become like wool.

> If you are willing and obedient,
>> you shall eat the good of the land;
> But if you refuse and rebel,
>> you shall be devoured by the sword;
>> for the mouth of the Lord has spoken."
>
> Therefore the Lord says,
>> the Lord of hosts,
>> the Mighty One of Israel;
> "I will turn my hand against you
>> and will smelt away your dross
>>> as with lye
>> and remove all your alloy.

(Isaiah 1: 18-20, 24-25)

ACT III—*Restoration to Responsibility*

> And I will restore your judges as at the first,
>> and your counselors as at the beginning.
> Afterward you shall be called the city of righteousness,
>> the faithful city."

(Isaiah 1: 26)

EPILOGUE—*Destiny—Righteousness and Peace*

> It shall come to pass in the latter days
>> that the mountain of the house of the Lord
> shall be established as the highest of the mountains,
>> and shall be raised above the hills;
> and all the nations shall flow to it,
>> and many peoples shall come, and say:
> "Come, let us go up to the mountain of the Lord,
>> to the house of the God of Jacob;
> that he may teach us his ways
>> and that we may walk in his paths."
>
> For out of Zion shall go forth the law,
>> and the word of the Lord from Jerusalem.
> He shall judge between the nations,
>> and shall decide for many peoples;

and they shall beat their swords into plowshares,
    and their spears into pruning hooks;
nation shall not lift up sword against nation,
    neither shall they learn war any more.

(Isaiah 2: 2-4)

C. The Epic of Israel's Deliverance from Egypt

Although both Hosea and Isaiah (8th century B.C.) anchored
their story in the covenant which the Lord had made with Israel
long before their time (13th century B.C.), their major emphasis
was placed upon the present situation and the prospect for the
future. They condemned Israel for her rebellion and infidelity
and assured her that, in his steadfast love, God would renew the
covenant; in his judgment he would purge her and restore her to
righteousness.

In the same period of Israel's national life, that is, as a divided
kingdom of Israel (922-722 B.C.) and kingdom of Judah (922-
586 B.C.), other prophets were recording and reinterpreting the
oft-repeated epic of the early years of their life as the people of
God, in which they had lived under the inspired and heroic leadership of Moses. These "teachers" produced the books of Exodus
(9th and 8th centuries) and Deuteronomy (7th century).

The book of Exodus tells the story of Israel's adventures during the lifetime of Moses and from the point of view of his leadership. The plot of this story is undoubtedly the original from
which Hosea, Isaiah, and others drew their inspiration.

PROLOGUE—*The Election of the Patriarchs*
God remembered his covenant
    with Abraham, with Isaac, and with Jacob.
He revealed himself to Moses as the Lord,
    who had chosen Israel as his people.

(See Exodus 2: 24; 3: 1-15; 6: 1-7.)

ACT I—*Israel in Egyptian Bondage*
God heard the groaning of his enslaved people
    and commissioned Moses to be the instrument
of his judgment by inflicting the plagues upon the Pharaoh.

(See Exodus 3: 16—11: 10.)

ACT II—*The Passover and the Exodus*

By the grace of God, Israel was saved from death
and delivered from the power of the Egyptians.

The Lord said to Moses:
"I will pass over you, and no plague
shall fall upon you to destroy you,
when I smite the land of Egypt."
And Miriam sang to [the people of Israel]:
"Sing to the Lord, for he has triumphed gloriously;
the horse and his rider he has thrown into the sea."

(Exodus 12–15; esp. 12: 13 and 15: 21)

ACT III—*The Law as Israel's Covenant Responsibility*

At Mount Sinai the congregation of Israel
was covenanted to God as a holy nation,
and received some of the rules of covenant responsibility.

(See Exodus 19–20; cf. 34.)

Then [Moses] took the book of the covenant,
and read it in the hearing of the people;
and they said,
"All that the Lord has spoken we will do,
and we will be obedient."

(Exodus 24: 7)

EPILOGUE—*The Destiny of Israel and the Mystery of God's
Presence*

The Lord said to Moses,
"Depart, go up hence, you and the people
whom you have brought up out of the land of Egypt. . . .
Go up to a land flowing with milk and honey."

"My presence will go with you,
and I will give you rest."

"But," he said, "you cannot see my face;
for man shall not see me and live."

(Exodus 33: 1, 3, 14, 20)

The book of Deuteronomy (the Second Law) is believed to have been written to encourage fidelity to the covenant of Moses during the reign of King Manasseh (687-642 B.C.), when Baal worship had become the predominant practice in Judah. Baalism is a form of primitive religion that persisted in Israel ever since the time of the early Canaanites. It is a fertility cult which was so bold in its promises and so satisfying in its cultic practices that many Hebrews were deflected away from the worship of the Lord of history. An agricultural civilization, so the argument went, needed the assurance of regular natural productivity of soil and herds. To assure their security and prosperity these people were encouraged to worship the principle of sexual reproduction. The symbol of the deity was a young bull, and the worship orgiastic. The prophets of the Lord, however, declared the cult of Baal an open act of infidelity to the covenant of him who is the Ground and the Goal of the whole creation. They condemned its cult and its gods as idolatry—the worship of an aspect of the creation in place of the Creator.

Long before Israel's prophets produced the book of Deuteronomy to combat this persistent evil in her life, however, the covenant story in its epic form had been sung as a cultic "confession of faith" in the Lord God of Israel. The full plot of this ancient confession is clearly recorded in Deuteronomy 6: 20-24 and in 26: 5-10. Both in its form and in its function this is the forerunner to our Apostles' Creed in the Christian church.

PROLOGUE—*Acknowledging the Lord's Covenant*

"I declare this day to the Lord your God
    that I have come into the land
        which the Lord swore to our fathers to give us."

ACT I—*Enslaved*

"A wandering Aramean was my father;
    and he went down into Egypt and sojourned there, . . .
And the Egyptians . . . laid upon us hard bondage."

ACT II—*Delivered*

"Then we cried to the Lord the God of our fathers,
and the Lord heard our voice,
and saw our affliction, our toil, and our oppression;
and the Lord brought us out of Egypt
with a mighty hand and an outstretched arm."

ACT III—*Restored*

"He brought us into this place
and gave us this land,
a land flowing with milk and honey."

EPILOGUE—*Thanksgiving to the Lord*

"And behold, now I bring the first of the fruit of the ground,
which thou, O Lord, hast given me."

D. Echoes of the Same Plot in the Lives of the Patriarchs

The book of Genesis is best understood if one takes it to be still another product of the genius of Israel's teachers in their effort to inculcate covenant loyalty to the Lord in each new generation. The stories of the patriarchs are presented as living examples of the divine-human covenant encounter.

In this book are woven together three strands of historical tradition. The two older ones originated as early as the ninth and eighth centuries (the time of Elijah and the time of Amos, Hosea, and Isaiah). The third is believed to have been the work of a teacher who was a member of the priestly profession in the period of Ezra and the post-exilic restoration of Judaism (5th century B.C.). Although the covenant motif is found in all three, it was most heavily underscored by the priestly writer. He referred to the covenant in the time of Abraham as "an everlasting covenant" and marked circumcision as its sign (Gen. 17: 11-13). The concept of "an everlasting covenant," as we shall see in chapter 4, was already the emphasis of Jeremiah, Ezekiel, and Second Isaiah in the sixth century.

The story of Israel's beginnings which we have just traced to her national origin in the exodus from Egypt is here pushed back two further steps: to the ethnic beginnings of God's chosen people as told in the legends of the patriarch Abraham and his descendants (Gen. 12–50); and to the beginnings of mankind in the universal myths or parables of Adam and Eve, Cain and Abel, Noah and his family (Gen. 1–11).

There is a twofold validity in our reading Israel's covenant history background in this fashion. First of all, it allows us to catch the perspective of her own prophetic teachers, whose purpose in recording their history was to recall "what God had done" in order to shed light upon "what he was doing" then and "promised to do" in the future. Since the "future" of Abraham and Moses in their times of decision was a part of Israel's past, she could learn from them how to face her future. Second, the main emphasis of covenant teaching in the book of Genesis represents the point of view of the priestly teacher who lived as late as the time of Ezra, about 450 B.C., nearly 200 years after Deuteronomy and 300 years after the time of Hosea and Isaiah. Thus, the earliest beginnings, in particular Genesis 1–11, are interpreted most completely by the latest strain of Old Testament covenant teaching.

In the three cycles of patriarchal stories found in Genesis 12–50, the plot of the covenant drama is everywhere evident. Most instructive for us, and for our twentieth-century effort to restore Christian education to its proper family setting, is the way in which the drama of the covenant *making, breaking,* and *renewal* repeats itself, generation after generation, in the family of Abraham and Isaac (Gen. 12–22), Isaac and Jacob (Gen. 27–35), and Jacob and Joseph.

JACOB AND JOSEPH

PROLOGUE—*Divine Election of the Family of Abraham*
    Jacob favored his younger son, Joseph.
          (See Genesis 37: 3.)

ACT I—*Family Rivalry and Conflict*
    Joseph vs. his brothers
    Joseph sold into slavery in Egypt
        (See Genesis 37: 4-36, 39-44.)

ACT II—*Divine Reconciliation*

> Joseph redeemed his brothers,
> saved the family from famine.
> Joseph said to them,
> "You meant evil against me;
> but God meant it for good."
> (Genesis 42: 6—45: 28; cf. 50: 19-20)

ACT III—*Renewal of Life Assured*

> God spoke to [Jacob] in visions of the night.
> "I am God, the God of your father;
> do not be afraid to go down to Egypt;
> for I will there make of you a great nation."
> (See Genesis 46: 2-3.)

EPILOGUE—*Destiny of the Family in the Mystery of God*

> Jacob blessed Joseph's sons, Ephraim and Manasseh.
> He blessed his own sons, constituting them
> the twelve tribes of Israel.
> (See Genesis 48—49.)

E. The Parable of Everyman and the Faithful Remnant

The earliest chapters of Genesis (1 to 11) are related to the Bible as a whole in the way the headline and first paragraph are related to the lead story in a newspaper. They give, in generalized terms, what the fine print will report in specific detail. All the human participants in the drama of life which the later history reports are caught up in a few characters, and ultimately one character, Adam, whose name means "Everyman," that is, mankind. In this context the plot of Israel's covenant history appears as the universal mythical drama of God and all mankind. Against the background of the specific historical encounters we have studied, the following account of the plot of the drama of Everyman gives us the clue for an outline of a system of covenant theology. (Cf. Part Two, "A Covenant Theology.")

Because of the universalized form the story takes here, there are two motifs of the covenant which come sharply into focus. Each motif is polar and paradoxical.

(1) Although the covenant is everlasting, one act of infidelity can break it. Even though the covenant is broken, one act of grace can restore it.

(2) Although the covenant is universal, only a remnant enjoys its blessing. Even though only a remnant is faithful, the covenant promise is meant for all.

PROLOGUE—*Divine Creation and Human Existence*
>Everyman has his origin and purpose in God:
>>Adam and Eve in the Garden of Eden
>>>>(See Genesis 1–2.)

ACT I—*Human Fall and Divine Judgment*
>One act of infidelity breaks the covenant troth:
>>The insinuation of the tempter
>>The pretension of Adam and Eve
>>Their expulsion from the Garden
>>The rivalry of Cain and Abel and their disastrous conflict

>The Lord saw that the wickedness of man
>>was great in the earth, . . .
>So the Lord said,
>>"I will blot out man whom I have created
>>>from the face of the ground, . . .
>>for I am sorry that I have made [him]."
>>>>(Genesis 3–4; 6: 5, 7)

ACT II—*Divine Deliverance and Covenant Renewal*
>God's troth is everlasting and is renewed
>>through the faith of a remnant.

>But Noah found favor in the eyes of the Lord. . . .
>And God said to Noah,
>>"I have determined to make an end of all flesh;
>>>for the earth is filled with violence through them;
>>behold, I will destroy them with the earth.

"Make yourself an ark of gopher wood; . . .
For behold, I will bring a flood of waters upon the earth . . .
But I will establish my covenant with you;
    and you shall come into the ark,
    you, your sons, your wife,
and your sons' wives with you."

(Genesis 6: 8, 13-14, 17-18)

ACT III—*Divine Restoration and Newness of Life*

God's one act of grace restores the covenant
    to all who live therein in confidence and obedience.

And God blessed Noah, and his sons, and said to them,
    "Be fruitful and multiply,
        and fill the earth."

"Behold, I establish my covenant with you
    and your descendants after you,
    and with every living creature
    that is with you."

(Genesis 9: 1, 9-10)

EPILOGUE—*Human Destiny in the Mystery of God*

God's covenant is everlasting and universal.

And God said,
    "This is the sign of the covenant
        which I make between me and you
        and every living creature that is with you,
        for all future generations:
    I set my bow in the cloud,
        and it shall be a sign of the covenant
        between me and the earth."

(Genesis 9: 12-17; esp. vs. 12-13)

FOUR

PROMISE AND FULFILLMENT OF THE NEW COVENANT

‾‾‾‾‾‾‾‾‾‾‾‾‾‾‾‾‾‾‾‾‾‾‾‾‾‾

T HE promise of a new covenant and the Messianic hope of a
   divinely chosen Deliverer arose together in the life of Israel.
They both belong to ACT II of the divine-human encounter. In
each historical era, Israel's prophets recognized that God had
chosen *a human mediator through whom to renew the covenant*
which his people had broken. This was the role of Noah in the
universal parable of Everyman. Joseph became the reconciler in
the family of Jacob, and Moses was empowered to set Israel free
from Pharaoh's bondage. Later, the tribal judges delivered the
people from their enemies, and kings were anointed (the Hebrew
word is *Messiah*) as the mark of their divine election as the
Lord's servant in the redemption of the nations. Recall David's
anointment at the hand of Samuel the prophet in 1 Samuel 16:
13.

A. Promise: The Death and Resurrection of Israel

As infidelity and the threat of slavery for Israel's kingdoms became increasingly more prominent, from the eighth to the sixth
century, prophetic "preachers" arose to give her hope that the
Lord would renew his covenant as in the days of old and would
anoint a king to deliver his people.

> The people who walked in darkness
>   have seen a great light;
>   those who dwelt in a land of deep darkness,
>   on them has light shined. . . .

For to us a child is born,
  to us a son is given;
and the government shall be upon his shoulder,
  and his name will be called
"Wonderful Counselor, Mighty God,
  Everlasting Father, Prince of Peace."
             (Isaiah 9: 2, 6; cf. 11: 1-16)

Equally important, within the context of the covenant drama, is the prophetic promise that, through the work of the divinely chosen Mediator, a remnant of Israel would be restored (ACT III). The remnant would fulfill the chosen people's role as "covenant to the nations." The extent of "purgation" and "regeneration" necessary to effect such a restoration of a faithful remnant in the land of Judah came, however, as a shock even to the prophets themselves.

A temporary restoration in the reign of Hezekiah, when in 701 B.C. the Assyrian Sennacherib was forced by a plague to lift the siege of Jerusalem, was followed by a long reign, marked by the predominance of Baal worship, under the apostate Manasseh in the seventh century. The flame of hope aroused in the time of King Josiah, because of his "reforms" begun in 621 B.C. on the occasion of the finding of the book of Deuteronomy, was dampened by the ominous threat of Nebuchadnezzar's Babylonian legions and Josiah's untimely death in a secondary conflict with Egypt.

At this low ebb in the national hopes of God's people appeared the spiritual giant of all the prophets to announce that the imminent destruction of Jerusalem was a part of God's own purpose. Jeremiah's heart was broken by the weight of doom in his message to the people he loved so deeply. Nevertheless, with full devotion to his calling he proclaimed the death of his beloved nation (605 B.C.).

Thus says the Lord concerning the house
  of the king of Judah:
"You are as Gilead to me,
  as the summit of Lebanon,

yet surely I will make you a desert,
    an uninhabited city.
I will prepare destroyers against you,
    each with his weapons;
and they shall cut down your choicest cedars,
    and cast them into the fire."

                       (Jeremiah 22: 6-7; cf. 25)

The clue to understanding such drastic action on the part of the Lord is given by the Deuteronomic editor of Jeremiah's sermons: "Because they forsook the covenant of the Lord their God, and worshiped other gods and served them" (Jer. 22: 9).

Jeremiah's most significant contribution to covenant theology, however, is his strongly influential use of the term "new covenant" in Jeremiah 31: 31-34. The passage reminds us of the dramatic confessions of faith in Deuteronomy (6 and 26). Jeremiah, too, recalls the old covenant event of the exodus, and he uses the traditional covenant formula:

        "You shall be my people,
           and I will be your God."

His most important emphasis, however, is eschatological; that is, his teaching looks forward toward a future consummation of the purpose of God in a "coming" event. This idea is not one of progress, onward and upward. Rather it is an expression of the hope which sees our known "present" and God's still-to-be-known "future" meeting one another. The covenant is a continuing renewal of the ancient promise, becoming *new* in that it bestows a new, inward motivation and power for fulfilling the covenant responsibilities which the people already know (the Law), but have failed to keep. That man whose sin is forgiven will become a "new creation." In the midst of his human bondage and in the face of the threat of death, he will be reborn.

        "A new heart I will give you,
           and a new spirit I will put within you."

                       (Ezekiel 36: 26)

A more picturesque interpretation of Israel's death and promise of resurrection is found in Ezekiel 37: 1, 3-5, 11-12, 26-27.

The hand of the Lord was upon me,
and he brought me out by the Spirit of the Lord,
and set me down in the midst of the valley;
it was full of bones.

And he said to me,
"Prophesy to these bones, and say to them,
O dry bones, hear the word of the Lord. . . .
Behold, I will cause breath to enter you,
and you shall live."

Then he said to me,
"Son of man, these bones are the whole house of Israel.
Behold, I will open your graves,
and raise you from your graves,
O my people,
and I will bring you home
into the land of Israel. . . .
I will make a covenant of peace with them;
it shall be an everlasting covenant with them; . .
and I will be their God,
and they shall be my people."

B. Fulfillment: The Death and Resurrection of Jesus

Two of the best known of Isaiah's servant songs have literally become a bridge between the new covenant "in promise" and the new covenant "in fulfillment." They are Isaiah 53 and 61.

The fulfillment of the Suffering Servant role (Isa. 52: 13–53: 12) in the life, death, and resurrection of our Lord Jesus appears to have been the basic motif in the theme of the earliest Christian preaching. Note, for example, the sermons in the book of Acts by the apostle Peter (Acts 2: 22 ff.; 10: 34 ff.), the witness of Philip to the Ethiopian eunuch (Acts 8: 26 ff.), and the confession of the apostle Paul in Philippians 2: 5-11. Moreover, we believe that this passage was consciously and voluntarily acknowledged by Jesus himself as the meaning of his existence (Mark 10: 45).

The Gospels and the Epistles make it quite clear that, although Jesus was revealed as God's Chosen One in the new covenant, and therefore was properly acclaimed as the Lord's Messiah, that is, the Christ, he is actually, even more significantly, the Remnant of Israel, a Remnant of One who seriously accepted her Suffering Servant mission.

What Israel had involuntarily betokened in her death (the Exile) and resurrection (the Restoration) she had not fulfilled, as is evidenced by her subsequent relapse into provincial nationalism and racial purism. This happened, however, despite prophetic efforts to keep the vision of Israel's redemptive mission ever before her eyes. New prophetic teachers arose to retell, in exquisite fashion, two stories drawn from Israel's early national history, in which her calling as a remnant servant was being tested. In one instance it was faithfully carried through; in the other, it was infamously rejected. The first is the story of the book of Ruth and of her redemption as a "foreign" Moabitess by the faithful Boaz. Through their marriage they become the ancestors of King David. In the second instance, Jonah, that is, Israel as a "dove," is sent to Nineveh to proclaim the love and righteousness of God, but refuses (chapter 1). Even after a "successful preaching mission" (chapter 3), prompted by his involuntary "death and resurrection" (chapter 2), Jonah shows that he still suffers from covenant infidelity (chapter 4). Both of these stories will be discovered to follow the plot of the covenant drama.

1. A PREVIEW OF JESUS' MISSION

Isaiah 61: 1-2 was our Lord's own choice of a prophetic word to use for a "keynote address" in his home-town synagogue in Nazareth (Luke 4: 16-30) not long after his baptism by John. In fact, this passage outlines the whole scope of his ministry: preaching, teaching, and healing. Indeed, Luke's Gospel begins the account of Jesus' public ministry with a dramatic sequence of events in Jesus' life, all of which may be taken as representative of many incidents to follow. Luke 3 and 4 appear to be like the opening section of the book of Genesis—a kind of newspaper-style, large-print, lead paragraph designed to encourage the reader to continue with the details of the story.

The most striking feature about Luke's arrangement is that these two chapters offer a complete synopsis of the plot of the new covenant in the mission of our Lord.

PROLOGUE—*Preparation*

The baptism of John
The blessing of God: "my beloved Son"
The genealogy of the covenant people of God

(See Luke 3: 1-38.)

ACT I—*Temptation by the Devil*

"If you are the Son of God,
    command this stone to become bread."

"If you, then, will worship me,
    all the kingdoms of the world
    and their glory shall be yours."

"If you are the Son of God,
    throw yourself down from here [the pinnacle of the temple];
[God] will give his angels charge of you,
    to guard you."

(Luke 4: 3, 5-7, 9-10. Adapted)

ACT II—*Commitment to Servant Mission*

"The Spirit of the Lord is upon me,
    because he has anointed me to preach good news to the poor.
He has sent me to proclaim release to the captives
    and recovering of sight to the blind,
    to set at liberty those who are oppressed,
    to proclaim the acceptable year of the Lord."

(Luke 4: 18-19; cf. Isaiah 61: 1-2)

ACT III—*Ministry of Teaching and Healing*
Jesus taught "with authority."
He healed a man with the spirit of an unclean demon.
He laid his hands on the sick and healed them.

(See Luke 4: 31-41.)

EPILOGUE—*Preaching the Kingdom of God*
"I must preach the good news of the kingdom
of God; . . . for I was sent for this purpose."

(Luke 4: 43)

There are other instances of the use of the plot of the covenant drama in Luke's Gospel. The story in Luke 5 of the call of Peter to discipleship is distinctly reminiscent of the account of Isaiah's call (Isa. 6). The famous parable in Luke 15, of the father and his two sons, commonly called "the prodigal son," gives an indication that Jesus' own thought about God and man was shaped by the great literary tradition of prophetic covenant drama (cf. Part Three, chapter 1).

2. THE PASSION STORY

Most significant for our purpose is the Passion story in Luke 19: 28—24: 49. This account is for the new covenant what the book of Exodus was for the old covenant. Here is the record of the crucial event which Christians confess as God's most complete revelation of his saving grace.

PROLOGUE—*Triumphal Entry*
The Servant is acclaimed King.
(See Luke 19: 28-40.)

ACT I—*Conflict with Evil Powers*
Jesus weeps for the city of Jerusalem.
Jesus cleanses the temple.
Scribes, Sadducees challenge his authority
They conspire against him.
(See Luke 19: 41—21: 38.)

Act II—*"The New Covenant in My Blood"*

> The Last Supper
> Gethsemane
> Arrest and trial
> Crucifixion and burial
> > (See Luke 22—23.)

Act III—*Resurrection and Newness of Life*

> Appearances
> Promises, and demands
> > (See Luke 24: 1-49.)

Epilogue—*Ascension*

> While he blessed them,
> he parted from them.
> > (Luke 24: 51)

The earliest Christian preaching proclaimed the life, death, and resurrection of Jesus as the fulfillment of the Suffering Servant role. The sermons in Acts 2: 22 ff. and Acts 10: 34-43, and the confession of Paul in Philippians 2: 5-11, are all distinctly molded by the covenant drama plot. They, in turn, give both form and content to the development of the Apostles' Creed, which has become the standard Christian confession of the church's covenant with the living God.

3. THE WHOLE DRAMA OF SALVATION

When one wishes to read the whole story of the covenant of God and man in Jesus Christ, from beginning to end, from "election" to "destiny," the New Testament offers him a continuous record written by a single author: the Gospel of Luke and The Acts of the Apostles. This inclusive theology of history, like its smaller segments, is structured by the plot of the covenant drama.

Prologue—*The Chosen One: Immanuel* (A New Election: Annunciation and Magnificat)

At the outset, before the curtain rises, it is announced that there is going to be a major substitution in the cast of covenant participants. God has determined to enter the covenant encounter on both sides. Jesus of Nazareth, called "the Son of God," replaces Adam, formerly of the Garden of Eden, in the lead role. This is the glorious gospel which permeates every part of the new covenant drama, for from the very beginning one is led to suspect that the Nazarene is the first-fruit of a new humanity. (Luke 1.)

ACT I—*Incarnation: New Beginning* (God's Son Identifies Himself with Enslaved Adam.)

Whereas the first event in the Old Testament drama portrays man's sinful infidelity and the correlative judgment of God, mediated through his righteous law, in the new covenant drama the accent is placed upon the identification of the new man with the old man's struggle against the powers of evil that have enslaved him. Jesus is born into "death," under an imperial tax burden and in the face of Herod's threat. He has a stable for a delivery room. He is tempted even as we are, yet without sin. He is the Word of God become flesh. (Luke 2: 1–19: 27.)

ACT II—*Atonement: New Covenant* (God's Victory over the Powers of Evil Through the Crucifixion of Jesus Christ.)

Again and again God has sent a deliverer to redeem Israel: Joseph, Moses, the judges, the prophets, and the promised Messiah. In the new covenant drama, the apostles proclaim, the promise in Isaiah 49: 6 has been fulfilled. Jesus Christ is much more than the man whom God has sent to redeem Israel; he is the Savior of all humankind. As such his mission is the fulfillment of Israel's own Suffering Servant role. In the show-down struggle between the servant of God's love and righteousness and the power of Satan, our Lord's death and resurrection become the *new exodus*, through participation in which all men may be set free from the bondage of sin and may share in the new creation. (Luke 19: 28–23: 56.)

ACT III—*Indwelling: New Life* (The Risen Christ Bestows the Holy Spirit upon the Church, His Body.)

The new life in Christ is at once individual and corporate. The gift of God's Holy Spirit both creates a fellowship of love which constitutes the church and sets each member apart to a Christian vocation of covenant responsibility. The "holy catholic church" is the sacrament of the Body of Christ on earth—the channel through which the recreative power of God's Holy Spirit may flow in faithful stewardship. (Luke 24; Acts 1: 1–28: 22.)

EPILOGUE—*Lordship over History* (The Consummation of the Kingdom of God)

The mystery of the future remains a mystery, but the hope it holds is both universal, that is, ecumenical, as against provincial, and intensely personal. The mystery (sacrament) of the Lord's Supper is the church's anticipation of full communion with God and his servants in the kingdom of heaven. (Acts 28: 23-30.)

FIVE

THE LIVING GOD AND THE
LIFE OF HIS PEOPLE

FROM the perspective of the covenant, God and man are so inextricably bound together that it is absurd to try to conceive of either one without the other. Indeed, the Bible is so thoroughly concerned with God "in action" in the midst of human affairs that it seldom ever singles out God "in himself" for separate attention. Therefore, the main focus of covenant theology is the interpretation of historical events in the life of God's people from the perspective of the revelation of his purpose in and through them. It is important to recognize clearly, however, that Christian theological studies involve three different levels of historical interpretation:

(1) the discovery of what was being believed about what was happening between God and man at any particular time in biblical history, for example, the exodus, the crucifixion;

(2) the recognition of what later interpreters, for example, the prophets and apostles, and church teachers through the ages, understood these events to indicate concerning the meaning of God's purpose as it related to their times;

(3) and, since religious truth can never rest in the past tense, a continual search for the significance of both levels for our own life in the covenant today.[1]

---

[1] Two excellent recent scholarly essays on biblical theology, including detailed studies of the significance of the covenant, are available to pastors and teachers who use *The Interpreter's Bible.*

Level (1) is discussed in "The History of the Religion of Israel," by James Muilenburg, Vol. 1, pp. 292-348.

Level (2) is discussed in "The Faith of Israel," by G. Ernest Wright, Vol. 1, pp. 349-389.

This book is an effort to reach level (3).

A. What the Covenant Teaches Us About God

In what follows we shall draw from the witness of both the life story of Israel and the life of the early Christian church to interpret the character of God.

1. THE MYSTERY OF GOD'S ELECTION

Israel, in the Old Testament, and the church of Jesus Christ, in the New Testament, are "the chosen people of God."

The mystery of human life is always deepest when we are involved in intimate personal relationships. The source of the mystery is most accurately identified when we acknowledge that we live and move and have our being in the love by which God has chosen to make us his own. Election is a special term in the language of faith to define our situation. Moreover, since living relationships are always two-way affairs, involving give-and-take, action and response, election is the symbol which the Bible uses to declare the divine initiative in establishing the everlasting covenant in which, generation after generation, we find ourselves participating. It is the acknowledgment that God is not only the source of our being but embodies within himself the reason for our being here. He is the Alpha and the Omega, the source and the goal, our origin and our destiny.

In religious terms election is a confession that the basis of our being chosen is hidden in the mysterious grace of God. We confess that it is God who has chosen us to be his people, not we who have chosen him. With prophets and apostles of old we recognize that God's people in all ages are called to participate in his covenant for the world's redemption through no merit or achievement of their own. In fact, apart from the grace of God they are utterly unworthy.

Moses (Deut. 7: 7-8) cautioned the people of Israel to remember: "It is not because you were more in number than any other people that the Lord set his love upon you and chose you, for you were the fewest of all peoples; but it is because the Lord loves you."

1 Peter (2: 9-10), quoting Hosea 2: 23, reminds the church of Jesus Christ:

> Once you were no people
> but now you are God's people;
> once you had not received mercy
> but now you have received mercy.

God's election-love (*'ahabhah* in Old Testament Hebrew, *agape* in New Testament Greek) is the innermost motive of his being. It is marked by freedom and spontaneity and is the source and goal of the mystery of life.

2. GOD'S PERSONAL SELF-REVELATION

Israel and the church know themselves to be chosen by virtue of God's own self-disclosure:

> *. . . by his Word of demand and promise,*
> "You shall be my people,
> and I will be your God."
> *. . . in his Mighty Acts of judgment and redemption,*
> the Egyptian slavery and deliverance
> the Babylonian exile and restoration
> the crucifixion of Jesus and his resurrection
> *. . . through the gift of his own Spirit,*
> inspiring the prophets of Israel
> indwelling the church of Jesus Christ

It is a commonplace in human experience that each person has a proper name. The living God, who enters into covenant with Israel and the church, glorifies this practice and exemplifies two of the basic truths of personal life:

(1) A person's name cannot be discovered. It must be revealed. The common experience in human encounter runs like this: "My name is So and So; what's yours?"

(2) When one gives one's name, one gives oneself away. The door is opened. The lines of communication are established. The intensity of personal relationship will, of course, depend upon the frequency and intimacy of encounter, but once two have met

they are no longer strangers. Each has a bit of claim upon the other.

One of the most dramatic events in Israel's history is the revelation to Moses at the burning bush. The Lord was laying a heavy responsibility upon this man's shoulders, and the man was loath to accept it. Remembering his own exile from his people and the need to identify himself to them, Moses asked God to give him the privilege of using his name for reference. The Lord obliged and announced his name as YAHWEH, meaning "I CAUSE TO BE THAT WHICH COMES TO BE."

The prophet who recorded this encounter, in Exodus 3: 13-15, interpreted the name YAHWEH, translated Lord in the Revised Standard Version of the Bible, as a mystery unfolded to Moses in terms of a play on the Hebrew root word "to be." None of the recent scholarly attempts at varying the tenses and the force of the more traditional I AM WHO I AM, such as the one we have used (cf. Muilenburg, op. cit., p. 301), can solve the mystery. However, this approach does indicate where the mystery lies—in the sovereignty of God's love and not in a verbal conundrum.

At the transfiguration of Jesus, witnessed by Peter, James, and John, when Moses and Elijah appeared in glory beside Jesus and spoke of his "exodus" which he was to accomplish at Jerusalem, a voice came out of the cloud that overshadowed them, saying,

> "This is my Son, my Chosen;
> listen to him!"
>
> (Luke 9: 35)

Through the new covenant in Jesus Christ the living God comes to be known and confessed as a personal triunity: the sovereign and righteous Father, the Holy Spirit of love, and the only-begotten Son, full of grace and truth.

3. GOD'S STEADFAST LOVE

By his Word, his Mighty Acts, and through his personal Gift, God has established with his chosen people a permanently binding relationship whose fundamental troth is "steadfast love."

We have already noted that our election is rooted in the mystery of God's love, that is, in the freedom of God to initiate a covenant with humankind. But what begins in "love as freedom" (election-love) comes to be "love as order" (covenant faithfulness). Love as freedom in the heart of God is clearly not what we mistakenly assume freedom to be in human life—unbridled license, doing as you please. Choosing involves an irrevocable commitment, an everlasting troth. Election implies an end-purpose and a steadfast will to its consummation. What the covenant says in effect is: "Once God has chosen to create a people, he is betrothed to them, for better or for worse."

On the other hand, being chosen demands, but does not guarantee, that God's people will maintain an equally faithful troth in return. Indeed, this mutuality of promise and inequality of fulfillment, God manward *and* man Godward, is the occasion for the dramatic plot of covenant encounter which we discerned to be the fundamental story of the Bible. In fact, God's unswerving loyalty to his covenant promises in the face of man's infidelity is the gospel, anticipated in the heart and mind of Hosea, Jeremiah, Second Isaiah, and the psalmist of Israel (cf. Ps. 89: 1-4), and incarnated in Jesus the Christ (cf. Rom. 5: 1-11).

The Old Testament Hebrew word to express God's covenant love is *chesed*. It is variously translated as "lovingkindness" or "mercy" in the King James version, and "steadfast love" or "faithfulness" in the Revised Standard Version. In the New Testament the equivalent Greek word is *charis* and is regularly translated as "grace." In both Testaments God's covenant loyalty is the dynamic in the story of the sustaining of human life, our unmerited redemption from sin, and our glorious re-creation in the newness of life.

4. GOD'S FAMILY STATUS: FATHER AND HUSBAND

The symbols of family relationships, father and son, husband and wife, are basic to the whole covenant pattern of life. They give the covenant both a normative and a realistic significance for understanding the divine-human encounter.

Normatively, the family symbols are used by Jesus, as well as by the prophets and apostles, to define the right structural relationship between God and his people. The biblical husband and father is the head of the family. Thus, God is the Husband (Hos. 2: 16; Isa. 54: 5) and Father (Hos. 11: 1; Isa. 1: 2) of Israel. In the New Testament the apostle Paul writes that Christ is the head of the church just as the husband is the head of the wife (Eph. 5: 23). Jesus, himself, teaches his disciples to pray, "Our Father . . ."

Fatherhood involves authority (cf. 5, below) but not mere sovereignty. Fatherhood is nothing apart from the sonship which is its counterpart. The intimate and fruitful kinship of the two rests upon the bond of fidelity which is inspired by the father's character as well as by his authority. A father is therefore the object of honor and love as well as of obedience. Moreover, the father's authority carries over to his obedient sons. A son is one who not only acknowledges his father's authority but comes to bear his father's character in himself (Matt. 5: 44-45).

In the Old Testament the Father-son relationship is sustained between God and the whole people he has chosen. In the New Testament Jesus is the Son of God, first of all, and then his disciples become sons of God, and through them, in turn, the church of the Apostles. In one sense, God the Creator is the Father of all mankind, that is, by the implication of the new covenant promise. In a functional family sense, of father-son rapport, however, God is the Father only of those who acknowledge their sonship in the covenant.

Realistically, in the sinful failures of human experience, these same symbols of intimate personal family relationship mark the breakdown of love and fidelity. Broken family fidelity, between spouses and between parents and children, strikes to the depths of human sin and misery. Here it is, however, that the significance of the divine-human analogy of God the Father and his human family is actually heightened. God's steadfast faithfulness and well-spring of forgiving love are a rock of assurance to a people or person enslaved by infidelity and made miserable by estrangement.

Jesus' parables regarding the healing of our broken covenant with God rest not upon the achievement of perfect human family concord but upon a rough analogy coupled with his "how much more."

> "If you then, who are evil, know how to give
>   good gifts to your children,
> how much more will your Father who is in heaven
>   give good things to those who ask him?"
>
> (Matthew 7: 11)

This makes it possible to see the golden thread which ties together the two senses of God's fatherhood, mentioned above. Just as in our broken human families, so in the family of God: even though the Father is still consciously fatherly toward the son who has rejected his authority and character, the father-son reunion awaits the return of the son from the far country, pleading for the status of a servant (Luke 15). When he comes, however, he becomes for the first time truly a son, begotten of his father a second time, once in the flesh but now in the spirit.

5. GOD'S SOVEREIGN AUTHORITY: KING AND LORD

The symbols which express "righteousness" in the covenant relationship emphasize the correlative but equal status of God and man, as King and people, Lord and servant.

God's sole kingship in Israel was assumed from the time of the exodus, only to be challenged by his people's desire to have a king they could idolize as their pagan neighbors were doing. When the people came to Samuel with this request, the prophet was displeased and tried to forewarn them of the oppression and exploitation to which a human king would subject them. But the people insisted, and when Samuel took it to the Lord, he said to Samuel,

> "Hearken to their voice,
>   and make them a king."

The way in which Samuel's reluctance to comply with the people's wish was finally put aside may indicate something of the mystery of God's grace in his sustaining our human freedom even when it brings us suffering and distress (1 Sam. 8).

For the biblical testimony the symbol of kingship personalizes the concept of God's sovereign righteousness as the corresponding father symbol expresses the steadfast love of the living God. Since he is himself righteous, God the author of justice and the judge of man's obedience can be trusted and his authority respected.

Jesus phrased the fulfilled covenant as "the kingdom of God." In his parables, over and over again, he described the righteousness of God's kingship and the people's inability or reluctance to accept its rigorous but ultimately glorious terms.

Lord and Servant

One aspect of the genius of biblical theology is the ability of its authors to point to the unity in God of attributes which seldom function well together in humanity. Indeed, their greatest contribution is the confession that in Jesus Christ the divine love achieved the zenith of righteousness by taking the whole of what threatens the unity of love and righteousness in the human situation into the divine life and overcoming it, once for all. The Lord himself became a servant, suffering the death, guilt, and meaninglessness of human life for our redemption and glorious deliverance.

The sovereignty of God's love is "holiness," the power and will to heal the brokenness of human life. His service on our behalf is not meant, however, to make our service unnecessary. Rather, his new Lordship over life as Suffering Servant makes our service through suffering possible by creating within us the courage to have the mind in us which was in Christ Jesus.

Have this mind among yourselves,
    which you have in Christ Jesus,
who, though he was in the form of God,
    did not count equality with God a thing to be grasped,

but emptied himself, taking the form of a servant,
  being born in the likeness of men.
And being found in human form he humbled himself
  and became obedient unto death, even death on a cross.

Therefore God has highly exalted him
  and bestowed on him the name which is above every name,
that at the name of Jesus every knee should bow,
  in heaven and on earth and under the earth,
and every tongue should confess that Jesus Christ is Lord,
  to the glory of God the Father.

(Philippians 2: 5-11)

Our identification with Christ and with his service to the world brings to life his purpose in identifying with us.

B. What the Covenant Teaches Us About Ourselves

Granting that it is impossible, in biblical terms, to talk about God "in himself," it would be equally meaningless to attempt to define man "in isolation." By virtue of the Lord's election and covenant troth, Israel and the church are not merely people, they are "the people of God." Just as the biblical doctrine of God is a "confession of faith," the covenant teaching about man is also confessional, ultimately a double confession of faith and of sin. Our confession of faith acknowledges "what we are meant to be." Our confession of sin acknowledges "that we are not what we are meant to be."

The biblical understanding of man, in covenant with the living God, suggests a number of propositions, each of which is inherently bipolar. Each proposition is polar because it refers to an inner ambiguity, a twofoldness in man's nature and in his situation. The basic polarity in man results from the fact that, although he is only a finite creature, he is nonetheless chosen for divine responsibility. As a creature he comes to be and expects to pass away, but the mark of "the image of God" upon him suggests that he has an eternal destiny. Expressions of this polar tension run through all that the Bible tells us about man, and give it tone and color. Although each pole expresses in itself a fundamental truth about man, the deeper truth is found when both aspects functioning together are recognized at once.

1. GOD'S GIFT AND MAN'S TASK

God's covenant is a gift, which, when accepted, bestows freedom and peace upon his people, while it demands of them their undivided loyalty and responsible service. This is the truth that is so admirably expressed in the German language by the words *Gabe* and *Aufgabe*, in which the *Gabe* is God's gift, and the *Aufgabe* is our task (something given to us to do).

The covenant is a gift of grace, which may be accepted or rejected by man. We may respond with a yes or a no to God's call. Acceptance or rejection is voluntary, but not a matter of indifference. By accepting God's gracious gift of life in his love and righteousness, Israel and the church experience the joy of responsible participation in God's work. And their periodic fits of infidelity and flight from responsibility are marked by disheartening loss of liberty and disastrous social conflict.

2. RELIGIOUS FAITH AND EXISTENTIAL FREEDOM

God's correlative "promise and demand" constitute the warp and woof of the covenant relationship and establish for us the basic poles of our life: religion and existence. "Religious faith" and "existential freedom" are rooted, respectively, in the biblical revelation of man as a creature and as the bearer of the "image of God."

Religious Faith

We become religious when we acknowledge our dependence as creatures and accept the fact that we need to put our trust in another for our security and the assurance of belonging. Religiosity is the common human capacity to respond to "that power which makes for security" with devotion and trust, that is, in worship.

Human piety may find its satisfaction, however, in the worship of any one of a great variety of idols. Idols are false gods, the satisfaction of any aspect of our life which, when distorted, claims to be the whole of it and to be the ultimate source of its significance.

The fundamental Christian expression of the religious role of our lives arises out of our covenant encounter with the God of history. Christian worship is strongly confessional in tone: *confession of faith*, motivated by ever deepening gratitude for God's steadfast love and sovereign righteousness, and *confession of sin*, motivated by despair of our idolatrous infidelity and the sense of guilt which flows therefrom. Despite our infidelity, our devotional life is both "recreative" and "empowering" in its effect.

Existential Freedom

When we affirm our independence as creatures endowed with God's own image, and become concerned for our personal identity and the use of our creative talents, we discover our existential freedom. This is our capacity to decide "to be what we will be."

The Christian life in the new covenant is unique in that it does not claim that religion alone can give full meaning to human life. The freedom of the Christian man is equally as divine as his worship. Indeed, the freedom to be oneself is God's most precious gift, the gift of his own creative power for the fulfillment of life.

A distorted form of dependence, we noted above, may lead a man to idolatry and pseudo-religion. Human freedom is likewise subject to distortion. In its creativity are conceived all the monsters of human perversity (for example, pride, arrogance, contempt) which result from a man's inordinate desire to rise above all dependence. Inevitably he deifies himself, falsely, and demands that all others become "religious" toward him.

Clearly both forms of idolatry, religious prostitution and inordinate self-affirmation, are distortions of God's more inclusive purpose for our lives. They become possible for us, oddly

enough, because he gives us the power and the motivation by
which to live by faith—either in responsible faith in him or in
irresponsible faith in such idols as his creation can afford us. In
any case we live by his grace alone.

In our life according to the holy covenant of love and righteousness, however, we are neither puppets condemned to a life
of mere dependency, nor are we permitted to subject others to
such indignity. A healthy Christian faith incorporates both responsible self-affirmation and religious dependence in the unity
of God's purpose for us in our Lord Jesus Christ. The courage
to be oneself in intimate personal encounter with one's peers and
the willingness to accept a vocation of "suffering service" to anyone in need are Christian expressions of the existential pole of
human life.

The two dimensions of the great commandment, as Jesus is
reported to have summarized the whole old covenant teaching,
indicates the tension between the two poles of our religious
devotion and our moral responsibility.

One of the scribes asked him:

"Which commandment is the first of all?"

Jesus answered,

"The first is,

'Hear, O Israel: The Lord our God, the Lord is one;
and you shall love the Lord your God
with all your heart,
and with all your soul,
and with all your mind,
and with all your strength.

"The second is this,

'You shall love your neighbor as yourself.'"

(Mark 12: 28-31; cf. Deuteronomy 6: 4-9
and Leviticus 19: 18)

The rhythmic beat of our Lord's own *promise* (peace and rest)
with his *command* (service and mission) sharpens the tension
even more.

"Come to me, all who labor and are heavy-laden,
   and I will give you rest.
Take my yoke upon you, . . . for my yoke is easy,
   and my burden is light."
                                        (Matthew 11: 28-30)

3. THE PEOPLE OF GOD AND THE PEOPLE
OF THE WORLD

*Participation in God's covenant involves Israel and the church
in a mission of "suffering service" to the world.*

The world, its culture and institutions, is largely the product
of our own human minds and effort, added to the work and
thought of countless generations. It is continually being threatened by self-destruction because our loyalties, like our hearts,
are tainted by the spirit of selfishness, greed, and ruthless rivalry.

The people of God, who compose the household of faith, on
the other hand, are called to be an entirely different kind of
body. Their concern is to communicate God's own spirit of love,
to bind up the brokenhearted, to bring healing and emancipation to those who have come out on the short end of the economic, political, and social competition and conflict which domi-
nate the world.

Since the people of God are also creatures who live in the
world, their status is always ambiguous. In every generation
they are faced with a decision: to be the servants of God or to be
the slaves of the world; to serve the Lord or the Baals; to worship
God or Mammon. In Israel and in the church there are always
many who want it both ways. But when the crucial moment
comes, although they are born or baptized into the covenant
community, they will sell their birthright for worldly security,
power, and prestige. In Israel only a remnant, at one time a
remnant of one, Jesus of Nazareth, seriously acknowledged the
call to be the "suffering servant of the Lord."

By our Lord's death and resurrection, however, he is proclaimed the mediator of the new covenant—the victor over the
powers of evil which still threaten to destroy us. Christ is,

thereby, the Lord of the world as well as of the church. In this context the vocation of the Christian church is clear. She is to minister to the world and its desperate needs in the name of the spirit of their one Lord. Her mission is twofold:

(1) To bring the people of the world into the life of the people of God. This involves the church's ministry of evangelism and world missions. Her task is to extend the community of love, by which she lives in covenant with the living God, to include all mankind.

> And [the Lord] said to me, "You are my servant,
> Israel, in whom I will be glorified.
> It is too light a thing that you should be my servant
> to raise up the tribes of Jacob
> and to restore the preserved of Israel;
> I will give you as a light to the nations,
> that my salvation may reach to the end of the earth."
>
> (Isaiah 49: 3, 6)

(2) To bring the love and righteousness of God into the life of the world, revolutionizing the world's social structures and reconciling the world's people to each other and to their God. This latter involves the church's ministry of prophetic preaching, social service, and social action. Our churches are utterly remiss in their social responsibility if they do not confess, with the prophet Isaiah (61: 1-2):

> "The Spirit of the Lord God is upon me,
> because the Lord has anointed me
> to bring good tidings to the afflicted;
> he has sent me to bind up the brokenhearted,
> to proclaim liberty to the captives,
> and the opening of the prison to those who are bound;
> to proclaim the year of the Lord's favor,
> and the day of [judgment] of our God."
>
> (Luke 4: 18-19)

4. COMMUNION AND A COMMONWEALTH

Human fidelity to the divine-human covenant promises a double bond of fellowship:

(1) Communion of the faithful with God: the church

(2) The community of the faithful in God: a commonwealth

When the ancient Hebrew tribes covenanted with YAHWEH at Mount Sinai they also covenanted with each other. Thus, the covenant is the basis of Israel's community-consciousness as it is the heart of her religious cult. The relative strength or weakness of their confederacy through the centuries was determined by the measure of their loyalty to the Lord, who had first set them free from Egyptian bondage.

"The true community does not arise through people's having feelings for one another [though indeed not without it], but through, first, taking their stand in living mutual relation with a living Center, and second their being in living mutual relation with one another."[1]

By the same token, just in so far as there exists a common loyalty to the Lord Jesus, so shall the new covenant people, as family, congregation, or ecumenical church, be bound together as a divinely inspired community of love and righteousness. Communion and commonwealth are correlative and indicative. Each becomes a barometer for measuring the other's vitality.

The apostle Paul reminded the Gentiles of their reconciliation with Israel through the new humanity created in Jesus Christ:

> Therefore remember that at one time you Gentiles
>   in the flesh . . . were . . . separated from Christ,
>   alienated from the commonwealth of Israel,
>   and strangers to the covenants of promise,
>   having no hope and without God in the world.
>
> But now in Christ Jesus
>   you who once were far off
>   have been brought near
> in the blood of Christ.

---

[1] Martin Buber, *I and Thou*, trans. by Ronald Gregor Smith. Edinburgh, Clark, 1952.

For he is our peace,
>who has made us both one,
>and has broken down the dividing wall of hostility, ...
that he might create in himself
>one new man in place of the two, so making peace,
and might reconcile us both to God
>in one body through the cross,
thereby bringing the hostility to an end.

(Ephesians 2: 11-16)

5. THE OLD MAN AND THE NEW MAN

God's everlasting loyalty and man's persistent infidelity present the occasion and the need, respectively, for God's judgment of his people and the renewal of the covenant in each new generation.

From the beginning the covenant dialogue became a lifetime drama of divine-human encounter, with episodes involving

(1) man's rebellion and estrangement from God;

(2) God's judgment and his redemption of man;

(3) man's renewal and responsible participation.

In each generation there is always a remnant in whose hearts covenant loyalty is reborn and through whom the historical continuity of God's purpose is assured.

The new covenant in Jesus Christ is the good news that God's sovereign righteousness and steadfast love have brought about a redemption for mankind that is universal and "once for all." Not only is each generation assured of covenant renewal, but history itself has entered upon a New Era. The Savior is a second Adam, and his church a new creation.

For as in Adam all die,
>so also in Christ shall all be made alive.

Thus it is written,
>"The first man Adam became a living being";
>the last Adam became a life-giving spirit.

(1 Corinthians 15: 22, 45)

C. The Story of the Bible, Generation After Generation

Taking account of the fact that, throughout the story of humanity's encounter with the living God, the same plot has been repeated, generation after generation, we can reconstruct the whole biblical drama of human history as follows:

PROLOGUE—*Divine Creation and Human Existence*

In the beginning, God makes a covenant with his people. The creation of Adam out of the dust, the call of Abraham from Ur of the Chaldees, the election of Israel in Egypt, the birth of Jesus in Bethlehem, are different ways of announcing and reaffirming God's troth: "You shall be my people, and I will be your God." He gives humankind the assurance of his love and of his righteousness, and he asks of them loyalty and faithful service.

ACT I—*Human Sin and Divine Judgment*

The first Act of man opens with a scene that is as surprising as it is disappointing. Adam and Eve fall prey to the serpent's temptation and are expelled from the Garden of Eden. Rivalry, dishonesty, greed, violence, and disaster mark the generations of Isaac, Jacob, and his sons. Israel rejects her Lord for the Baal landlords. God and his people are estranged (Isa. 1). The marriage is broken (Hos. 1). The children of God are lost in a far country (Luke 15). Even Jesus is born in exile and suffers temptation. But God is faithful to his troth. He continues to sustain and govern his world with love and righteousness, even though the people's infidelity brings down judgment upon their heads.

ACT II—*God Raises Up a Deliverer to Redeem His People and Sets Them Free*

The second Act portrays the most astonishing incident in the whole drama. The covenant people have rejected their heritage and are enslaved by the powers of evil. This and more they have fully deserved. In the midst of their misery they find that, by no merit of their own, God has raised up a deliverer to save them. God has sent a redeemer to buy his people back from bondage. In one situation this redeemer is symbolized by a Noah and his ark. In another he is a Joseph, bringing his brethren and his father into the security of Egypt. In one age he is a Moses leading Israel out of bondage; in another it is the judges who save them, generation after generation, from their enemies. And at long last, all of these presage the coming of the Messiah, who is God's redeemer sent not just to save Israel, but by vanquishing the powers of evil to bring freedom to all humankind (Isa. 49). This is the mightiest act of all. It is the mystery of Jesus Christ, the Word become flesh (John 1: 1-17), and the Suffering Servant (Phil. 2: 1-11).

ACT III—*God's People Are Restored and Acknowledge Their Covenant Responsibility*

The third Act announces the restoration of a remnant covenant community, among the people of God who have been redeemed. This is the meaning of the rainbow for Noah, of Canaan for Abraham, and the promised land for Joshua and the children of Israel. For the generation of the exile in Babylon it is the promise of the re-establishment of the remnant of Israel. Reduced to a remnant of one, in Jesus Christ, there arises out of him a new covenant fellowship among his people. This is the Christian church, to whom the Holy Spirit was originally given at Pentecost, whose vocation is to live in the Spirit of the Redeemer and to be faithful in the stewardship of his love and righteousness in the world.

EPILOGUE—*The Coming Age of God's Kingdom Is Assured*

And, finally, there is the anticipation of the consummation of God's kingdom, the promise of universal peace, of God's final victory over the powers of evil and the estrangement of our human life. "Jesus Christ is Lord of the church and of all the world." (Cf. Isa. 2, Daniel, Matt. 25, the book of Revelation.)

This is the story of the Bible, generation after generation.

What amazes each new generation of us who live within the Christian church is the discovery that the story of the Bible is our story, that the Bible is our covenant book. It is just like

opening the old family album to trace back our social and biological heritage, to find that it takes us back to great-great-
grandpa's and great-great-grandma's marriage certificate. When
we open the church's family album (the Bible) to trace back
our moral and spiritual heritage, we find that it leads us to another marriage—the covenant of God made with the chosen people of Israel and renewed with the disciples and apostles of Jesus
Christ as the Christian church. The word by which God has
plighted his troth is affirmed again and again:

> "I will take you for my people,
> and I will be your God."
> (Exodus 6: 7)

This shows us why the Bible of the old and new covenant is
recognized as our ultimate source of authority when questions
concerning the meaning of our life are faced. It is not primarily
because of the ideas about God and man which are to be found
within the Bible, but rather because of the conversations that are
recorded there—the promises and demands which God himself
makes and the responses which come from his people. By identifying ourselves with our spiritual forebears, we are able in the
reading of these conversations to hear God speak to us as he
spoke to them. We hear him say to us: "You shall be my people,
and I will be your God." We too hear him ask, "Whom shall I
send, and who will go for us?" Coached by Isaiah's answer, we
learn to say, "Here I am. Send me."

The Bible, therefore, when taken as our family covenant album, is as important for what God tells us about ourselves, when
we read his conversations, as for what he is revealing about himself. When we read the Scriptures in this light, we discover that
the focal point of our biblical heritage is the unfolding of "The
Story of Our Life in Covenant Encounter with the Living God."

PART TWO

A Covenant Theology
The Story of Our Life in Encounter with the Living God

The covenant drama begins and ends in mystery. It begins in the mystery of God's election in creation (the PROLOGUE), and points toward the consummation of his purpose in the glorious kingdom of God (the EPILOGUE).

In between these two, the Alpha and the Omega of "The Mighty Acts of God," the Christian church confesses the story of our life in covenant encounter with the living God, revealed in Jesus Christ.

THE PROLOGUE
DIVINE CREATION AND HUMAN EXISTENCE

In which we ask:
Who are we meant to be, in the purpose of God?

To which our Christian faith answers and confesses:
We believe in one God the Father Almighty,
Maker of heaven and earth,
And of all things visible and invisible.
We acknowledge that we are the children of God,
Creatures vested with responsibility,
And endowed with creative powers.
We are meant to be stewards of creation,
And servants of peace and righteousness
in the covenant community.

Thus says God, the Lord,
who created the heavens and stretched them out,
who spread forth the earth and what comes from it,
who gives breath to the people upon it
and spirit to those who walk in it:
"I am the Lord, I have called you in righteousness,
I have taken you by the hand and kept you;
I have given you as a covenant to the people,
a light to the nations.

(Isaiah 42: 5-6; cf. 40: 28; 48: 12-13)

"In the beginning . . . God created man in his own image."
This is the way our biblical drama opens. Here, we confess, the
story of the life of each one of us begins. Nonetheless, the meaning of our beginning is still an enigma to human thought.
Throughout the ages some of the best minds have been inspired
to try to cope with this mystery. Early Greek mythology and
later philosophic thought have coalesced to give us the picture
of a "golden age" in the past, from which the present has de-
generated. The Hebrew prophets tell of a pristine "age of inno-

cence" in the Garden of Eden, where Adam was "what man was meant to be" before he fell away from God's will. On the other hand, some modern scientists and philosophers speculate that human history is the story of the "ascent of man" from more primitive stages of life to the one we now enjoy.

Humanly speaking, any knowledge of our creation involves us in a feat of retrospective imagination and vicarious reminding achieved through reading the story of our life backward.

A. Reading Life Backward from the Middle

Take, for example, the experience of coming in late to a movie or a play. The action has already begun. How disconcerting! We keep wondering what has already happened. Our fate accepted, we settle down and identify ourselves with the present action. Finally, when the play reaches its climax, we are able to read backward what the opening scene revealed about the plot.

This is a parable of our life. Though in the world from birth, only much later do we first become aware of the meaning of what took place in the beginning. I am quite sure I did not understand childhood when I was living in it, as now I have come to appreciate its significance in the lives of our children. In fact, each of us lives a childhood twice. Through a kind of "flash-back" experience we relive our lives, again and again, through our children or those young people who are close to us in our mature years. The striking thing is that nearly one third of life is past before we become seriously concerned to ask, "What does it mean?" "Why was I put here?" "What is God's purpose for me?" From this perspective, therefore, we set about to read life backward, hoping to discover the meaning of what happened "before we came in."

The truth expressed in this parable is the reason for our presenting the Christian doctrine of "the creation of man" as the PROLOGUE to the drama of our life in divine-human covenant encounter. The first of the mighty acts of God happens "before we come in." It is, however, the fundamental basis for understanding all that happens in the personal dialogue with God which follows. Thus, we acknowledge that God's act of creation is first not merely in time but also in significance.

We have other symbols of this "coming into the middle" and understanding life backward. The greatest of these is our calendar. Our Christian civilization reckons time from the middle of history. It dates from the central event of human history: God's redemptive act in the birth, life, death, and resurrection of Jesus Christ. Thus, we count time in two directions—as we live it forward, *Anno Domini*, in the year of our Lord, and as we read it backward, B.C., that is, before Christ.

It is then from the middle of life, from the perspective of Christ in our life, that we are able to go back to its beginning, asking and answering, meaningfully, the basic questions concerning God's purpose in creation. Although, traditionally, systematic theology has always started from the beginning, from God's point of view, Christian faith understands much better from the middle, where we actually live.

We have already observed that the Hebrew people had the same experience in understanding the meaning of their national life. As the prophets looked back upon the most important events in their history, they singled out one creative act of God as the one by which their national existence had been determined. The exodus, they declared, was the occasion which marked the beginning of God's activity in their national life. God had chosen them. God had loved them when they were unlovely, thereby creating out of nothing a people for himself. In fact, however, the exodus, as a point in history, came long after the beginning of life. Therefore, the prophets proceeded to think farther back to the beginnings, not just of their national history but of all human history, of universal history. They wrote a gloriously imaginative account of the beginnings of the world in the first chapters of Genesis. "In the beginning God created the heavens and the earth. . . . And the Spirit of God moved over the face of the waters. And God said, "Let there be light and darkness . . . a world in the midst of the firmament . . . living things . . . human beings. And God saw everything that he had made, and behold, it was very good" (Gen. 1: 1-31).

To be sure, in the generation in which I was a student, the doctrine of creation was a controversial issue. At that time there was a tremendous conflict going on, because there were those who wanted to have not only an explanation of the meaning of our life but to find within the biblical structure that which would stand up to modern scientific theories of biological evolution and relativity physics. It comes quite clear to us now that the interest of the Hebrew prophets in understanding the beginnings of the world was not at all a scientific inquiry into the origin of the natural universe. Their chief concern was to ask: "What explains human existence?" "What is the meaning of our being here?" In this regard the prophets have their own basic principle of interpretation. It is the covenant election by which God has chosen to make "everyman" his own. We should not ask the prophets to be experts in another field.

This is not to depreciate the concern and the contribution of natural science, for which we are so deeply indebted to our Greek heritage. It is rather to say that natural science was not the Hebrew prophets' calling. Moreover, to adopt the prophetic perspective is not at all to deny the importance of scientific knowledge about the beginning of the natural universe and of the human species. Rather, it is to acknowledge a fundamental division of labor among our intellectual disciplines, and to affirm that Christian theology's task is primarily concerned with a Christological interpretation of history.

Actually, it is in the New Testament that we learn this method of understanding our creation through the redemptive work of God at the center of history.[1] The opening chapter of John's

---

[1] "The gospel does not depend on whether the earth is round or flat or whether it is supported on the backs of elephants or 'on the waters under the earth,' or on whether the universe is finite or infinite, expanding or contracting. The spatial terms of the New Testament, the 'up' and 'down,' do not affect the validity of the gospel which was proclaimed in that world any more than it has been substantially affected by the change from the physics of Newton to that of Einstein. As far as precision of location is concerned, it does not matter whether Christ sits 'at the right hand of God' or whether he is diffused throughout space. The efficacy of the Atonement and the proclamation

Gospel declares that the Word (God's covenant promise and demand) which became flesh in Jesus Christ and dwelt among us, full of grace and truth, was in the beginning with God. All things were made through the Word, and without his Word was not anything made that was made (John 1: 14, 2-3).

This is the pattern by which the Christian church has taught us to interpret the meaning of our existence. We acknowledge that the covenant of love and righteousness, in which we live through faith in Jesus Christ our Redeemer, is grounded in God the Father, the Creator of heaven and earth, and will be consummated in his glorious kingdom of heaven. If we are asked to explain our origin or our destiny, we confess that we live and move and have our being in the mysterious purpose of God's holy love and that the God and Father of our Lord Jesus Christ is the same yesterday, today, and forever.

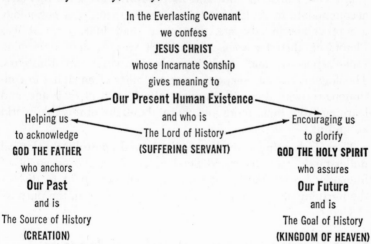

In the Everlasting Covenant
we confess
JESUS CHRIST
whose Incarnate Sonship
gives meaning to
Our Present Human Existence

Helping us   and who is   Encouraging us
to acknowledge   The Lord of History   to glorify
GOD THE FATHER   (SUFFERING SERVANT)   **GOD THE HOLY SPIRIT**
who anchors   who assures
Our Past   **Our Future**
and is   and is
The Source of History   The Goal of History
(CREATION)   (KINGDOM OF HEAVEN)

In summary may we say, therefore, that: (1) The Christian doctrine of creation is a confession of faith, not a cosmological

---

of salvation are not affected by whether, depending on the point of observation, the earth goes round the sun or by whether, as may well be possible in relativity physics, the sun goes round the earth."—Geraint V. Jones, *Christology and Myth in the New Testament* (Allen and Unwin, Ltd.)

theory. It is expressed in terms of a universal covenant myth or parable, arising out of the Christological interpretation of history.

(2) The Christian doctrine of creation universalizes the prophetic conception of God as the Ground and Goal of Israel's existence (election and destiny). It differs from the classical philosophical arguments which rest upon a temporal-causal interpretation of the natural universe. In place of "God as the logical First Cause," Christian faith posits "God as the eternal Ground and Goal of existence." God is thereby infinitely more than a remote instigator of a cosmic process. He is the ever present active initiator and providential director of historic events (for example, call of Abraham; exodus; fall and restoration of Jerusalem; birth, life, death, and resurrection of Jesus; the rise and servant mission of the Christian church).

(3) Our Christian faith and its interpretation of history may accommodate to itself whatever scientific theories of cosmology are prevalent in any age. For more than 1,000 years it was Platonism, then for some centuries it was Aristotle's teaching (scholasticism), and more recently Darwin's and Einstein's. Theologians cannot escape the responsibility of engaging in continuous conversation with the natural scientists of their age, and learning from them more and more about the observable world around us.

Thus, in keeping with the prophetic and apostolic theological understanding of history, defined in terms of the covenant of humankind with the living God, we shall set about to discuss the meaning of the origin of man and of his place in the purpose of God.

B. The Meaning of Creation: The Analogy of Procreation

What our biblical heritage tells us, and what our own experience indicates, is that the creation of Adam (humankind) is very much like, and is well symbolized by, the birth of a child. In truth, each one of us was created just that way, as a little child. This view implies that our faith in the divine creation is not derived from information about an incident which happened once upon a time, way back when, and which can be dated either by studying geology, anthropology, archaeology, or by guessing. Our faith involves our understanding that creation is actually a continuing activity of God, including the bringing forth of little children by means of one generation procreating another. Each of us is created, not way back there, but at the time of his own conception and birth.

There are two very significant characteristics about the birth of a child. One of these is symbolized by the umbilical cord, the other by the navel, the umbilical scar after the cord is cut. The umbilical cord symbolizes our creatureliness, our utter dependence upon parents for our procreation. On the other hand, the cutting of the umbilical cord symbolizes our being put here in a world in which, sooner or later, we will have to stand on our own feet and become individual, separate persons. These are the two basic aspects of our human life as we know it: one, our *creatureliness* and *dependence;* the other, our *freedom* and *creativity.* One represents our need for security; the other our capacity for responsibility. The truth of the matter is that we can never destroy the reality of either of these characteristics.

Human life is inherently basically bipolar. Our biblical account of the creation affirms the fundamental tension that lies at the heart of our human situation in the words:

> God created man in his own image,
> in the image of God he created him.
> (Genesis 1: 27)

These two aspects of our life are inherently ambiguous, creatureliness and "the image of God."

There is also a very simple but profound parable which is told by the prophet who wrote Genesis 2: 7. We may suppose that this is the way many Hebrew parents told it to their little children, generation after generation, in ancient times.

> The Lord God formed man of dust from the ground,
> and breathed into his nostrils the breath of life;
> and man became a living being.

Here, in quite different language, the same ambiguity is being declared. To be formed of the dust of the earth, the symbol of nature, is the mark of our creatureliness, our dependence. On the other hand, the gift of God's own spirit marks our endowment with personal character and responsible individuality.

The biblical view of man as "a unity of nature and spirit" must be carefully distinguished from the Greek mythological conception of man which, although verbally similar, is in reality quite different. This other tradition in our western culture claims that man's internal conflicts arise from the fact that his existence unites two disparate substances: soul—essentially good and divine in origin; and body—temporal and essentially evil. The good life is presumed to depend upon the rigorous discipline of "mind over matter."

The biblical view, by contrast, makes it quite clear that in both aspects of our given human situation we are divinely derived but nonetheless temporal. Our "creatureliness" incorporates all our being, including the "image of God" reflected by us. The divine origin even of our bodies, on the other hand, marks our whole being as fundamentally "good." The biblical heritage underscores God's expression of satisfaction with his creative work. "Behold, it was very good." Both good and evil are therefore functional. The responsive spirit is good; the rebellious, evil. By the same token authenticity and pretension are the yardsticks of good and evil in regard to all our creaturely functions.

What is God's intention for us, in making us as he has, "creatures in his own image"? It would be conceited of us to claim to know.

The biblical confession, that our life's center of gravity is established in the mystery of God's election, simply affirms his holy righteousness and love as our origin and our destiny without uncovering the blueprint of his plan. One hypothetical explanation is that these ambiguous characteristics would serve as checks upon each other to keep us from overestimating either our limitations as creatures or our possibilities as the stewards of his spiritual gift.

The difficulty with this explanation, however, is patent. Our actual human situation, apart from the grace of our Lord Jesus Christ, indicates that finiteness (the threat of death) and freedom (the urge to live) are helpless to effect stability in human beings. It is precisely the extravagant demands that each and both place upon the faithfulness of man that keep him everlastingly in the state of tension which is called "anxiety" (the insecurity of faith continually tempted to unfaith). Cf. ACT I, Scene 1.

1. RELIGION

Our creatureliness always reminds us that we are dependent upon God not only for the source of our existence but for the goal of it. This is his world; our end, like our beginning, lies with him. We are led, thereby, to acknowledge that it is his life he has put into us, and that we are bound always to be amenable to his will in using it and in fulfilling it. This is the basis of religion in human life. As in the symbolism of the umbilical cord, our finiteness reminds us that our safety depends upon our being properly "bound back" to the source of our life in worship. Religion, derived from the Latin word *re-ligare*, means "to bind back."

Being religious, therefore, expresses our need of, and our lifelong search for, security and re-creation. Every man, like his brother, is religious, including the communist and the capitalist, the churchman and the atheist, the primitive man and the sophisticated modern. Every man seeks for security, and that in which he finds, or thinks he finds, a dependable security functions for him as "god." But religiousness is only one half of life; when taken by itself it inevitably leads to some form of idolatry. Sooner or later, all our idols of creaturely satisfaction, knowledge, or virtue, are discredited as "homemade gods" and inadequate to our fundamental needs.

2. EXISTENCE

The other half of our human life is actually more distinctively human, but equally as vicious when distorted. The definitive word for it is *existence*, that is, personal existence. This word, like religion, defines itself. Existence comes from the Latin *ex-sistere*, which means "to be put out," "to be placed over against." In biblical terms this is the description of man created *in the image of God* and endowed with *response-ability*. Thus, the image of God is symbolic of the fact that, since we are cut off from our source of procreation (the meaning of the umbilical scar), we must stand out here subject to face-to-face encounter (1) with the world around us, (2) with other people, and (3) most basically of all, with him who created us, and who holds us responsible for his gift of creative power.

Simply put, the uniqueness of God's purpose for us as human beings is that we are meant to be creative and responsible animals. We *are* animals—that we must always remember. Our natural origin stamps it indelibly upon us. But we are unique animals, marked by God's own image. We are the only animals who know that we are animals, and can get away with calling ourselves by animal names in jest. Think of the number of animal epithets that we use for ourselves when we call each other, in disrepute, skunk, hog, cat, snake, squirrel, wolf. It goes up and down the line, does it not? We are aware that we are animals, and yet we have a capacity to see ourselves from a perspective beyond our animality. And so we can either laugh at ourselves, as we are doing right now, or very seriously condemn one another by using these animal names. This is the first mark of our capacity for personal responsibility as human beings—that we are made to be more than animals.

G. K. Chesterton seems always to have a story appropriate to any occasion. He is reported to have told this one in an effort to distinguish the basic difference between man and the animals. When you find a man, he said, who has just downed his tenth whisky, you would, even so, very likely slap him on the back and say, "Be a man!" On the other hand, however, if you were to meet a crocodile that had just downed his tenth missionary, you wouldn't pat him on the back and say, "Be a crocodile!"

What may be normal animality for animals becomes debauchery in man and as such is basically a sickness. And it must be treated as a sickness, so that the person is not merely condemned but is brought to a state of healing. No matter what form the misery of human bondage may take, whether it be of body, mind, or spirit, there is still the mark of God's own image upon us by virtue of which the therapist may expect that his healing work will bring response. This is undoubtedly what Harvey Cushing meant when, in *The Life of Sir William Osler*, he affirmed that "the desire to take medicine is perhaps the greatest feature which distinguished man from the animals."

We are made for fellowship with God. We are made to stand "over against" him that we may engage in conversation with him and take directions from him in fulfilling his purpose. Even when we are most recalcitrant and unresponsive, we are aware of our destiny and are chastened by it to return to our responsibility. The image of God in the creature, however much it may be besmirched, is still the Creator's gift of his own creative spirit and our sole source of worth as human beings.

3. OUR PROPER ROLE

In Jesus Christ, in whom we see ourselves "as we ought to have been" most clearly, we envisage the character of human responsibility in its fullness. We are meant to be:

(1) the recipients of God's blessing of love and righteousness in the family and the intimate covenant community.

(2) the servants of his peace and justice in the expansion of "community" throughout the world.

(3) the stewards, that is, responsible guardians, of his entire creation, both human and natural.

C. The Providence of God's Holy Love and Sovereign Righteousness

The ambiguous character of our life in God's covenant reflects the fact that his own nature is bipolar, that we need to use two words together to express his inner character. The essence of God cannot quite be expressed in one word at a time. At least, in so far as we are able to understand him, we are unable to express all his nature in a single concept. In the New Testament one of the greatest words we find to describe God is contained in the verse that we first teach to little children: "God is love." Yet we are aware that this is not all that God is, nor all that God stands for in his covenant relationship with us. His love may say, "You shall be my people, always." But one has to find some other word to say the sterner thing which he is affirming when he says, "and I *will* be your God." The Scripture expresses this element of firmness and determination in the word "righteousness." God is righteous as well as merciful. He stands for all that is right and good and true, as well as for care, concern, helpfulness, and mercy.

We are surprised that in God these two capacities, rigorousness and gentleness, righteousness and love, discipline and nurture, freedom and order, are capable of operating together without contradiction, because we find it so difficult to keep them in balance in ourselves. This is why we are both serious-minded and facetious when we refer to the woodshed incident, in which father says, "This hurts me more than it does you." Seriously this implies that even the human father's firmness does not cover up the fact that his love goes out to the transgressor. This is something of the experience that we all have with our parents when we are still young, and later as parents with our own children.

The witness of the Old Testament prophets and New Testament apostles concurs in reporting that God has revealed himself in his covenant as the Holy Spirit of love and the sovereign vindicator of righteousness. In the power of his righteousness we are disciplined for freedom and creative individuality. By the power of his love we are nurtured for security and an orderly pattern of life.

Although it would be a mistake for theologians to blur the distinction between love and righteousness, it is their duty not only to clarify the polarity between them but to explain as clearly as possible the form of God's unity which incorporates both characteristics. In biblical language the unity of God is his holiness. The prophets call him the Holy One of Israel. His worshipers sing his praises: "Holy, holy, holy is the Lord of Hosts." The followers of our Lord Jesus received the gift of the Holy Spirit at Pentecost.

Holiness represents the "divineness" of God, his own transcendent power and integrity through which he expresses the wholeness of his purpose for the world and by which he maintains his sovereignty over it. In the power of his holiness we account not only for the polar unity of love and righteouness, but also for the polarity of power with righteousness and of love with power. The polar unity of love and righteousness in the Being of God, as manifest in his mighty acts of judgment and redemption, points "backward" to the polarity of power with righteousness in the creation (God the Father) and "forward" to the polarity of love and power in the consummation of his covenant purpose (God the Holy Spirit).

The classical diagram of the doctrine of the Trinity (cf. the EPILOGUE, p. 139 ff., where this teaching is discussed in more detail) allows us to acknowledge these various manifestations of his love, power, and righteousness, while affirming their ultimate unity and co-equality in the holiness of his Being.

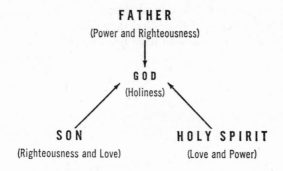

FATHER
(Power and Righteousness)

GOD
(Holiness)

SON
(Righteousness and Love)

HOLY SPIRIT
(Love and Power)

ACT I

OUR HUMAN SIN AND THE DIVINE JUDGMENT

In which we ask:
What have we done?

To which our Christian faith answers and confesses:
Through infidelity, we have rejected God's covenant
of love and righteousness.
We are estranged, and enslaved to the shadows
of our own pretensions.
We acknowledge that we are subject to the judgment
of God's holy will.

Thus says the Lord:
"For three transgressions of Israel,
and for four, I will not revoke the punishment;
because they sell the righteous for silver,
and the needy for a pair of shoes—
they . . . trample the head of the poor into the dust of
the earth,
and turn aside the way of the afflicted;
a man and his father go in to the same maiden,
so that my holy name is profaned;
they lay themselves down beside every altar,
upon garments taken in pledge;
and in the house of their God they drink
the wine of those who have been fined."

(Amos 2: 6-8)

In the context of the biblical covenant we are retelling the story of our life in dialogue with the living God. The first act of God is his creation, in which the Lord has bound us to himself for time and eternity. We were there, but we have to confess that our understanding of it is largely a matter of retrospective imagination informed by the re-creation in the person of Jesus Christ. From the perspective of human history, therefore, the creation is the PROLOGUE of the drama of our life. It raises the question, "Who are we meant to be, in the purpose of God?"

To this question our Christian faith answers and confesses that we are the children of God, creatures of his, who are endowed with his own creative powers and vested with moral responsibility. We are meant to be the stewards, that is, the responsible guardians, of his entire creation, both human and natural. We are called to be servants of peace and justice in and through the covenant community.

The first episode in which we become conscious participants, however—our ACT I in the covenant encounter—is the story of how we mess up the plot. The beautiful theme of the Garden of Eden music is distorted and nearly drowned out by discord and confusion when man begins to conduct the show. This is undoubtedly disconcerting to God. It is very painful to man. In distress he cries out: "What have we done?"

SCENE 1
THE FALL OF MAN

Someone has observed that man is his own worst enemy. Nothing could be closer to the truth. Take poverty and want, for example. They have dogged the heels of men and civilizations from the beginning of history. This has been so, not because the good earth has failed to produce an adequate supply of food to assure the children of men the basic essentials of livelihood. Rather, the responsibility lies with man himself, for it is he who persists in building and maintaining the economic, political, and social barriers which produce the evils of plenty versus want, luxury versus poverty.

Again, take war. It is not atomic energy by itself which threatens to destroy us in this generation. On the contrary, by the ingenuity of our human minds *we* have constructed atoms into bombs, and by virtue of the sickness of our human wills *we* propose to drop them upon each other. It is neither our knowledge nor our ignorance which makes us a threat to each other and to ourselves. It is the willful confusion of our knowledge by fear and pretension that makes us such despicable fools.

Probably no one has given us a more vivid picture of the inexorable logic of our human perversity than has Frances V. C. Hitchcock[1] in a piece called "The Creation in Reverse":

And the earth had been beautiful and light shone upon it, but the spirit of man moved upon the earth and man's darkness grew and increased and man saw that it was growing darker and he was pleased, and it was the seventh day before the end.

And man said: "Let us have power in the earth." So man divided nation against nation and man made one nation to war against another nation and it was so. And man called this "civilization," and this was the sixth day before the end.

And man said: "Let us gather together our resources into one place and let us bring forth more tanks and more guns and more ships." And it was so. And man saw his power increase, and it was now the fifth day before the end.

And man said: "Let us name the great nations to be our 'security,' and let us call the lesser ones 'secure.'" And man was pleased with this. And it was now the fourth day before the end.

And man said, "Let our 'security' bring forth abundantly, more cars after their kind, more radios after their kind, more of everything after its kind." And man was pleased with this abundance of things.

And man ordered that the number of all these things be in-

<hr>

[1] Presbyterian missionary to Colombia, South America. From *Colombian Clippings*.

creased a thousandfold, and it was now the third day before the end.

And man said, "Let us continue to smash the atom, that more and more power shall be ours. We shall increase our abundance of things and shall quickly destroy those who oppose us." And man continued his experiment with the atom and was pleased. And it was now the second day before the end.

And on the last day there was a great noise upon the face of the earth. And there was no more man to be pleased and rejoice in his works.

This satirical paraphrase on man's reversal of the purpose of creation is a caricature. Like every caricature, it takes one feature of a person or one aspect of a situation and enlarges it out of perspective. This one, for example, portrays man's faithless pretension in the distortion of God's purpose.

And the earth had been beautiful and light shone upon it, but the spirit of man moved upon the earth and man's darkness grew and increased and man saw that it was growing darker and he was pleased . . . .

As such, this is a superb parable of our life. But it reckons without the power of God to fulfill his purpose, despite and even including our defection. In fact, this story takes no account of the covenant. It treats what we call ACT I of the covenant drama as if it were the last Act, in contradiction to the theme of the PROLOGUE, making no place for the redemptive and re-creative work of God in our history. On the contrary, our human situation as creative creatures must ultimately always be kept in the perspective of God's purpose and of the power of God's love, as revealed in Jesus Christ.

There is, nonetheless, a tremendous truth expressed in "The Creation in Reverse." It is an indication of what man, taken apart from God, is threatening to make of man. It portrays how utterly destructive infidelity can be and how completely our human hope must be rooted in the assurance that God is faithful, even though man is not.

It has been the genius of Christian thinking to trace the root of all evil in our human life to infidelity and rebellion, that is, to our willful rejection of God's intention that his people live together in righteousness and peace. Infidelity, rebellion, disobedience, are the common words used by our prophetic heritage to describe Israel's response to God and his covenant. We know what they mean in our own experience. Put in psychological and social terms they describe the common human predilection for greed and lust, for jealousy and rivalry, for exploitation and war, the idolatrous worship of Baal, Mammon, and Mars.

A. A Parable of Everyman

The creation story, in the book of Genesis, carries a sequel, which is a parable of what Everyman (Adam) does when God puts him in the Garden of Eden "to till it and keep it." Adam and Eve are portrayed as having all they need, even though they do not have everything. God has given them the whole garden, with the exception of the fruit of one tree. And it was not until the serpent slyly insinuated that they were missing out on something that they began to want it all.

The Lord God commanded the man, saying,
"You may freely eat of every tree of the garden;
    but of the tree of the knowledge of good and evil
        you shall not eat,
    for in the day that you eat of it
        you shall die."

And the man and his wife were both naked,
    and were not ashamed.

Now the serpent . . . said to the woman,
    "Did God say,
        'You shall not eat of any tree in the garden'?"

And the woman said to the serpent
    [all that God had said].

But the serpent said to the woman,

"You will not die.

For God knows . . ."

So when the woman saw that the tree was good for food,
and that it was a delight to the eyes,
and that the tree was to be desired to make one wise,
she took of its fruit and ate;
and she also gave some to her husband,
and he ate.

The Lord God called to the man, and said to him,

"Where are you?"

And he said,

"I heard the sound of thee in the garden,
and I was afraid, because I was naked;
and I hid myself."

(Genesis 2: 16-17, 25; 3: 1-6, 9-10)

Perhaps we show the subtlety of our human pretension most of all in the confusion we allow ourselves regarding the boundary line between what we need and what we want. It is so easy on the surface of things to equate wants and needs. This is because we are generally inclined to define our needs in terms of our wants. The striking thing is that this "sickness" is as evident in children as it is in adults. When Grandma came to visit her two little grandchildren at Christmas time, she brought them both gifts. She knew that there might develop some jealousy between them, so she decided to bring them each the same gift but in different colors. When she opened the package, she said, "Now, Mary, which one do you want?" Mary thought for only a second, and said, "I want Johnny's!"

It is so easy to lose sight of the boundary line between our wants and our needs. Our wants are limitless. We want so many things that we do not need, and yet we can convince ourselves that we need them very much. Remember the children's story called "The Fisherman and His Wife."

A fisherman lived with his wife in a wretched hovel by the

sea, and every day he went out fishing. Once, as he was sitting with his rod, looking at the clear water, his line suddenly went far down below and, when he drew it out, up came a big flounder.

Said the flounder, "Hark, you, fisherman, I pray you put me back in the water. I am no common fish; I am a fish who can grant people their wishes."

"Come," said the fisherman, "deliver me from a fish that talks!" With that he put the flounder back into the water, and down went the flounder to the bottom of the sea. Then the fisherman went home to his wife.

"Have you caught nothing today?" said the woman.

"I drew up a flounder," said the fisherman, "but he said he was no common fish—he was a fish who granted people their wishes, so I put him back in the water."

"Well, and what did you wish for?" asked the woman.

"Oh!" said the man, "what should I wish for? I wished for nothing. I'm quite content with what I have."

"Ah, you stupid good-for-nothing!" cried the woman. "It is surely hard to have to live always in such a wretched hovel; you might have wished for a pretty cottage. Go back and call the fish. Tell him we want a pretty cottage; he will surely give us that."

The man did not quite like to go, as he could see no reason why he should trouble the fish again. But his wife insisted, so at last he went. The water was all green and yellow now and no longer smooth as it had been before, but the fisherman stood by the sea and said:

> "O Fish of the Sea, come, listen to me,
>   For Alice, my wife, the plague of my life,
>   Has sent me to get a boon of thee."

Up came the fish. "What does she want?" he said.

"Ah!" said the man, "she says I should have asked you to grant us a wish. She does not like to live in a wretched hovel any longer. She would like a little cottage."

"Go," said the fish, "she has it already." . . .

In rapid succession and in increasing tempo the fish was called upon to grant her wants—"a stone mansion," "a palace," "to be king!" The fish was obliging in each instance, albeit with growing disgust, until the man came again with another request.

"What does she want now?" said the fish, and his voice was strange and threatening.

"She wants to be Lord of the sun and the moon, so they dare not rise save at her command!"

"Go!" said the fish. "She is back in the hovel."

And there they live to this very day.[2]

Whatever else we may think about the serpent in the Garden of Eden, at least this much is true. The serpent represents the aspect of our human existence that tends to blur the boundary line between needs and wants, driving us to want more and more until we want to be "like God." But more than this, does it not represent the temptation that tickles an inveterate obstinacy in human nature, an everlasting *un*willingness to accept life as it is given to us, without attempting to manipulate it to some other end?

At any rate, Adam and Eve "fall" for the serpent's suggestion that they could run the Garden more efficiently and more equitably than God had proposed. And their "fall" has become a by-word in theology to express what we mean when we acknowledge that we are not "what we are meant to be." Knowing that we are meant to be "creative creatures," faithful stewards of God's Garden, we try desperately to fulfill our pretension to be its lords. But when the Lord comes into the Garden we run and hide behind the bushes, because we are naked. And with good reason, for the Lord God soon makes it quite clear that he plans to run the Garden according to the original rules, and that arguing with the Umpire is the most disastrous of pretensions.

---

[2] Adapted from Grimms' *Household Tales* by Olive Beaupré Miller. From *My Book House.* Used by permission of the author and The Book House for Children, publishers.

B. Life vs. Death: Anxiety

The explanation for the fall of man is difficult to find. That the occasion of our fall is the ambiguity of our given situation as "creatures in God's own image" is fairly clear. We are an uneasy combination of freedom and dependence,[3] of separation and reunion, of creativity and the need for re-creation, of existence and religion. But why the fall should have happened and how it comes to affect us all in such a disastrous way is hard to explain. To say that its meaning is hid in the mystery of God's holy purpose is at once to say all that is confessionally possible, and at the same time a temptation to hide from facing up to the knotty intellectual problems that arise out of the actual limitations of all human knowledge.

Depth psychology, here as elsewhere, offers a hypothesis that helps a great deal. Incipient in life from its very beginning, this view affirms, is "the threat of death." Birth is itself a "life or death" matter. There is no in-between, and yet death always hovers over, even when life is established. To what extent this knowledge, available to all from observable human experience, is a part of the common "unconscious" of the race is difficult to establish. At any rate, our first "conscious" human reaction to life is one in which we are shocked into the awareness of "insecurity" and of the reality of what has come to be called a "dreadful freedom." Birth is a crisis experience, of distinctly traumatic proportions. The infant is not only involved in forcing his way out of his fetal security, from which he shall soon be permanently cut off—he is literally "shocked into existence." He is forced to breathe, that is, to live, by a timely slap on the back. Significantly, the infant's first reaction to life is a cry.

The inevitable expression of our ambiguous status in regard to life (and its entrancing promises) vs. death (and its ominous threat) is the state of tension which is technically known as

---

[3] Here and throughout ACT I the author acknowledges his debt to Reinhold Niebuhr's *Nature and Destiny of Man*. Cf. Volume 1, page 181: "Man is both strong and weak, both free and bound, both blind and farseeing. He stands at the juncture of nature and spirit; and is involved in both freedom and necessity."

anxiety. Anxiety is not simply "fear," for fear arises only when something immediately threatening appears. Anxiety, that is, psychological insecurity, is always with us and has no specific object, because everything is its object. Without continual rapport with forces in a man's environment which are friendly to him, his anxiety becomes inordinate and uncontrollable. This is what makes it so awful. We remember the account given by a practicing psychiatrist regarding the therapy administered to fliers who "cracked up" internally under the unabated tension of successive bombing missions over enemy cities during World War II. The therapy was a hypnotist's simple suggestion to the patient of an actual object of fear; for example, that there was a venomous snake in his bed. The physical effect, he reported, was shattering. When, however, the patient recovered from the shock, his inordinate anxiety was cured.

A normal state of anxiety mothers all our acts and desires, including those which are right and proper, on the one hand, and those which lead us into irresponsibility, on the other hand. No man can live without anxiety. It is the most definitive trait of the human being. A man without any psychological tensions is dead. Our struggle for livelihood, for social security and significance, our desire to be loved and to serve the needs of others, our drive to create and our motivation to seek for recreation—all are conceived in the matrix of human anxiety.

Furthermore, no man can do anything significant in life if he is either "unconcerned" or "too sure of himself." A mother's endless watchfulness over the lives of her children, careful attention to one's task in shop or office, the uneasiness of the farmer about tomorrow's weather, the hustle of the ball player and even frenzied build-up for track and field competition, the rapid heart-beat of the public speaker or singer just before an appearance—all these are normal and healthy expressions of anxiety.

C. Beguiled into Sin: Infidelity and Pretension

Our anxiety becomes activated whenever a decision is to be made or the responsibility of a former decision is to be carried out. This is the point at which the reality of what our biblical heritage calls *sin* appears. We cannot explain its origin logically. We acknowledge that we are responsible for it, and yet we suspect that we have been beguiled into it. In so far as we can see, it is because we are creatures and cannot ever guarantee a perfect balance between our resources and our needs, between our God-given freedom and creativity and our creaturely limitations, that our will is inevitably caught in a state of imbalance and internal disorder. The apostle Paul confesses what we have all experienced:

> I can will what is right,
>   but I cannot do it.
> For I do not do the good I want,
>   but the evil I do not want is what I do.
>   (Romans 7: 18-19)

Sin is functionally this distortion of the inner structure of my being. But it is also the concomitant distortion of my relationship to other beings, and ultimately to the ground of my being in the Creator and Sustainer of life. Since both the first two are merely symptoms of this last, it is the nub of the whole situation. Sin is fundamentally the state of being out of communication with the living God. Morally expressed, it is the *infidelity* to God's love and the *rejection* of God's righteousness which anxiety begets in the decisions we make regarding the use of our freedom and our pursuit of security. The psychological scar of infidelity is pretension, and by it our status is greatly worsened.

To recapitulate: theologically sin is infidelity, that is, failure of faithful response to God's love and open rebellion against God's righteousness; psychologically it is pretension—the falsification of freedom into license and of individuality into self-sufficiency, on the one hand, and the perversion of dependence into parasitism and of creatureliness into murky sensuality on the other. Distorted by pretension, our given ambiguity of spirit and nature, already in a state of anxiety, falls prey to confusion and desperation, making the threat of death all the more evident and ominous.

At this point it must be acknowledged that the Christian doctrine of the fall of man rests upon an apparently unresolvable ambiguity of power. As a creative creature, endowed with spiritual power from on high, that is, with a will to make decisions regarding his own existence, man is held responsible for the way in which he responds to his circumstances. At the same time, however, the total situation of his life, surrounded by incipient and immediate threats of death, inevitably tempts him into infidelity and pretension, thus transforming his divine gift of power into a demonic distortion.

The extremes to which man is driven by demonic pretension purport to offer him opposite but correlative statuses—absolute independence and completely encompassing security. Both carry a morbid fascination, but are in sober truth "unreality."

Living under an inordinate awareness of the threat of death, man's freedom becomes dreadful and his creative powers demonic (witness the atom bomb). He is beguiled into pretending that sovereign authority and full independence are the possible possession of a mere creature or group of creatures. *This is the sin of pride.* It is the inordinate expression of the freedom and creativity of our "existence" and leads logically to the pretense of *self-deification.*

On the other hand, under the same inordinate awareness of the threat of death, man's search for security and re-creation manifests a comparable but contrasting sickness. His insecurity beguiles him into blurring the proper distinctions between want and need, and drives him into an obsessed desire for creaturely comforts and satisfactions. *This is the sin of sensuality.* It is an insatiable dependency and an unhealthy religiosity, and leads logically to utter irresponsibility and *self-abdication.*

The extent to which we attempt to simulate the reality of these unreal pretensions is indicated by the extravagant expression in our human life of the phenomenon known as *idolatry.*

SCENE 2

OUR IDOLATROUS PRETENSIONS: PRIDE AND SENSUALITY

When Israel was a child, I loved him,
and out of Egypt I called my son.
The more I called them,
the more they went from me;
they kept sacrificing to the Ba'als,
and burning incense to idols.

(Hosea 11: 1-2)

The best exemplification of the sins of pride and sensuality and their confused interrelationship is in the popular religion that existed in Israel called Baalism. Indeed, it was both a religion and a theology. It offered religious "security" and the promise of prosperity to all men, and to a few it gave a respectable opportunity to play god with impunity. Baalism was a natural religion. It concentrated its worship upon a power of Nature, specifically the power of fertility, the capacity of creatures to reproduce. The prophets of the Lord quite correctly recognized and declared its cult to be a religiously sanctioned prostitution. But it is a "natural" religion in still another sense. It is as natural as it is for fallen and confused human beings to distort a God-given function and the accompanying creaturely satisfaction into a pump-priming activity whereby to coerce the deity into assuring us of security and perhaps even of success! Baal worship is the original and still champion religion of successful achievement as an end in itself. The Baals were the exploiting absentee landlords in ancient agricultural civilization of Israel. They were the few people who could "play god" and not be challenged, at least not by their tenants. Remember Naboth's vineyard. The Baals represent the philosophy arising everlastingly in the human breast, which whispers, "You can have all the things you want, and perhaps a bonus, if you will only try a little harder!"

And what is more, it pays off. Our distorted (fallen) human perspective always suggests that we look around and see how successful this one is and that one is. He or she did it; why can't we? And we fall for it, just as the minnows in Pestalozzi's story fell for the line that was passed out by the head pike. The story is that once there were living together in a pool of water a school of pike and millions of little minnows. The pike fed on the minnows; finally the minnows organized and objected. The head pike took their complaint under advisement and quickly handed down a decision that seemed to be acceptable: "We will allow one out of every million minnows to become a pike."

The truth is that a few men do seem to get away with playing God. That is what the pike were doing, and so were the Baals. This encourages the rest of us shamefully. Our young people view with envy these pike in the pool of life, and who knows that they were not, one day, little minnows whose cult of success had paid off?

Sensuality as a form of sin is "prostitution" not just of the sex function in life (which is one of the most obvious forms of expression) but of all the functions of life. It is the distortion of life from the service of God to the service of self. It is the corrupt religion of the success-hound, who, like the little minnow, is sooner or later swallowed up by his own ambition. One always seems to wind up like Hosea's wife, Gomer, as the prostitute and never as Baal. Hell is full of little would-be Baals who lost their soul in the struggle for success, and now have neither success nor a soul to be troubled about. The mark of this Hell is emptiness, and although the place is crowded, its inhabitants are terribly lonely.

Pride is the mask of the "successful" sinner. It is surprising, in the light of what we have just said, that a second look at our human situation discloses a myriad of shadows chasing around in the emptiness still searching for success. Poor fools, they thought they had it once, and then for sure! He had risen to be president of his company, and she was the center of the social whirl! Their income had increased from $5,000 per year to nearly $50,000 in a little over 10 years. The only trouble is that they too are horribly lonely, but cannot admit it, at least not to themselves.

94 · A COVENANT THEOLOGY

SCENE 3
OUR MISERY AND THE JUDGMENT OF GOD

Our biblical tradition leads us to diagnose our willful infidelity and rejection of God's plan for our lives as at once involving us in acts of irresponsibility and reducing us to a state of misery. Thus two aspects of our human situation have come to be called sin. Sin is a kind of "activity," that is, pride and sensuality, but it is also a "state of spiritual ill-health." Men not only sin but are sinners; they are sinful. In both aspects sin is broken covenant. As an act sin is "broken faith," that is, un-faith. As a state it is "broken fellowship," that is, estrangement and enslavement.

A. Estrangement from God and Enslavement to Satan

The prophet Jeremiah, in denouncing Israel's apostasy from her Lord, wrote,

> Hear the Word of the Lord:
>
> Has a nation changed its gods,
> even though they are no gods?
> But my people have changed their glory
> for that which does not profit.
> Be appalled, O heavens, at this,
> be shocked, be utterly desolate,
> for my people have committed two evils:
> They have forsaken me,
> the fountain of living waters,
> and hewed out cisterns for themselves,
> broken cisterns, that can hold no water."
>
> (Jeremiah 2: 11-13)

The prophet observed that when we reject the love and righteousness of God, we set about diligently to "make believe" that a worthless substitute can take his place and satisfy our needs. The truth is that whereas in the eyes of God sin is first of all infidelity and rebellion, in our own experience it is also estrangement from the Source of our being and enslavement to the shadows of our own pretension. This demonic perversion of the power of the human will the Bible calls the serpent, Satan, or the devil.

Moreover, the threat of death is reality-based. When the apostle Paul writes that "the wages of sin is death," he is acknowledging the truth that just as the organs of the body cannot live without receiving blood from the heart and then returning it, so as human beings we cannot live without receiving love from God and then returning it. Permanent estrangement from God means the death of the soul. Persistent "pretension" on man's part leads ultimately to destruction in every phase of life, disintegration within the self, war between selves, hell between the self and God.

Death, sin, and Satan are a formidable triumvirate of evil powers in our biblical theology of man. Taken all in all but by themselves, they constitute that complex of factors which represents man's fall into infidelity and pretension, whereby the structures of our life are corrupted and distorted and marked for destruction, spelling out the apparent failure of God's covenant purpose in human history.

B. Man's Extremity Is God's Opportunity

In terms of what God's sovereign purpose is for man, however, death, sin, and Satan represent *the judgment of God.* The sovereign will of God is at work even in our human distortion to sustain "wholeness" and to maintain "righteousness" as against all efforts toward perversion. The demonic powers, which are the distortion of the heavenly gift of power to be a child of God, dragging him down to destruction, are, at the same time, the instrument of God's righteous purpose. They are the "wrath of God" driving man to despair of himself, to confess the guilt of his pretensions, and to reach back for the courage to ask for help.

Clearly our human misery is an enormous distortion of the inner structure of God's purpose for man. But why, one asks, should the distortion be possible and so inevitable? The clue which comes out of our Christian faith at this point is drawn not from our analysis of the human situation itself but from the revelation of the eternal purpose of God in the man Christ Jesus.

Life and death must be faced together. The life and death of our Lord Jesus Christ indicate not only the ultimate victory of life over death, but the power of God to make of the acceptance of death the schoolmaster of courage. Courage[1] is the form of human faith which most nearly represents the faithfulness of God, because it is so utterly devoted to the welfare of others. Courage is faith purified by the cauterizing heat of God's own love. That is to say, faith at its best is the courage to affirm oneself as a servant of God's love and righteousness.

Our human security and freedom, as well as life itself and any hope of a destiny other than death, are all dependent not upon our birth to life but upon the faithfulness of Him who gives us not only life but faith. Faith is the disposition to accept his purpose for our life as it is declared in his covenant troth: "You shall be my people, and I will be your God." When purified it becomes the courage to face the inevitability of death, dying to self and all its pretensions as well as its puny insecurity, and rising in the security of his service.

Almighty and most merciful Father, we have erred and strayed from thy ways like lost sheep. We have followed too much the devices and desires of our own hearts. We have offended against thy holy laws. We have left undone those things which we ought to have done; and we have done those things which we ought not to have done, and there is no health in us. But thou, O Lord, have mercy upon us, miserable offenders. Spare thou those, O God, who confess their faults. Restore thou those who are penitent, according to thy promises declared unto mankind in Christ Jesus our Lord. And grant, O most merciful Father, for his sake, that we may hereafter live a godly, righteous, and sober life, to the glory of thy holy name. Amen.

---

[1] Cf. Paul Tillich, *The Courage to Be*, Yale University Press, 1952. We shall elaborate on this theme on page 180 ff.

ACT II

JESUS CHRIST AND OUR CHRISTIAN FREEDOM

In which we ask:
　What can be done, by the grace of God?

To which our Christian faith answers and confesses:
　God has remained faithful and steadfast,
　　Even though his people are faithless and weak.
　God has raised up a Deliverer to redeem his people.
　　While we were yet helpless, Christ died for us.
　　For freedom Christ has set us free.
　We rejoice in God through our Lord Jesus Christ,
　　Through whom we have now received our reconciliation.

> In the beginning was the Word,
>   and the Word was with God,
>   and the Word was God.
>
> And the Word became flesh
>   and dwelt among us,
>   full of grace and truth;
>
> We have beheld his glory,
>   glory as of the only Son
>   from the Father.
>
> And from his fullness
>   have we all received,
>   grace upon grace.
>
> (John 1: 1, 14, 16)

The central act in our biblical covenant drama, ACT II, is the one in which God raises up a Deliverer for his people. This is "the event" which we call the gospel of Jesus Christ, the good news that God has renewed, "once for all," the covenant which his people have broken. The plot of the story so far is simply told:

An everlasting covenant binds the Lord and his people.
The covenant is broken by the people's infidelity,
　leaving them estranged and enslaved.

God's love has remained faithful and steadfast even though
his people are faithless and weak.

In our interpretation of the story of our life in covenant with
the living God, we have been asking ourselves a series of questions:

In the PROLOGUE we asked, "Who are we meant to be, in the
purpose of God?" And the answer of the scriptures, to which our
own mature faith bears witness, is clear. We are meant to be
creative creatures. We are meant to be God's servants in his
world, to be the channels through which his kingdom of peace
and righteousness is established.

In ACT I we asked, "What have we done?" We have had to
answer honestly, when we looked inside ourselves, that we have
subverted God's purpose at every turn. "We have been pretending to be gods!" The authority of God, vested in us as his servants, stands as a continuous temptation for us to "play God" in
the lives of the people around us. And failing the achievement
of so pretentious a claim, we have sought to flee into oblivion, at
least temporarily, in order to have the "relief from responsibility"
which comes through an inordinate indulging of our sensual
desires.

Sooner or later, however, and one by one, we come to admit
that all our pretense is vain, that neither God nor anyone else has
been fooled, not even we ourselves! Our vain pretensions gone,
we confess in the words of the General Confession:

Almighty and most merciful Father, we have erred and
strayed from thy ways like lost sheep. We have followed too
much the devices and desires of our own hearts. We have
offended against thy holy laws. We have left undone those
things which we ought to have done; and we have done those
things we ought not to have done; and there is no health in us.

It is in this mood, then, that we plead: "By the grace of God,
what can be done?" The answer of Christian faith is specific.
"God has judged us, God has redeemed us, and reconciled us to
himself and to each other, in the man Christ Jesus."

SCENE 1

THE MAN OF GOD'S OWN CHOOSING: *Christus Victor*

For to us a child is born,
  to us a son is given;
And the government will be upon his shoulder,
  and his name will be called
"Wonderful Counselor, Mighty God,
  Everlasting Father, Prince of Peace."

Of the increase of his government and of peace
  there will be no end,
upon the throne of David, and over his kingdom,
  to establish it, and to uphold it
with justice and with righteousness
  from this time forth and for evermore.

The zeal of the Lord of hosts will do this.

(Isaiah 9: 6-7)

The earliest disciples knew Jesus of Nazareth as a man, first of all. He was a carpenter and a carpenter's son. He was a teacher and a preacher. He was a healer—not only of their bodies but of their minds; not only of their bodies and minds but of their self-centered souls. He was a friend of sinners and a foe of the self-righteous. He was a prophet of God's will, and withal, the fulfillment of God's will in himself. He was an unusual man, to say the least. Indeed their Jesus, it was thought, must be *what God means by Man.*

But some of these same disciples had seen this man die and had discovered that death could not hold him. He not only carried the day on Black Friday, judging his judges at his trial and forgiving them from the cross, he confronted his disciples on Easter with new hope. Whatever else Jesus might have been, from that moment onward he was their Savior. In him their weakness became strength; their ignorance, wisdom. In him their fears were transfigured and their hatred was dissolved. In him their sins were forgiven and their sinfulness healed. They had experienced an incarnation. They too were no longer ordinary men. They were men in whom the Spirit of Christ dwelt.

After some time, however, these disciples began to remember that this One, who had functioned so divinely, was also very human, even as they. Indeed he was a better man than they, but all the more Man. Could it be? Had this man, the carpenter's son, the teacher and preacher, the healer and prophet, been related to God as they had been related to him? Was God incarnate in Jesus, even as they had experienced Jesus' Spirit to be in them? Was Jesus to become for all mankind not only what God means by man, but *what man means by God?*

Martin Luther, the father of the Evangelical Reformation, has written a number of great hymns. The one for which he is best known among us tells the story of our human struggle with evil, assuring us that the victory is ours because the right man is on our side, "the man of God's own choosing." You remember the words, inspired by those of the 46th Psalm:

A mighty Fortress is our God,
　A Bulwark never failing;
Our Helper he amid the flood
　Of mortal ills prevailing.
　　For still our ancient foe
　　Doth seek to work us woe;
　　His craft and power are great;
　　And, armed with cruel hate,
　On earth is not his equal.

Did we in our own strength confide,
　Our striving would be losing;
Were not the right man on our side,
　The man of God's own choosing.
　　Dost ask who that may be?
　　Christ Jesus, it is he,
　　Lord Sabaoth his name,
　　From age to age the same;
　And he must win the battle.

The imagery which Luther used in his "Ein' Feste Burg" is borrowed from the field of battle. The sides are sharply drawn: Man and the Prince of Darkness vs. God and the Man of His Own Choosing. Man's ancient foe, that demonic source of pretension and fear and hatred, by which he has already enslaved us, is now threatening to destroy us. We are helpless. Our only hope is in God and the Man whom he has chosen to do battle with the powers of evil.

> And though this world, with devils filled,
>   Should threaten to undo us,
> We will not fear, for God has willed
>   His truth to triumph through us.
>   The prince of darkness grim,
>   We tremble not for him;
>   His rage we can endure,
>   For lo! his doom is sure;
>   One little word shall fell him.
>
> That word above all earthly powers,
>   No thanks to them, abideth;
> The Spirit and the gifts are ours,
>   Through him who with us sideth;
>   Let goods and kindred go,
>   This mortal life also;
>   The body they may kill:
>   God's truth abideth still;
>   His kingdom is forever.

Our Reformation heritage is sharp in its diagnosis of our human perversity. It has been equally as confident in the divine victory. Our heritage proclaims that human sin and its power are not the last word in a world which was created by God in faith and for faith. The crucifixion of Jesus, which seemed to be Satan's victory, was rather the price of self-sacrifice by which the steadfast love of God won a resounding victory over its enemies —fear, pretension, greed, hatred—and redeemed humankind from enslavement to them. His resurrection on Easter is the assurance of the renewal of faith and love in a redeemed humanity.

SCENE 2
CRUCIFIED AND RISEN FROM THE DEAD

Since all have sinned and fall short of the glory of God,
    they are justified by his grace as a gift,
through the redemption which is in Christ Jesus,
    whom God put forward as an expiation by his blood,
to be received by faith.   (Roman 3: 23-25)

God was in Christ reconciling the world to himself,
    not counting their trespasses against them,
    and entrusting to us the message of reconciliation.
           (2 Corinthians 5: 19)

The crucifixion of Jesus was a historical event, incident to the policy of Roman military government in first-century Palestine. But the cross upon which our Lord was crucified is more than an instrument of punishment used by the Roman government in ruling her colonies. It has become the standard symbol of the new spiritual movement which was born of his travail.

To be sure, the cross has no meaning apart from the character of him who was crucified upon it. But it is equally true that we do not understand Christ until we are confronted by our crucified Lord. The cross is not only the church's central symbol; it is her definitive message, the heart of her gospel. Specifically, the cross of Christ marks that watershed event in human history in which the supreme violence of human sin and the consummate fullness of divine love meet.

The "seven last words," which constitute Jesus' final message to mankind, have often been portrayed in terms of a threefold relationship: *down* from the cross to his friends, encouragement; to his enemies, forgiveness; *across* from one crucified "criminal" to another, assurance of pardon; and *up* to his Father in heaven, absolute obedience and self-surrender.

These three spatial relationships fail in themselves, however, to express the definitive truth of the gospel. They leave unexplained what Christian art has tried to express by making the central cross highest. It is actually not likely to have been higher than the others. But the Spirit which was incarnate in him that was hung upon it was and is greater. Just as the three dimensions of space are inadequate by themselves, apart from the dimension of time, for determining the location of any historical event, so the three human dimensions of the cross are meaningless apart from the fourth dimension of eternity. "God was in Christ reconciling the world to himself" explains the source of the power by which Jesus forgave his enemies and offered the assurance of pardon to his fellows. It is the fourth dimension which gave to the other three their dynamic character.

The meaning of the cross therefore involves both the manward movement of God in Jesus Christ and the Godward movement of the man Christ Jesus. Our Lord is representative of both movements, of God's love to man and man's faith to God. To man, Jesus is Savior, and to God he is the first-fruits of the new humanity. Otherwise stated, Christ is what man means by God and what God means by man. Unique among men, he is not a god. Incarnate of God, he is not just a man. Jesus Christ is that man in whom God acted to redeem us from the power of sin and to reconcile us into fellowship with himself.

In the course of Christian history, the saving work of God in Christ crucified and risen from the dead has found expression in three biblical words whose precise meanings are not always clearly distinguished: atonement (for the guilt of sin), redemption (from the enslavement of sin), and reconciliation (from the estrangement of sin).

A. Atonement

The widest scope of meaning is covered by the word "atonement." Its history traces back to the high priestly ceremony of "covering" the sins of man by an offering required by God once each year (cf. Leviticus 16 for the ritual of Yom Kippur, Day of Atonement). In Christian usage its meaning faces in two opposite directions at once. Relative to sin, death, and the powers of evil, it denotes "expiation," that is, cleansing or purifying. When used as a verb the object is always *sin* and the subject *God,* or the *power of God.* Atonement by expiation is not to be mistaken for pagan rituals of "propitiation," whereby the devotee seeks to appease or curry the favor of the deity. In our biblical heritage, moreover, the priestly teaching regarding "expiation" is often blended with the prophetic proclamation regarding the redemptive work of God on man's behalf. In Romans 4: 7 Paul quotes Psalm 32, in which the two are used in poetic parallel:

> Blessed are those whose iniquities are forgiven,
> and whose sins are covered.

Relative to God, on the other hand, atonement means "to be reconciled with," that is, "to be at one with God."

Each of these two aspects of our Christian experience yields, in turn, to further analysis.

B. Redemption

The fact of the divine initiative on behalf of our redemption or emancipation from the power of sin must in no wise blind us to the gravity of our rebellion and the consequent judgment of God upon us. Nor should it lead us to underestimate the necessity for the right human response in terms of renewal of faith and repentance. Thus the representative work of Christ is widened at both ends. His "Father, forgive them for they know not what they do" came as a word of assurance of pardon to the thief, in whom the flame of faith had been rekindled. On the other hand, our Lord's cry of dereliction, "My God, my God, why hast thou forsaken me?" was an actual representation of the experience of humankind before divine judgment, an encounter in which our representative offered the only therapeutic antidote to human despair: "Father, into thy hands I commend my spirit." The seal of our Lord's resurrection to full sonship was already implicit in this act of absolute self-surrender.

The most significant aspect of the redemptive transaction, apart from the fact of the divine love and righteousness as its source, is the truly miraculous event of "reconciliation."

C. Reconciliation

It is obvious that persons who are enemies are a problem to each other. What appears to be not so obvious is that their basic problem is not each other but their enmity. Yet so long as each assumes that his enemy is his problem, there is no solution save for each to destroy the other. By this procedure death becomes the ultimate destiny of mankind, and enmity is victor over all.

The capacity of divine love, on the other hand, to destroy enmity by reconciling the enemy is the secret of the cross. And its power to break the hold of sin without destroying the sinner is the clue to Christ's victory over death. Rome chose the cross (we use the electric chair, or perhaps, worse, the wasting of a life in prison) to destroy her enemies—thieves, revolutionaries, delinquents. Jesus chose the cross to reconcile both Rome and her enemies to the great destroyer of all enmity. The cross is not only a revelation of the self-sacrificing character of God; it is a decisive act of redeeming the world from self-love and consequent death by reconciling mankind to himself through the power of self-sacrificing love.

Reconciliation with God, however, like its counterpart, redemption from sin, is only possible and not actual until we acknowledge that Christ has not only done something *for us*, but can and will do something *in and through us*. The Christian experience of the meaning of the cross reaches its finest focus in the insight that "our Lord's victorious self-sacrifice was not achieved in order to make our own unnecessary, but to make it possible." The cross has established the spiritual principle that those who through repentance and renewal of faith have been "justified by grace" are under obligation to participate in the continuous process of his vicarious work. "God, who through Christ reconciled us to himself, gave unto us the ministry of reconciliation."

> I listen to the agony of God—
> I who am fed,
> Who never yet went hungry for a day.

I see the dead—
The children starved for lack of bread—
I see, and try to pray.
I listen to the agony of God—
I who am warm,
Who never yet have lacked a sheltering home.
In dull alarm
The dispossessed of hut and farm,
Aimless and "transient" roam.
I listen to the agony of God—
I who am strong,
With health, and love, and laughter in my soul.
I see a throng
Of stunted children reared in wrong,
And wish to make them whole.
I listen to the agony of God—
But know full well
That not until I share their bitter cry—
Earth's pain and hell—
Can God within my spirit dwell
To bring his kingdom nigh.
—Georgia Harkness, "The Agony of God"[2]

Specifically, this means that the positive goal of the atonement process involves two sets of dimensions: the divine-human and the human-human or social. It is not enough to assume that an individual's sins and redemption from sin are purely a matter between him and God. It becomes clear that, since a person is the center of a network of relationships, sin not only causes enmity between a man and God but builds social barriers between him and other men in terms of race and class and nation. The injection of the redemptive power of the cross into the social pattern of our life is therefore necessary to the completion of the redemption of each one of us.

---

[2] From *The Glory of God*. Copyright, 1943, by Whitmore & Stone. Used by permission of Abingdon Press.

In a word, *the ministry of reconciliation in every human social relationship becomes a major function for all those who belong to that community of the Spirit of the crucified and risen Christ, known as the Christian church.* Such a ministry in our day will mean, among other things, that as churchmen we must not only work for the legal implementation of our national policy of racial integration, but we must undercut the foundations of prejudice with a program of wholesome interracial community experiences.

In the cross of Jesus we have been reconciled to God and made sons by adoption. In the same cross and through the power of his resurrection we must, therefore, find our reconciliation with one another and be made brothers in the family of God. Such is the twofold character of the process of reconciliation about which Paul, a Jewish Christian, wrote to his Gentile converts at Ephesus: "For [Christ] is our peace, who has made us both one, and has broken down the dividing wall of hostility, . . . that he might create in himself one man in place of the two, so making peace, and might reconcile us both to God in one body through the cross, thereby bringing . . . hostility to an end" (Eph. 2: 14-16).

Scene 3
The Author and Perfecter of Our Faith

Let us also lay aside every weight,
  and sin which clings so closely,
and let us run with perseverance
  the race that is set before us,
looking to Jesus the [author] and perfecter of our faith,
  who for the joy that was set before him
    endured the cross, depising the shame,
  and is seated at the right hand of the throne of God.

(Hebrews 12: 1-2)

God knows that the only cure for the spiritual sickness called sin is to restore faith. This is as obvious as the truth that the cure for any sickness is to restore health! The gospel which gives spiritual content to this truth declares that in Jesus Christ God has already defeated the power that has hardened our hearts and diseased our wills. The One whom God has sent to redeem us is "the author and perfecter of our faith."

Quite properly, therefore, our prayer of confession shifts in the middle from the admission of our "unfaith" to a declaration made "in faith":

But thou, O Lord, have mercy upon us. Spare thou those, O God, who confess their sins. Restore thou those who are penitent; according to thy promises declared unto mankind in Christ Jesus our Lord. And grant, O most merciful Father, for his sake, that we may hereafter live a godly, righteous, and sober life, to the glory of thy holy name. Amen.

Like all health as against its distortion in illness, Christian faith is restorative, re-creative. How we become new creatures in Christ is mysterious, but it is not magical. Forgiveness of sins as the healing of "unfaith" is the miracle which often blesses personal relationships. It is the miracle of the spiritual life that, being trusted, even when one is untrustworthy, begets trust in return and finally produces trustworthiness.

It is one of the greatest insights of our Christian faith that each one of us is so interdependently related to others and to God himself that ultimately our safety does not depend upon what we can do alone but upon what others can and will do for us. Clearly, what is being said is that one does not simply become a Christian; one is made a Christian by the work of our Lord. The beginning of new life for us is the receiving of a gift, no less remarkable than the original gift of life itself, for the free gift of God is eternal life in Christ Jesus our Lord (cf. Romans 5: 15-21).

There is a problem hidden underneath this acknowledgment of Jesus Christ as the author, or pioneer, of our faith. It is one that has split Christian thought into controversy many times in history. The problem is this: "How can Jesus be the author of my faith and it still be *my* faith?" A good share of the difficulty is met, at once, in the recognition that all that we are or ever hope to be we owe to God! Every breath we draw we owe to him, yet the use to which we put our breath is our responsibility. But how can all be grace and yet we be responsible?

There is an interlocking of activities here that makes it possible to say that *any* faithful act may at once be God's and mine. A Scotsman was asked how many it took to convert him. "Two," he replied. "Two! How was that? Didn't God do it all?" his friend inquired. "The Almighty and myself converted me," he said. "I did all I could against it, and the Almighty did all he could for it, and he was victorious." This is undoubtedly an honest confession, but is not an entirely accurate description. The philosopher Huxley is quoted as having said that "it doesn't take much of a man to make a Christian, but it does take all of him." And that is very true. Although we cannot be converted by our own will, we cannot be converted against it. The paradoxical truth is that our will must surrender itself, and yet it is incapable of doing so without the grace of God.

Paul was well aware of this double authorship of our faith. He expounded the meaning of "justification by grace through faith" in various ways. In Galatians 2: 20 he said of himself:

It is no longer I who live,
but Christ who lives in me;
and the life I now live in the flesh
I live by faith in the Son of God.

To the Philippians (2: 12-13) he declared:

Work out your own salvation with fear and trembling;
for God is at work in you, both to will and to work.

God's forgiveness is both a state and a power. We become aware of the healing power of forgiveness only after we experience the resulting state of forgiven-ness. Forgiven-ness is the state of being accepted by God. "While we were yet sinners Christ died for us" (Rom. 5: 8). The awareness of this acceptance prompts us to "accept our acceptance," to borrow Paul Tillich's useful play upon words. To accept our acceptance is faith, and it is our faith, but it is not ours until our Lord has given it back to us in forgiven-ness.

Bernard of Clairvaux, of the twelfth century, put it succinctly when he wrote:

In his first work (creation) God gave me myself;
In his second work (incarnation) he gave me himself;
And when he gave me himself, he gave me back myself.

This puts the problem of our freedom and responsibility as over against God's grace in the right perspective. There is no conflict when we realize that our only real freedom is in response to our Creator's love. What we often call freedom, "doing as we very well please," is no freedom at all. It is the perversion of freedom by unfaith. It is what Martin Luther called it, the enslavement to pretension, which is sin.

The answer to the problem of human freedom is all bound up with the form in which the question is put—*freedom from what and to what?* Western civilization has tended to confuse the issue by emphasizing *freedom from* in such individualistic terms that unfaith seemed to be made a virtue. Freedom *from* tyranny, in the struggle for which western civilization, as we know it, was born, tends to slip over into freedom from authority and then to license for the "rugged" individual will.

In Christ we are set free from the slavery of pretension and fear. In Christ we are set free "for freedom" within the capacity of the love of God. One of the finest forms we have of confessing our new life of freedom in the Lordship of Christ is George Matheson's hymn:

Make me a captive, Lord,
And then I shall be free;
Force me to render up my sword,
And I shall conqueror be.
I sink in life's alarms,
When by myself I stand;
Imprison me within thy arms,
And strong shall be my hand.

My heart is weak and poor
  Until it master find;
It has no spring of action sure,
  It varies with the wind;
It cannot freely move
  Till thou hast wrought its chain;
Enslave it with thy matchless love,
  And deathless it shall reign. . . .

My will is not my own
  Till thou hast made it thine;
If it would reach a monarch's throne
  It must its crown resign;
It only stands unbent
  Amid the clashing strife,
When on thy bosom it has leant,
  And found in thee its life.

*O Lord, heavenly Father, almighty and everlasting God, thine
is the kingdom and the power and the glory. Thy throne is for
ever and ever, and thy faithfulness unto all generations. Thou
lookest in compassion upon the children of men; in wisdom and
love thou dost draw near to us all and work evermore for our
good. Thou didst send thy beloved Son into the world that we
might live through him, and hast also given us thy Holy Spirit to
guide and help us throughout the whole course of our life. Let
thy name be known throughout all the world. Make manifest
among every people thy saving power. Kindle in the hearts of
all men the love of justice, mercy, and truth, that thy healing
may spring forth speedily and thy blessed kingdom may go forward; through Jesus Christ our Lord. Amen.*

—Adapted from *A Book of Pastoral Prayers*
by Ernest Fremont Tittle. Abingdon Press.

ACT III

THE CHURCH AND OUR CHRISTIAN VOCATION

In which we ask:
Who are we, now?

To which our Christian faith answers and confesses:
We are forgiven sinners
And a new creation in Jesus Christ.
By the gift of God's Holy Spirit,
We are incorporated into the fellowship
of the New Covenant church.
We are, now, grateful to accept the role:
Servants of God and stewards of his kingdom
of peace and righteousness.

In Paul's Second Letter to the Corinthians, he proclaims: "From now on, therefore, we regard no one from a human point of view; even though we once regarded Christ from a human point of view, we regard him thus no longer. Therefore, if any one is in Christ, he is a new creation; the old has passed away, behold, the new has come. All this is from God, who through Christ reconciled us to himself and gave us the ministry of reconciliation (5: 16-18)."

SCENE 1
THE RHYTHM OF OUR NEW LIFE IN CHRIST

"Come to me, all who labor and are heavy-laden,
and I will give you rest.
Take my yoke upon you. . . . For my yoke is easy,
and my burden is light."   (Matthew 11: 28-30)

"Go therefore and make disciples of all nations, . . .
Lo, I am with you always, to the close of the age."

(Matthew 28: 19-20)

In the previous ACT, when we were trying to explain the meaning of Christ's work for the redemption of our lives, we referred to the ancient allegory of Christ's self-sacrifice in the struggle for the release of our souls from bondage to the powers of evil. No matter how much or how little that figure may have carried meaning to your mind, the experience of having been helped when you were helpless—and at a price to your benefactor that you can never repay—will live long in your hearts. It will act as a prompter to the deepest passion that the human heart can express—the spirit of gratitude. True it is that no one is quite so much "on the spot" as a person who, thinking himself to be an atheist, feels a spirit of gratitude and knows not whom to thank.

Indeed, does not our own experience simply verify what the gospel repeatedly avows, that *gratitude is the mainspring of the whole Christian life?* The response we make to an unexpected favor that has come from someone who did it at a cost of tremendous self-sacrifice indicates the quality of heart within us. This is the story of the "steadfast love of God" as it redeems broken and worthless lives, only to motivate in them the power to seek and save the least and the last of the lost.

This is the story of Alcoholics Anonymous. And I believe that Dr. Gerald Heard is right when he says that this group is functionally one of the best examples we have today of the New Testament church. When we invited a member of AA to speak at Eden Seminary to a class in the psychology of religion about the philosophy of this movement, it was pointed out that the healing of an alcoholic follows a well-tested pattern:

(1) The alcoholic must acknowledge that he is helpless, that alcohol is his master.

(2) He is encouraged to confess that his own will is too weak to accomplish the defeat of the tyrant, and to seek God's help.

(3) He finds himself accepted in the fellowship of a group of others like himself who have swallowed their pride and have asked for help.

(4) For the first time in a long time, perhaps for the first time in his life, the patient is able to accept himself as he is.

(5) Then comes the most crucial point of all: he is given the responsibility to take care of someone who is worse off than he is.

An alcoholic who has begun to respond to cure, the representative explained, must become vitally concerned about the welfare of others like himself or his cure will be short-lived. It is not difficult to understand what he meant when he concluded: "In Alcoholics Anonymous, we thank God for drunks!" What would happen to our church if we were seriously to thank God for sinners?

When we ask, "Who are we, now?" the answer is clear, "We are sinners anonymous!" One doesn't know which word shocks us the more, to be called a sinner or to be asked to be anonymous. At any rate, the early church clearly understood itself to be a community of forgiven sinners, and our Lord cautioned his first followers, again and again, to a kind of anonymity with regard to good works of healing that they did for others. "Do not let your left hand know what your right hand is doing" (Matt. 6: 3).

The little word "now" in our question is more crucial than one may think. In our language it has a number of meanings. In the first place, it quite clearly means immediately, at once. There is an unmistakable urgency about it. The news report of a plane crash near the airport at Fort Leonard Wood declared that the plane would have landed safely if it had had ten seconds more. Ten seconds is usually time we can waste, but in certain instances it is the difference between life and death. "Now, is the appointed time." Now, we must decide, not ten seconds from now, not a year from now, but right now!

There is, however, another meaning, one that arises out of our compounding "now" with the word "that." Now that your mother-in-law has come to live with you, what are you going to do? Now that you are going to become a millionaire . . . Now that you have your job back . . . Now that you have graduated
. . . .

"Now that" refers to some definitive event that, as we say, changes things. Somewhere in the past, in the relatively recent past, a crucial event has occurred that changes our entire future. "From now on, therefore . . ." This is what happens in the story of our life in covenant with the living God. Now that God has sent his Son, our Lord Jesus, to redeem us from the powers of evil, and now that we have acknowledged him, from now on everything is different. The original "before" and "after" advertisement was very likely inspired by the Christian calendar. *Before Christ,* sin, death, and Satan threatened to destroy us. *After Christ,* love, light, and peace are victorious. How marvelous is the new covenant and the outlook for those who belong to the "renewed" humanity in Jesus Christ! "The old has passed away; the new has come."

One finds, however, that old habits and patterns of life die hard. Past history leaves its mark and intertwines itself with the new history like the thistles and the wheat in our Lord's parable. The Emancipation Proclamation came in 1863, but . . . . I acknowledged Jesus Christ as my Lord and Savior thirty years ago, but . . . . This is not to deny that crucial events make a difference. The difference is tremendous on all counts, but so long as we are human the inner ambiguity of our nature still rises to plague us. It was Paul, the mature man of faith, who wrote in the Letter to the Romans: "I do not do the good I want, but the evil I do not want is what I do" (7: 19). We are forgiven sinners, not gods. This we have to recognize and admit when we praise the Lord for his mighty acts. The "before" and "after" means just one thing, that our help is in the name of the Lord. Our lives are different, not only because of what he has done, but because of what he is doing and promises yet to do. Our salvation in Christ is not so much like a vaccination which would give us a guaranteed immunity against sickness as it is the assurance that our "doctor" is on duty and is available to all who call upon him.

For those of us who are called to various forms of the healing ministry, the Gospel of Luke tells an unforgettable story (9: 18-43). Jesus had led his disciples to Caesarea Philippi for what we have come to call a "retreat." Here it was that Peter's confession, "Thou art the Christ of God," had taken place.

"Now about eight days [later, Jesus] took with him Peter and John and James, and went up on the mountain to pray. And as he was praying, the appearance of his countenance was altered, and his raiment became dazzling white. And behold, two men talked with him, Moses and Elijah, who appeared in glory and spoke of his [exodus], which he was to accomplish at Jerusalem. Now Peter and those who were with him were heavy with sleep but kept awake, and they saw his glory and the two men who stood with him. And as the men were parting from him, Peter said to Jesus, 'Master, it is well that we were here; let us make three booths, one for you and one for Moses and one for Elijah'— not knowing what he said. As he said this, a cloud came and overshadowed them; and they were afraid as they entered the cloud. And a voice came out of the cloud, saying, 'This is my Son, my Chosen; listen to him!' And when the voice had spoken, Jesus was found alone. . . .

"On the next day, when they had come down from the mountain, a great crowd met him. And behold, a man from the crowd cried, 'Teacher, I beg you to look upon my son, for he is my only child; and behold, a spirit seizes him, and he suddenly cries out; it convulses him till he foams, and shatters him, and will hardly leave him. And I begged your disciples to cast it out, but they could not.'

"Jesus answered, 'O faithless and perverse generation, how long am I to be with you and bear with you? Bring your son here.'"

It appears that Jesus is having to put up with us for a long time. Even though we have mountaintop experiences which lift us out of our very boots in devotion to the living Christ, we find that when we come back from the Mount of Transfiguration to "the valley of disfiguration," we are woefully powerless to help those who are still suffering from the world's ills. Like Peter we want to "permanentize" our glorious visions and bask in his glory. But a cloud suddenly wipes out the vision and we are back in B.C. again, with the same old world and the same sick people pleading for help. Fortunately, we have learned from these hapless disciples that *there is a steady beat in the rhythm of the Christian life.* For every "retreat" there is a "return"—not retreat to escape, but withdrawal for renewal. Many church bulletins emphasize the rhythm with the injunction: "Enter to worship—depart to serve." Some are more subtle but equally emphatic: "The service begins when the Service ends!"

Our Lord Jesus set the pace for the Twelve when, in the midst of his holy impatience, he said: "Bring your son here." And he "rebuked the unclean spirit, and healed the boy, and gave him back to his father."

Moreover, our Lord's two most striking commands begin with the simple words "come" and "go." He invited his disciples to share with him fully in both dimensions of his life, his healing power and his healing mission. "Come to me, all who labor and are heavy-laden, and I will give you rest." This is our salvation. "Take my yoke upon you. . . . Go therefore and make disciples of all nations." That is our vocation. And they are one in him. In the repetition of "retreat" and "return" we shall grow in grace and in the confidence of our calling.

As this is being written, we have before us, in memory, the full and completed life of Ruth Isabel Seabury. I can think of no one whose life better represents this rhythmic functioning. She was a person of deep devotion and humility. And from this devotion and commitment to Christ she found a springboard of courage for prodigious Christian action. She was both a disciple and an apostle of Christ's life of suffering service. The title of her last book, *So Send I You*, recently published by The Christian Education Press, 1955, records both the source of power and the direction of her life. So may it be with us all!

In her memory and for our rededication we pray in the words of Francis of Assisi:

O Lord, may we have thy mind and thy spirit—
Make us instruments of thy peace;

where there is hatred, let us sow love;
  where there is injury, pardon;
where there is doubt, faith;
  where there is despair, hope;
where there is darkness, light. . . .

O Divine Master, grant that we may not so much
  seek to be consoled as to console;
to be understood as to understand;
  to be loved as to love;
for it is in giving that we receive,
  it is in pardoning that we are pardoned,
and it is in dying that we are born to eternal life. Amen.

SCENE 2
THE COMMUNITY OF THE FAITHFUL

For as in one body we have many members,
  and all the members do not have the same function,
so we, though many, are one body in Christ,
  and individually members one of another.

Having gifts that differ according to the grace given to us,
  let us use them:
if prophecy, in proportion to our faith;
  if service, in our serving;
he who teaches, in his teaching;
  he who exhorts, in his exhortation;
he who contributes, in liberality;
  he who gives aid, with zeal;
he who does acts of mercy, with cheerfulness.

(Romans 12: 4-8; cf. 1 Corinthians 12; Ephesians 4)

The opportunity to find our vocation within the life of the church is structured by the Christian year. It begins with the gift of the spirit of promise and anticipation which belongs to Advent and Christmas. Our appreciation is deepened during the season of Lent by observing our Lord's struggle, on our behalf, against the powers of evil, and it reaches a tremendous climax as we identify ourselves with him in his victory on Good Friday and Easter. But this is only the completion of the first half of the Christian drama. Its fulfillment in the church, in which now we can identify ourselves among the participants, begins at Pentecost and points ever toward the future.

The heritage of our Christian faith which Jesus pioneered and perfected was not so much a body of beliefs as a body of believers. Our Lord left not just the exemplary faith of one man but a community of faithful followers. And the community of the faithful has been an essential factor in Christianity throughout its history. It transcends any effort to establish a false division within the Christian life, such as between individual and social, as, for example, in the so-called personal and social gospel. In the biblical word *koinonia* these two are united as one. *Koinonia* means community in a personal sense. *It is a fellowship of persons, bound together by a common spirit and concerned with a common purpose.*

Fellowship comes in two dimensions. In depth we call it communion; in breadth we call it community. True fellowship can be only as broad as it is deep. Social community rests upon and flows from spiritual communion—the fellowship of the Holy Spirit—and is a gift of God's gracious love. By the same token "broken" community is a symptom of spiritual anemia.

In social terms community implies a profound conception of equality. It is the Christian faith that, in contrast to general practice among men, there is a genuine equality of all men before God. This equality does not mean a dead level in ability, contribution, or character, but an equality in the fundamental right of all men to be persons and to engage in personal relationships.

Before God our human distinctions of race, nationality, and social status are as nothing. The spectacle of a small number of people in every age appropriating, because of their military, political, or economic power, the chief sources of wealth and leaving the masses without the same access to the means of health and to the opportunities for developing the possibilities within themselves—this is, in the sight of God, a great blasphemy.

In a really Christian community there would be no occasion for any man to worry about food and clothing and shelter. "Look at the birds of the air: they neither sow nor reap nor gather into barns, and yet your heavenly Father feeds them. Are you not of more value than they?" (Matt. 6:26). The peculiar note in Jesus' teaching is not, as the twentieth century declares, its "impracticality." It is our Lord's insight that the birds, not being rational creatures, have not intelligence enough to defeat the heavenly Father's plans. "There is none among them capable of organizing a 'corner' in worms or fruits of the field, none to seize the woods as his possession and charge 'rent' for all who would roost in them, and so they all come alike to the table that God has spread for them."[1]

One of the greatest tragedies of our time is that a secular movement, *communism,* has stolen and perverted and thereby put a stigma upon the great Christian word *community.* By its appropriation of this biblical concept and the equalitarian hope it engenders, communism has temporarily taken the initiative from Christianity as the most revolutionary movement in human history. By its declaration that community rests basically upon material equality and is a product of a natural process of conflicting forces, communism has shown itself to be a Christian heresy. And by its adoption of the ruthless tactics of military aggression in power politics and the calculated oppression and destruction of personal and civil liberties in its institutions and policies, communism has become the world's greatest threat to the very objective of community it has promised to fulfill.

The church—the community of the faithful—is, therefore, challenged today both by the desperate state of the world's broken community and by the competition of a false, but vital, secular "gospel."

When we face up to this challenge we recognize that human-

---

[1] From *Socialism and the Ethics of Jesus* by Henry C. Vedder. The Macmillan Company, 1914.

ity's difficulty is not merely broken community, with the threat of conflict, but *impersonality*, bearing the threat of meaninglessness with regard to life. The results of conflict between nations, races, economic and cultural groups are not merely death and the destruction of the body, but the more subtle dangers to the life of the spirit for those who must continue to live in broken community. Enmity, loneliness, fear, despair—these are worse than death. They contribute to a living death.

Modern man is threatened most acutely with the fact of impersonality. *Given the condition of broken community,* all that men have to bind them together is their partisan loyalty to institutions. And institutions tend to treat each other as things not as persons. When a larger "we" is broken up, institutionally the personal relationships are reduced to a smaller "we" vs. "they" distinction. But "they" is just a short step from becoming "it." The machinery by which institutions attempt to offer security to their members tends to become their master, and impersonality reigns supreme, reducing persons to things.

The church in our heritage has always had to meet this challenge by making a double confession: of sin and of faith. The church, both in its membership and its organizational form of expression, is as surely a part of the problem as are other institutional forms of community. Therefore we must confess sin.

Were this all that the church could say, there would be no hope. The church, however, is both divine and human. We are the fellowship of the Holy Spirit, and when we confess our faith with the family of the faithful we recognize that the real challenge confronting us comes not from the world but from our Lord. The world's challenge is only an echo of his call to repentance and faith. Before the challenge of the world we are hopeless, because the evil is also within us. When our Lord confronts us there is hope, for we are empowered by his Spirit to be and to do what God intends by community.

The sharpest way to express this difference is by interpreting three words used in the New Testament to refer to the church in God's purpose.

A. Ecclesia

Ecclesia means church as *congregation.* It corresponds to the Old Testament conception of the chosen people. Literally it declares that *the church is "called out" from the world of broken community to be God's people and to live in his covenant.*

Again and again prophets and reformers within our heritage have had to remind the church of the true meaning of her being chosen. We human beings are inclined to make choosing between two persons or things the basis of rejection of that which was not chosen. We have had to learn the hard way that God's election is not partisan. Israel was chosen *not* for special privilege as against correspondingly unprivileged neighbors. She was chosen to be God's means of sharing the same blessing with her neighbors (and enemies) that God's favor had already bestowed upon her. She was called out to go back as a servant.

Both the parable of Jonah and Isaiah 53 underscore the truth that all who are chosen to serve the Lord must accept suffering as their union card. The cross of Jesus is the verification. When the church *is* the church it hears with reverence the words of Paul: "Do not be conformed to this world but be transformed by the renewal of your mind, that you may *prove* what is the will of God" (Rom. 12: 2). The call of God is not a one-way street. We are called out that we may be prepared to go back to serve! There is no place for indifference and accommodation to the world in the New Testament norm for the church.

But there is indifference, and it is often mated with arrogance on the part of those who are "called." The Jews had the Gentiles, the Greeks the barbarians, Americans have "foreigners," and the clergy have the laity, as the symbol of their "unfinished business." This is the recurring story of people who, having been called out, forget to come back! The Reformers' insistence upon the "priesthood of all believers" (often misconstrued in individualistic terms to mean that every man is his own priest) needs ever and again to be recovered as the deeper meaning of *ecclesia:* every believer a minister, a servant of peace and righteousness.

B. Koinonia

The congregation that is called with the motive of service will become a koinonia of the Holy Spirit, a fellowship of those who are bound together by a common spiritual bond and purpose. This is the church's cure for broken community. Just as the cure for unfaith is the restoration of faith, so the cure for broken community is the restoration of community. God has given the church a job like that of yeast in bread dough. Paul spoke of the *ministry of reconciliation,* and the unknown author of the second-century *Epistle to Diognetos* saw clearly that it is the church's responsibility to "hold the world together," declaring that "what the soul is to the body, Christians are in the world."

Our ministry in this universal priesthood is to bring to each other comfort for the broken-hearted, recovery of sight for the blind, liberty for the enslaved, reconciliation for enemies, and restoration of community wherever it has been broken. The church as the *koinonia* is like the heart in our bodies, the reservoir of life-giving blood, which works day and night to restore vitality to a depleted social organism.

It is significant to note that our generation is confronted with the glorious opportunity to be the bearers of *koinonia* in a sense that has never before been true. By virtue of the spiritual vitality engendered in the ecumenical movement, our divisive denominations and partisan sects are beginning to give way to the purpose of God expressed in the Apostles' Creed: one holy *universal* Christian church.

C. Kuriakos

Kuriakos is used infrequently in the New Testament, but often enough to represent the third meaning of the church. It means "that which belongs to the Lord," a synonym for the oft-used term "the body of Christ."

The importance of continuous witness to the lordship of Christ in the body of his believers makes this a key word. Moreover, language scholars point out that both our German *Kirche* and our English *church* come from the Greek *kuriakos.*

The church's responsibility in witnessing to her Lord appears on the surface of things to be as harsh as her reconciling work in the power of the spirit seems to be soothing. In the name of her Lord the church is called to pursue *a ministry of revolution.* The pastor who "comforts the disturbed" must also be the prophet who "disturbs the comfortable." The fellowship of the Holy Spirit stands not only for the restoration of community but for the destruction of false community. Fellowship is also a word that has been depreciated by its casual users, and needs, like community, to be redeemed in our usage.

The truth of the matter is that the church's prophetic ministry of revolution is deeply imbedded in our "evangelical" heritage. Bearing witness to the Lord, whose love is righteous, is at once to proclaim judgment upon the idols which we worship in place of the Lord and at the same time to proclaim the true Lord in whom we are given the life which is the light of men.

Thus both community and personality are proper fruits of the church's function. Just as the Holy Spirit heals broken community, so the acknowledgment of the lordship of Jesus Christ restores personality. The hope for men who, having set out to establish their own lordship in God's world, wind up enslaved to those "things" which they have mastered lies in repentance and faith—faith in *the Lord,* who is Lord of all, in bondage to whom is our perfect freedom.

Scene 3
The Faithful in "Broken" Community

"The Spirit of the Lord is upon me,
because he has anointed me to preach good news to the poor.
He has sent me to proclaim release to the captives
and recovering of sight to the blind,
to set at liberty those who are oppressed,
to proclaim the acceptable year of the Lord."

(Luke 4: 18-19; cf. Matthew 25: 31-40)

The Christian church is a gift from God. It is the fellowship of persons who have found reconciliation, within and without, in the Spirit of our Lord Jesus. *The church is the body of Christ.* It is not an institution, although it is embodied in an institution. She is not the membership, although her existence as a community requires that she have members. The church is "the community of the faithful," whose faith is fed by the communion of God's Holy Spirit.

The church is not of the world, but she exists in and for it. The lives of the "community of the faithful" must be lived in the midst of the world's broken communities. The church is God's gift to the world, and therefore is nothing if she fails to function in a way that is relevant to the world's need for community.

Our world is, in fact, many broken communities. It is broken by all manner of expression of human pride and egocentricity—racial, economic, political. The fact that I am a Caucasian, middle-class American tends to exclude me from community with millions of people whose provincial experiences of community require other labels to describe them. Racial segregation, class exclusiveness, nationalism, are all evil, not merely because of the inequalities of opportunity and privilege that are usually intended and achieved thereby, but because these barriers destroy something basic in the spirits of those who live on both sides of our "iron curtain." The major symptom of broken community is loneliness. It points to the fact that the lines of personal communication are out of order.

When we become aware of the brokenness of our community we say that we are in a *crisis.* Crisis is the breakdown of community. We speak of an economic crisis: in the 1930's it was called depression, in the 1950's it has been called inflation. We speak of the international crisis of East and West, or of a critical stage in race relations, just as we are inclined to speak with awe of the crisis in a dreadful illness. This term which the world has learned to use in so many ways is a Greek word taken over into English from the New Testament. In the English Bible *krisis* is translated judgment, meaning the judgment of God.

Although crises are terribly destructive, they are even more ominous as symptoms than deplorable as facts. That is, when they explode externally in violence and destruction—race riots, strikes, wars, and the like—they merely manifest the "sickness unto death" that exists within. A crisis is, as it were, the violent fever which results from the conflict of forces which takes place within the "body" of community. Because these forces are a judgment of God, however, the world's crises are not really hopeless. Indeed, they offer hope, for therein we see God's purpose for community breaking through the shackles of our provincialism and false divisions. The hope in any crisis may be measured by the extent to which there is found, by the grace of God, an active center of unbroken faith in the midst of the broken community.

The objective toward which the church works in the world, therefore, is the restoration of community. But this objective is sterilized by ineffectiveness unless we employ the proper strategy. *The Christian life is a vocation.* It is centered in the imperative: "Love one another." We are called to be servants. Community is the objective of Christian service; love is the strategy. Without love there is no real foundation for community. Where love is present, there the healing powers of community re-creation are already at work. The church is a dynamic resource of fellowship in the midst of the world's brokenness. The world's hope, however, is not in us but in God, for God *is* love. It is he who first loved in Christ and gave us the community of his Holy Spirit. "If we love one another, God abides in us and his love is perfected in us" (1 John 4: 12).

A realistic understanding, however, of the relationship of "strategy" and "objective" suggests that in dealing with human life we are not in a position merely to blueprint an objective and then set ourselves to its reproduction in fact. From the very outset servants of community must come to grips with the problem of evil, the fact of the universal recalcitrance of our human nature, individually and collectively, and the evil institutions and practices which result therefrom.

Our scientific generation has made the so-called "law of cause and effect" almost an axiom of everyday wisdom. Yet in dealing with the problem of evil in human relationships, our world has been singularly blind to the truth that grapes are not gathered from thorns nor figs from thistles. The *Washington Post,* a few years ago, carried a striking cartoon. Against the background of hordes of hungry people, massed on the shores of the other continents, President Truman was shown confronting the representative of the American people with the cost of his Point IV program for assistance to underprivileged and underdeveloped areas of the world. The cost was marked at 35 million dollars. But our spokesman replied, "Nah, let's wait until they go communist, then spend a few billions fighting them."

Clearly our world has not learned what Christian faith continually rediscovers—that it is impossible to treat the symptoms of evil on the human scene without getting at the conditions and causes which produce the symptoms. It reminds one of trying to cure an itch by scratching the place where it itches! Hitler, Stalin, communist aggression, race riots, city slums, are only symptoms of more deep-seated evils. The Christian church knows that the world can never defeat communism by propaganda or by bullets, and that it cannot avert race riots by doubling or tripling the police force. Indeed, the power of these evils can be checked only by a more thoroughgoing redemption of man from the evils underlying broken community, from economic poverty, social insecurity and injustice, personal fear and hatred, inordinate self-interest and pride.

To live the Christian vocation as a suffering servant of the Lord, in the midst of the world's crises, is therefore not a simple matter. The issue, broadly speaking, is centered upon the conflicting claims of *citizenship,* subject to the strategy of the political state, and of *churchmanship,* subject to the strategy of the body of Christ. The most striking instance of this problem is the decision with which Christian young people are faced regarding national military service, with its avowed strategy of enmity and its goal of human destruction, as against their Christian training to love their enemies and to seek the welfare of all mankind.

Are they to be "conformed to this world" or are they to take seriously the demand of their faith to be the servants of God in the transforming of this world into the kingdom of Christ?

In our generation war, either hot or cold, has come more and more to be accepted by the world as the fundamental condition of life, and militarism has little by little enthroned itself as "the way of life." Pacifism, in the meantime, has been claimed by a few as a total philosophy of life. By the many, however, it is considered a crack-pot view, a luxury which may be permitted to the few only on condition that it remain harmlessly irrelevant.

By a customary distinction Christians call themselves either pacifists or nonpacifists in regard to their political philosophy. But their common commitment to Christ as Lord makes this a distinction different from pacifism vs. militarism. All Christian action is ultimately directed toward peace-making, that is, toward community-building, social reconciliation, and personal healing. The Hebrew word for peace *(shalom)* means wholeness, community, health. Therefore, as against militarism, *all* distinctively Christian action is pacifistic. Political pacifism is, however, not the only Christian position that is antiwar and antimilitaristic. In fact, political nonpacifism is a term not to be identified with militarism, which is used to define the view of those who emphasize the Christian's responsibility to restrain evil, as itself a part of the community welfare.

Christians, pacifists and nonpacifists alike, know full well that peace-making as community building and rebuilding must be given top priority or we face the peril of total disaster to human-kind. At the same time Christians know, from a realistic acquaintance with human nature, that pacifism cannot be a total philosophy of life for mankind in its present perverted estate. *Neither militarism nor pacifism, as a political philosophy, is realistic regarding the contradictions of this world, at once perverted by human sin and sustained by God's love.* Each falls prey to a human pretension.

Complete militarism cannot be the honest, working philosophy of anyone but a thoroughgoing atheist, for militarism is the world's strategy for the world's evil, that is, original sin, prescribing the destruction of Adam for the "cure" of his illness, destroying the evil by liquidating the evildoer. Militarism reckons without the redemptive power of God's love.

Complete pacifism, on the other hand, cannot be the honest, working philosophy of anyone but a citizen of the heavenly kingdom, for it reckons without the demonic power of evil in the world. It offers utopia on conditions that cannot be met so long as the "old Adam" persists.

Although pacifism and militarism are contradictory political philosophies, the one "angelic" and the other "demonic" in its pretensions, Christian pacifism and Christian nonpacifism are actually opposing vocations, or, better, polar aspects in the vocation of the Christian man, undergirded by the bipolar unity of God's love and judgment.

The church's membership, therefore, is made up of "citizens" whose political responsibilities require some to be less pacifistic than others, for our sinful nature requires government to control our inordinate self-interests. For this purpose cities, states, and nations curb freedom in the attempt to keep order. This is the negative condition of community, and responsible Christian citizens will accept the "restraining of evil" as a Christian duty.

It is necessary, however, to distinguish between the duty to restrain evil, that is, to share in *the policing function of government*, and what has traditionally been known as military action, that is, war between governments. Without presuming to stand in judgment concerning other men's convictions, we may attempt to define objectively the distinguishing marks of these two types of coercive activity.

Policing, as the restraint of evil, becomes a Christian duty when it is the function of a community whose government accepts responsibility for the welfare of the evildoer. On the other hand, the motive of war has always been a conflict of national self-interests, coupled with the normal human drive for self-preservation, regularly resulting in ruthless aggression and aggrandizement on the one side and equally ruthless reprisal and retaliation on the other. War, as a national policy, persists in the world so long as there is acknowledged no higher arbiter than the conflicting parties themselves. It is in this sense, indeed, that we must understand the apostle Paul's teaching in Romans 13 that "governing authorities have been instituted by God." In the international stage of historical development this would mean that the policing role undertaken by the United Nations, albeit all too hesitant, is clearly ordained of God. The evil of war roots in the provincial character of the absolutes which command the loyalty of its partisans. War, therefore, cannot claim responsible participation by the Christian because it is a manifest expression of man's deification of the nations as the ultimate determiners of human destiny, making government a function of the perversion of community. *War is broken community perpetuating and extending its brokenness. In a word, the aim of war is judgment without redemption. Policing, on the other hand, must aim to minister redemption in the administration of judgment.*

The church as the body of Christ, however, must be completely pacifist as against militarist, and predominantly pacifist as against nonpacifist. *Reconciliation, through suffering service, is the church's strategy, by the grace of God, for her own life in the redemptive community; she can see, therefore, in reconciliation the hope of peace beneath the "crises" of broken community in the world.* Reconciliation is the positive and creative aspect of community. To live as citizens and churchmen in the world of broken community, under continual crisis and hope, underscores for us the conflict in our own souls, where sin and law, as against faith and grace, continue their struggle for possession. So long as sin persists, there is law (order) to restrain and check it; where there is faith, grace (freedom) has begotten it and does not cease to nourish and sustain it.

The church will properly have both "restrainers" and "reconcilers" in her membership, although her own primary function is reconciliation. This tension, whether between individual members or within a single person, continues to keep the church sensitive to the fact that her membership is continually being confronted with the temptation to pretension. "Restrainers" who are aware that their Christian purpose subjects their restraining to the end of reconciliation must be disturbed continually by the problem of means and ends. "Reconcilers," who are aware that evil men must be restrained before they can be reconciled, dare not be naïve about the problem of power and will have to accept responsibility for organizing power to restrain evil.

The church as the people of God, moreover, knows that at best the restraining of evildoers is but a curbing of evil. The positive task which is her birthright is *to destroy evil by redeeming the evildoer.*

Although the example which we have chosen to present the problem of broken community is one of the most controversial, it is not unique. The same pattern of interpretation would apply to other areas of life, such as economic relations, race relations, civic responsibility, and family life.

Our heritage of life-giving faith is the story of the sovereign righteousness and holy love of God and of his everlasting covenant with humankind. Its plot is recorded in the Bible and re-lived, in each new generation, by the community of the faithful who acknowledge that Jesus Christ is Lord.

In order that the faith-community may fulfill the role entrusted to her, she must bear a threefold witness:

(1) to help the world to acknowledge the *sovereignty of God,* warning mankind of impending judgment and of the insanity of attempting to resolve human conflict purely on the political level and with military power as the sole arbiter.

(2) to reassure mankind of the *providence of God,* in order that the present mood of hysteria and craven fears may not lead to fatalism and reckless disregard for moral responsibility. This is a time for crisis; therefore there is hope, for God is working in these times to effect his will.

(3) to bear witness in fact to the *redemptive love of God,* that is, to be the channel which provides the margin of healing energy that can tip the balance toward recovery and new life.

THE EPILOGUE
THE KINGDOM OF GOD AND OUR HUMAN DESTINY

In which we ask:
>What is our hope?

To which our Christian faith answers and confesses:
>The kingdom of the world
>>shall become the kingdom of our Lord
>>>and of his Christ,
>
>And he shall reign forever.
>
>God, who has revealed himself in Jesus Christ,
>>is the same yesterday, today, and forever.
>
>Through the mystery of the Lord's Supper,
>>we live in joyful anticipation
>>>of his eternal fellowship.

Then I saw a new heaven and a new earth;
>for the first heaven and the first earth
>>had passed away, . . .

and I heard a great voice from the throne saying,
>"Behold, the dwelling of God is with men.
>
>He will dwell with them,
>>and they shall be his people, . . .
>
>He will wipe away every tear from their eyes,
>>and death shall be no more,
>
>neither shall there be mourning
>>nor crying nor pain any more,
>
>for the former things are passed away."

And he who sat upon the throne said,

>"Behold, I make all things new. . . .
>I am the Alpha and the Omega,
>>the beginning and the end."

(Revelation 21: 1, 3-6)

The story of our life in covenant with the living God runs through five episodes. The drama opens with a PROLOGUE, in which we are assured that we are created by the living God to be stewards of his world and the faithful servants of his love.

This is followed by three ACTS of covenant encounter between us and our Creator:

(1) We begin by rejecting our covenant calling. As a result of our infidelity and pretension, we find ourselves enslaved to the powers of evil—powers that threaten to unseat the authority of God's love in his world and that have their abode in our own hearts. These powers are legion: rebelliousness, pride, greed, envy, hatred, contempt . . .

(2) And then, a glorious thing happens. There comes the man of God's own choosing, the man Christ Jesus, who brings deliverance to the rest of men. He releases us from our enslavement and renews our faith.

(3) By virtue of this re-creation of our hearts we are restored to our covenanted responsibilities and given a second chance. Out of gratitude for our restoration to freedom, we commit ourselves to do battle against the evil powers at every turn. The battle rages everywhere—in our own hearts (already healed, but still subject to further infection); in our families; in our congregations; in the community and world around us, in which we face a confusion of conflicting races and nations and ideologies.

Finally, in the EPILOGUE, we ask: What is our destiny? What is our hope? What assurance is there that we shall be victorious over these evil powers?

Christian faith, rooted as it is in the covenant faithfulness of God, offers us both hope and assurance. So much of our human hoping is without assurance. We naively assume that everything will come out all right, or we bet on the law of averages, or we hope for the best and expect the worst. "Blessed be the God and Father of our Lord Jesus Christ! By his great mercy we have been *born anew to a living hope*" (1 Peter 1: 3).

A. We Are a Colony of Heaven

The covenant story is a way of affirming the historic teaching which the church has called the doctrine of God's providence, or sometimes predestination. By this we declare that our destiny, like our origin, lies with the Lord. He is the Alpha and Omega—the beginning and the end. Our future, like our past, is hid in the mystery of God's steadfast love and righteousness.

Our creation (the PROLOGUE) is understood by reading life's story backward—a feat of "retrospective imagination," as in the way we figure out the beginning of a movie into which we come a little late. By the same token, knowledge of the conclusion of the drama of our life, insight into our destiny, is reached here and now by a comparable act of "anticipation," for we are a "colony of heaven." In both instances, however, the clue for finding out the purpose of God—in our creation and for our destiny—is what we have come to call the central event in all history and the most crucial event in our lives. It is the coming into the world of the Man of God's own choosing, "the new covenant" in the body and blood of Jesus Christ.

Standing "beneath the cross of Jesus" offers us an excellent position from which to get perspective upon ourselves: our past, our present, and our future. The cross which looms overhead gives us a perfect focus, for it stands precisely in the middle of our human horizon and permits us to see ourselves through His eyes. "And I, when I am lifted up from the earth, will draw all men to myself" (John 12: 32).

From this position we can look back upon Lent, which commemorates the struggle of our Lord Jesus with the powers of evil, and his suffering to save us from destruction at their hands. We can also look forward to Easter and envision our Lord's victory over death, sin, and Satan, and our hope of re-creation through his Spirit.

In a broader scope, we can look from the cross back to Christmas when we celebrated the divine incarnation in our Savior's birth, the beginning of God's full identification with our troubled and broken human situation on earth. At the other end of our horizon we foresee Ascension Day, our Lord's glorious return to the right hand of God, the first-born of the new humanity, living in full fellowship with God in heaven. In a word, *the cross marks at once the depth of our Lord's involvement in our human misery, and the height of our hope of sharing in his glory.*

Throughout the centuries the church has celebrated this dramatic sequence of divine-human activity, from the incarnation to the ascension, once each year. The purpose has been to give us a continuing reminder of the overarching significance of these events for our lives and to help us to find our role in the drama of God's covenant with his people.

This same concern has motivated the church to produce a biblical theology of history by which to interpret the whole meaning of life and of human history from the perspective of the cross. Ultimately the vista carries us back to the beginning of time and forward to its consummation in eternity.

The last book in the New Testament, the book of Revelation, is a heightened expression of what is generally said in the Bible as a whole. It is concerned with the mystery of human destiny in the purpose of God. Just as in the entire biblical covenant drama, this book centers upon a key personality through whom the ultimate mystery of life is revealed. This person is referred to as "the Lamb who was slain" (Rev. 5: 12).

The symbol of the Lamb is derived from an interpretation of our Lord's death on the cross as an expiatory sacrifice whereby God's children are redeemed from every tribe and tongue and people and nation, and restored to his kingdom of love and righteousness. The Lamb is a symbol of Jesus Christ, the revealer and consummator of God's purpose in the events of human history. Indeed, he is the risen and glorified Lord of history, to whom an ever increasing chorus of voices raises its praise:

> Worthy is the Lamb who was slain,
>   to receive power and wealth
>   and wisdom and might
>   and honor and glory and blessing!

In the same way that the cross has come to be the symbol of
the center of history, the Alpha and the Omega, the first and the
last letters of the Greek alphabet, have come to be symbols for
the beginning and the end of human history. Although the concept of God as "the first and the last" had already been taught
by the prophet Second Isaiah (44: 6 and 48: 12), it is not until
the last book of the New Testament that the symbols themselves
are used to express this universal span of God's activity as seen
from the perspective of the cross.

Most inclusive of all the symbols for God and Jesus in this
book is the one that affirms the universal scope of God's activity
in terms which correspond to the unity undergirding the three
tenses in our human existence: present, past, and future. In the
opening chapter (1: 8) the apostle witnesses to the eternal God
as the Almighty who declares:

> "I am the Alpha and the Omega, . . .
> who is and who was and who is to come."

In the last chapter (22: 13) it is the Lamb, speaking for God
whose throne he shares, who declares:

> "I am the Alpha and the Omega,
> the first and the last,
> the beginning and the end."

In these terms, therefore, the Bible rounds out at once its report of God's eternal purpose, implicit in his creation and made
explicit in his Son our Lord Jesus Christ, and of man's eternal
destiny, implicit in the election of Israel and made explicit in our
Lord's death and resurrection. In Jesus the Christ, crucified and
risen from the dead, *we have received, at one and the same time
the full revelation of God to man and of man to himself.*[1]

As the embodiment of the sacrificial love of God in history
(the Eternal Word of God) Jesus Christ points to the sovereign
authority of God as the source and author of our existence (God

---

[1] Cf. the opening affirmation of the Message of the International Missionary Council, Jerusalem, 1928, "He is the revelation of what God is and of
what man through him may become."

the Father) and to the everlasting faithfulness of God as the goal and fulfillment of our existence (God the Holy Spirit). This, we believe, is the deepest biblical insight into the triunity of God's character (cf. section B, following).

On the other hand, our Lord Jesus is the perfect embodiment of human obedience. His is the perfectly centered life. He is the norm of the faithful human stewardship of life, in the service of the neighbor and to the glory of God. Before his authentic humanity our lives are judged as counterfeit, threatened by death, sin, and Satan. We cannot say, as he says, "*I am* who I am, who I have been, and who I will be." By his standards our past is a nightmare of failure and shame, our present a momentous pretension (sometimes we are more and sometimes we are less than we pretend), and our future hope-less.

Jesus Christ is our Judge and our Redeemer. His judgment is itself redemptive, and his redemption comes to us as divine justification. No wonder that the apostle Paul refers to our Lord's life and word as "the mystery of the gospel" (Eph. 6: 19). Christ's judgment, taken by itself, however, can but lead us to utter despair. The irony is that if it does not lead us to despair of our pretensions, the other side of the coin of his revelation of perfect manhood, the bestowal of his own righteousness for our forgiveness and recreation, goes by default. Indeed, his acceptance of us as we are brings about no change in us until we acknowledge that "*we are* who we are." When, however, we acknowledge his judgment as righteous, his redemptive work is being done. Our spirits have not yet been wholly transformed, but our lives have been restored to their lost center.

This, then, is our hope: The goal of our being, like its source and its center, is in the living God. In Christ we confess the gift of eternal life and testify to his victory, through death and resurrection, over the powers that threaten to undo us. Note, in the following chart, the correlation between the last phrases of the Apostles' Creed and the biblical meaning of the victory of Jesus Christ over the powers of evil.

The Church's Confession of Faith		The Biblical Meaning of the Victory of Jesus Christ	
LIFE EVERLASTING	Communion of Saints - Fellowship of the Holy Spirit	vs. Status of permanent estrangement (Hell)	THE POWER OF EVIL
	Forgiveness of Sins - Redemption to authentic selfhood	vs. Enslavement to pretension (Satan)	
	Resurrection of the Body - Rebirth of personal encounter	vs. Individual extinction (Death)	

Indeed, the church of Christ in history acknowledges that, by the blood of the new covenant, we are *already* citizens of the eternal kingdom, but that we are *not yet* at home in Zion. We are a "colony of heaven" (Phil. 3: 20, Moffatt), whose work is on earth. We are colonists entrusted with the responsibility of witnessing to the lordship of Christ on earth, as it is already acknowledged in heaven.

> Whenever there is silence around me
>   by day or by night—
> I am startled by a cry.
> It came down from the cross—
>   the first time I heard it.
> I went out and searched—
> And found a man in the throes of crucifixion,
> And I said, "I will take you down,"
> And I tried to take the nails out of his feet.
> But he said, "Let them be
> For I cannot be taken down
> Until every man, every woman and every child
>   come together to take me down."
> And I said, "But I cannot hear your cry.
>   What can I do?"
> And he said, "Go about the world—
>   tell everyone that you meet—
> There is a man on the cross."
>
>   —Elizabeth Cheney[2]

---

[2] Quoted by Gaius Glenn Atkins: *From the Cross: the Seven Last Words*, p. 57. Harper & Brothers, 1937.

B. Confessing Our Faith in One God: Father, Son, and Holy Spirit

There are many ways to express the meaning of the mystery of the Being of God in terms of what the Christian church has traditionally called the doctrine of the trinity. They all attempt to explain the unique situation which has produced the Christian faith, that is, the personal revelation of the eternal God in the midst of historical time. To some it may appear arbitrary that the key number in interpreting the temporal aspect of God's personal revelation should be *three*, not two or four or some other. In reply it must be acknowledged at the outset that this doctrine is the work neither of scientific investigation nor of speculative reasoning. It arises as a "confession of faith," out of the personal confrontation of the early Christian church with the presence of God in the man Christ Jesus.

Although the depth and character of God's own inner life will always remain a mystery, the unfolding biblical drama gives us the following clues for discovering why the church has consistently declared the Being of God to be three-in-one, that is, a triunity:

1. *The three dimensions of personal encounter in our relationship to God in Jesus Christ, expressed confessionally.*

Jesus Christ, we confess, is our Judge, Redeemer, and Recreator. This threefold confession defines our status in relationship to God, who "was in Christ reconciling the world to himself" (2 Cor. 5. 19):

> God is over-against-us, as Judge,
> God is with-us, as Redeemer,
> God is within-and-among-us, as Re-creator.

One of the oldest symbols that the church has used to represent the trinity is a circular diagram showing the unity of God at the center and denoting the co-equal threeness of his character or function by three equal radii. When we express our confession diagrammatically in this form we are portraying one of the most basic meanings of trinitarian teaching, God's functional three-in-oneness.

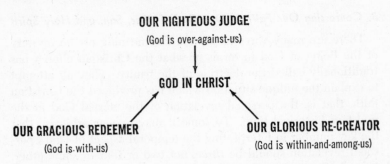

OUR RIGHTEOUS JUDGE
(God is over-against-us)

GOD IN CHRIST

OUR GRACIOUS REDEEMER
(God is-with-us)

OUR GLORIOUS RE-CREATOR
(God is within-and-among-us)

2. *The self-revelation of God as the Eternal Being in relationship to the three tenses of our human existence in historical time.*

"I am [he] who is and who was and who is to come."
(Revelation 1: 8)

"Jesus Christ is the same yesterday and today and for ever."
(Hebrews 13: 8)

Our biblical heritage makes prominent use of time categories in expressing both our relationship to God and his relationship to us. Among these the measure of a lifetime, the span of human history and eternity, are of primary importance.

One's lifetime, like history, must always be seen from the perspective of the present, bounded on the one side by the past and on the other by the future. The apostle Paul's great trilogy of Christian graces—faith, hope, and love—covers the whole of life when it is analyzed in terms of the measure of a lifetime. Figuratively we may say that faith is the past tense of love, and hope is its future tense.

History, too, is best understood from the perspective of its center. In the midst of human history God revealed himself in the man Christ Jesus as the authentic meaning of our human existence (I am who I am) and the embodiment of *love* and righteousness. From this position *faith* confesses God as the Source of history (the Alpha) and the Author of our existence (I have always been who I am). At the same time *hope* con-

fesses God as the Goal of history (the Omega) and the fulfillment of our human destiny (I will ever be who I am).[3]

This line of interpretation of the Christian teaching regarding
the three-in-oneness of God is of special significance, because it
gives us the assurance that God has involved himself so deeply
in our life that all history has been transfigured by him.

As a clue to the meaning of the trinity we use the following
diagram. It represents the threefoldness of the dramatic sequence of covenant encounter without, however, distorting the
unity of God's eternal perspective.

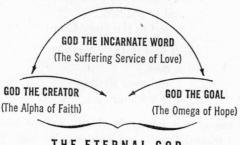

GOD THE INCARNATE WORD
(The Suffering Service of Love)

GOD THE CREATOR
(The Alpha of Faith)

GOD THE GOAL
(The Omega of Hope)

THE ETERNAL GOD

So faith, hope, and the suffering service of love abide, these
three, and the greatest of all is the eternal faithfulness of God
which begets and sustains all of them.

3. *The personal interrelationship of roles within the family
constellation as an analogy to God's own inner personal life.*

Fatherhood, motherhood, and childhood constitute together
the inner spiritual situation in which the meaning of human
existence is revealed. In each family where Christ is Lord and
Savior, "fatherhood," "motherhood," and "childhood" become
sacramental symbols of the divine life in human terms.[4]

---

[3] Here we are using the clear teaching of Revelation 1:8 to define the content of the mysterious announcement of God about himself, I AM WHO I AM,
in Exodus 3:14.

[4] This view is supported by the interpretation of the well-known second-
century Christian theologian, Clement of Alexandria, in a homily entitled
Quis Dives Salvetur. "The ineffability of God is Father, but his sympathy toward us is Mother; by loving [us] the Father becomes female."

The concepts of fatherhood as God's sovereign "righteousness," sonship as the "suffering service" of God, and motherhood as the "steadfastness" of God's love not only help us to understand each of our family roles as sacramental symbols of the divine life, but they likewise correspond to the tenses of God's eternal self-revelation. We confess, in the Gloria Patri that God our heavenly Father, who came to us in his Son, Jesus Christ, is with us now and forevermore through the Holy Spirit. This is the way in which the church has sung his praise throughout the ages:

> Glory be to the Father,
> and to the Son,
> and to the Holy Ghost;

> As it was in the beginning,
> is now,
> and ever shall be;
> World without end.

The doctrine of the trinity is clearly not so much a secret mathematical formula[5] as it is a glorious doxology, praising the eternal God and reaffirming the whole covenant story of what he has done, is doing, and promises yet to do.

---

[5] Nonetheless, the classical formulations of the Christian doctrine of the trinity involve certain paradoxical expressions regarding the internal mystery of the Being of the living God. These arise in regard to the three and one as three-in-one. The result is a careful balance, between affirmations regarding the threefoldness of God's nature and corresponding affirmations regarding the three-in-oneness of his Being.

Classical Christian theology affirms:

(1) the priority of the Father over the Son (begotten) and the Holy Spirit (proceeding) and the co-eternity of all three (Father, Son, and Holy Spirit, ever one God);

(2) three distinct personal manifestations of God (*tres personae,* meaning three persons, in the sense of legal status or as *dramatis personae*) and the equal divineness of each and all (*una substantia, homo-ousion,* one in essence);

(3) that distinctive characteristics are revealed in each of the three *personae,* (for example, sovereign righteousness in the Creator, justifying love in the Reconciler, and empowering love in the Consummator of the Kingdom) and the presence of the whole trinity—Father, Son, and Holy Spirit (the Eternal God) in each act of divine-human encounter.

(4) that the Father is not the Son, the Son is not the Holy Spirit, and the Holy Spirit is not the Father, and yet God is One—Father, Son, and Holy Spirit.

We have already drawn several diagrams to express different facets of trinitarian interpretation. This final chart is meant to represent the whole covenant drama of God and man in trinitarian terms.

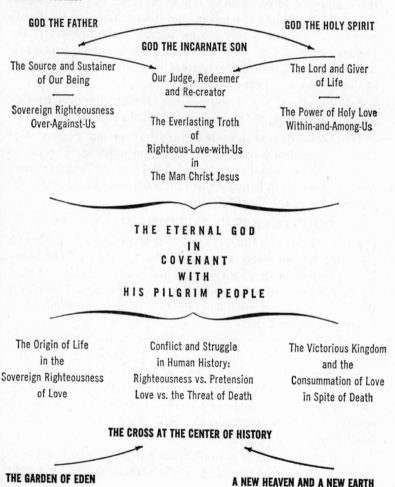

GOD THE FATHER   GOD THE HOLY SPIRIT

GOD THE INCARNATE SON

The Source and Sustainer
of Our Being   Our Judge, Redeemer   The Lord and Giver
                                 and Re-creator   of Life

Sovereign Righteousness
Over-Against-Us   The Everlasting Troth   The Power of Holy Love
                                      of   Within-and-Among-Us
                                 Righteous-Love-with-Us
                                      in
                                 The Man Christ Jesus

THE ETERNAL GOD
IN
COVENANT
WITH
HIS PILGRIM PEOPLE

The Origin of Life   Conflict and Struggle   The Victorious Kingdom
in the   in Human History: and the
Sovereign Righteousness   Righteousness vs. Pretension   Consummation of Love
of Love   Love vs. the Threat of Death   in Spite of Death

THE CROSS AT THE CENTER OF HISTORY

THE GARDEN OF EDEN   A NEW HEAVEN AND A NEW EARTH

C. Practicing the "Mysteries" of Our Faith

The Christian church practices two time-honored mysteries. Taken together they represent the relationship of Christ both to the origin and to the goal of our lives. They are called sacraments; the sacrament of baptism, and the sacrament of the Lord's Supper. Sacrament simply means "mystery," the mystery of the healing power of God's love and how it works once it gets inside the human heart, first in the heart of Jesus and then in the hearts of those of us who bear his name.

Baptism affirms the mystery of our election, the promise that from the beginning we are included in God's covenant love.

The Lord's Supper reveals the mystery of our destiny, that God's love is steadfast and his covenant everlasting. The Lord's Supper is the clue to the mystery of the end of our human drama, because it writes in letters six feet high a banner headline for the final edition of the *World Times:*

GOD'S LOVE IS VICTOR OVER MAN'S FEAR

The Lord Jesus on the night when he was betrayed took bread, and when he had given thanks, he broke it, and said, "This is my body which is broken for you. Do this in remembrance of me." In the same way also the cup, after supper, saying, "This cup is the new covenant of my blood. Do this, as often as you drink it, in remembrance of me."

Such love disarms pretensions and reveals the wantonness of infidelity. It throttles the rebellious will, strangling pride and greed, envy and contempt. Above all, Christ's love reassures us at the most vulnerable spots. He reassures us that our fear of extinction is unfounded. If he can die in order that we may be redeemed from a living death, death itself loses its demonic fascination.

There are four words in our Christian heritage which we have used to express the meaning of the sacrament of the Lord's Supper:

(1) Eucharist—or thanksgiving for the grace of our Lord Jesus Christ;

(2) Holy Communion—or fellowship with God through Christ;

(3) *Agape* (the Love Feast)—or the fellowship of those who are one in Christ;

(4) Victory Banquet of the Kingdom of God—or the food of eternal life.

First and foremost, we must understand our celebration of the Lord's Supper as an act of gratitude. It is occasioned by our remembering ("Do this in remembrance of me") of Christ's sacrifice ("my body which is broken for you") in redeeming us from the powers of evil. How can we possibly celebrate so great a sacrifice as his has been for us without making our celebration a sacrifice of praise and thanksgiving?

Our Lord's own words of institution imply that we give thanks as often as we break bread. Indeed, I think that the Iona Community, in the Church of Scotland, has maintained in its liturgy an essential element in the practice of the Eucharist. The bread for the Lord's Supper (the sacrament is celebrated every Sunday) is baked by the housewives of the community. In fact, the whole week's supply of bread is brought to the communion table with the morning offering. There it is blessed, some is broken and shared sacramentally, and the rest is taken home to hallow the whole week's work. The Eucharist is therefore the Christian community's sacrifice of praise and thanksgiving.

In the second place, and quite centrally in our lives, the Lord's Supper is the Holy Communion. It is our innermost experience of fellowship with God. One of the controversial issues in understanding the meaning of the Lord's Supper has grown out of differing interpretations of the "real presence."

Whatever our interpretation of the manner of the real presence of Christ and of his love in our midst, we cannot mistake his presence when we see him break the bread. Moreover, "the miracle of grace in the Lord's Supper is not any change in the nature of bread and wine, but it is the fact that the bread is *broken*, as Christ's body was broken, that the wine is *poured out*, as his blood was poured out, and that as these things are *given* to the people by God so they receive the sacrifice of God."[6]

As John Calvin clearly saw, the mystery is not how bread becomes His body. The mystery is that His body and blood, that is, his death and resurrection, become the bread and wine by which our spirits are fed.

> "On him must our spirits feed,
> O taste and see that the Lord is good."

Recall the story of the two disciples on the way to Emmaus. It was just three days after the Lord's crucifixion. These disciples were sadly returning home from Jerusalem when a stranger drew near and walked along with them. Their conversation was enlightening, but not until they had invited him to share the evening meal with them did he, in the breaking and blessing of the bread, reveal his identity to them. "Their eyes were opened and they recognized him" (Luke 24: 31). We cannot mistake his presence when we see him break the bread.

And we cannot escape his presence when we hear his words: "Come to me." One experience that Mrs. Miller and I shall never forget is our attendance at the service of Holy Communion at the Domkyrkan in Copenhagen, Denmark, at the time of the Lund Conference on Faith and Order in August, 1952. In this stately old Danish cathedral church the sculptor Thorvaldsen has placed huge likenesses of Christ and his disciples. The twelve disciples are arranged at intervals along the side walls, six on either side of the nave, and the Christ stands over the altar, with hands outstretched in compassion, saying the words which the church has rightly always associated with the celebration of the Lord's Supper: "Come to me, all who labor and are heavy-laden, and I will give you rest." When we knelt to receive the broken bread and a sip from the cup, Christ looked us right in the eye. We could not escape his presence!

In the early church there was an observance which has been lost from the celebration of the Lord's Supper for the most part, but which we would do well to restore. Even in the early days

---

[6] "Sacrifice and Sacrament" by Robert S. Paul. *The Chaplain*, April, 1956.

it seems to have been a separate practice. It was called the *agape*, the "love" feast. (My only acquaintance with this form of observance came in my youth in a little Methodist church in eastern Pennsylvania.) The central feature of the simple ritual is the act of each worshiper sharing his bread with his neighbor.

Just as we acknowledge that the presence of Christ in our midst is guiding us to communion with God, so his presence unites us in community with each other. We become a community because we are a people who have been bound together in communion with the living God. The love that redeems and re-creates us thereby seeks to inspire us to love, to bring healing into our "broken" communities. Therefore, we must add, the depth of our communion in the sacrament of the Lord's Supper is measured in the eyes of God by the breadth of our community during the remainder of the week. The demand *(Aufgabe)* that goes with the promise *(Gabe)* is clear. Fervently may we pray the prayer which the early church included in the *Didache*:

> As the broken bread was scattered over the mountains,
>> and being gathered together became one,
> So may the church be gathered from the ends of the earth
>> into thy everlasting kingdom. Amen.

This is the meaning of our Lord's parable concerning the day of final judgment and redemption.

"Then the King will say to those at his right hand, 'Come, O blessed of my Father, inherit the kingdom prepared for you from the foundation of the world; for I was hungry and you gave me food, I was thirsty and you gave me drink, I was a stranger and you welcomed me, I was naked and you clothed me, I was sick and you visited me, I was in prison and you came to me.'

"Then the righteous will answer him, 'Lord, when did we see thee hungry and feed thee, or thirsty and give thee drink? And when did we see thee a stranger and welcome thee, or naked and clothe thee? And when did we see thee sick or in prison and visit thee?' And the King will answer them, 'Truly, I say to you, as you did it to one of the least of these my brethren, you did it to me'" (Matt. 25: 34-40).

Thus through the *agape* the Lord's Supper comes finally to be an eschatological feast. It is a victory banquet, celebrating, in anticipation, the final consummation of God's purpose. The victory which God has already won, in the Man whom he has chosen to represent his healing love in human life, is our assurance that God's love will ultimately reign supreme.

When Jesus said to his disciples, at the time of his last supper, "I tell you I shall not drink again of this fruit of the vine until that day when I drink it new with you in my Father's kingdom" (Matt. 26: 29), our Lord was making the promise which led the apostle Paul to supplement his record of the words of institution with the injunction: "For as often as you eat this bread and drink the cup, you proclaim the Lord's death *until he comes*" (1 Cor. 11: 26).

The Toastmaster at the victory banquet of the kingdom of God is the One who was crucified for us, who was raised from the dead that we may be re-created, and who sits at the right hand of God the Father. He is the Lord of life.

Our Lord's victory is to be shared, however, only by those who will choose "life" over "death"—the community of love over the barriers of segregation and warfare, the suffering service of the neighbor over the compulsion to self-aggrandizement.

A modern parable has been written about "the heavenly banquet."

There are two great rooms, in which people are gathered around tables loaded down with food. The rooms and the tables of food are the same, and, at first sight, it appears that the people are the same, for each person is equipped with huge spoons, fastened to the arms, the handles extending all the way up to the armpits.

But with this the likeness ends, for in one room the people are starving. There is cursing and fighting and gnashing of teeth. In the other, there is peace and joy. A closer look discloses that in the room where confusion reigned, each one was trying to feed himself. In the other, the people had learned that in order to live in God's world they must feed each other.

O God, the Father of our Lord Jesus Christ, of whom the whole family in heaven and earth is named; we rejoice before thee in the blessed communion of all thy saints, wherein thou givest us also to have part. We praise thee for the holy fellowship of patriarchs and prophets, apostles and martyrs, and the whole glorious company of the redeemed of all ages, who have died in the Lord, and now live with him forevermore. We give thanks unto thee for thy grace and gifts bestowed on those who have thus gone before us in the way of salvation, and by whom we are now compassed about in our Christian course, as a cloud of witnesses looking down upon us from the heavenly world. Enable us to follow their faith, that we may enter at death into their joy; and to abide with them in rest and peace, till both they and we shall reach our common consummation of redemption and bliss in the glorious resurrection of the last day. Amen.

*Lord Jesus, for thee I live, for thee I suffer,
   for thee I die!
Lord Jesus, thine will I be in life and death.
Grant me, O Lord, eternal salvation! Amen.*
(Prayer of Commitment, *Evangelical Catechism*)

PART THREE

Christian Nurture and Discipline
Reclaiming Our Covenant Heritage in Christian Education

"Christian nurture *and* discipline" is obviously much more than a human enterprise. Its character is fundamentally rooted in divine-human encounter. That is to say:

(1) Christian education is the task of *nurturing* each new generation *in the discipline of the Lord.* We bequeath to our children what we ourselves have received—the gracious renewal of our being in the gospel of Jesus Christ our Lord.

(2) God himself is the main actor in all Christian nurture and discipline. It is his love and righteousness which he is entrusting to us to transmit from generation to generation.

The awesome task of communicating the love and righteousness of God from one generation to another, and at the same time of exemplifying that love and righteousness as the life and mission of the people of God, defines nothing less than the entire function of the Christian church.

Christian education enlists the participation of the whole congregation: parents, teachers, and pastors; children, adolescents, and adults. The nurture of God's love and the discipline of his righteousness are the warp and woof of the whole Christian life: confession of sin and confession of faith; decision and action; worship and work. Christian education is involved in every phase of the Christian ministry. The traditional "means of grace" —teaching, liturgy, preaching, and the sacraments—are all media through which the people of God relive their covenant with the Lord. They are the channels through which the church recapitulates for her people, day after day, week after week, year after year, and in every generation, the vital truth of the renewal, growth, and fulfillment of our being in Jesus Christ.

Hear, O Israel:
   The Lord our God is one Lord;

And you shall love the Lord your God
   with all your heart,
   and with all your soul,
   and with all your might.

And these words which I command you this day
   shall be upon your heart;

And you shall teach them diligently to your children,
   and shall talk of them
when you sit in your house,
   and when you walk by the way,
   and when you lie down,
   and when you rise.

And you shall bind them as a sign upon your hand,
   and they shall be as frontlets between your eyes.
And you shall write them
   on the doorposts of your house
   and on your gates.

                        (Deuteronomy 6: 4-9)

Children, obey your parents in the Lord,
   for this is right.

Honor your father and mother, . . .
   that it may be well with you
   and that you may live long on the earth.

Fathers, do not provoke your children to anger,
   but bring them up in the [nurture and discipline]
   of the Lord.

                        (Ephesians 6: 1-4)

THE TASK OF CHRISTIAN COMMUNICATION

Communication is the life blood of all personal existence. It is as essential to one's whole being as breathing is to the body. Awareness of this basic human situation has prompted penal officers and outlaws alike to devise solitary confinement as the most rigorous kind of human punishment. All evidence points to the truth that the functional unit of a healthy humanity is not the lone individual but the community of two or more persons engaged in a variety of expressions of personal communication with each other.

By the same token, the "iron curtain" is a symptom of a most deadly disease. It threatens the very existence of mankind in every generation. The break-down of communication is the basic source of all that is evil in God's world. The symptom is especially dangerous in our age. Our brokenness is all the more disturbing because we face it at a time when human invention has effected unbelievable improvements in the physical media of communication, effectually destroying distance, one of community's most formidable foes.

We live today in one world geographically, and we are deeply embarrassed that we are not one community socially and spiritually. Our political pretension that there are two worlds which are to be deliberately kept incommunicado is therefore doubly serious. We are like two persons living in the same room, each unwilling to share the room with the other, actually willing the destruction of the other, but each inescapably dependent upon the other for his existence.

Communication is not only the problem of international relations. It is also the problem of all other human relations as well—industrial, racial, social, family, and ecclesiastical. For lack of it racial antipathies become vicious and labor-management tensions become rigid and inflexible, just as individual men and women become neurotic and psychotic. Incommunication produces utter loneliness and meaninglessness; it is existence on the edge of "the abyss of nothingness." To be someone is to be in communication with someone else. To be alone, completely alone, is hell. The problem is fundamentally spiritual, and roots in the failure of communication between our spirits and the Spirit of God.

To save the world and its people from hell, from the consequences of their own deliberate separatism, God has entered into communication with humankind in a most spectacular and salutary way—*the Incarnation of His Word*. It is the genius of our biblical heritage in the life of the Christian church to bear witness to the fact that in Jesus Christ the lines of communication between God and humanity are basically re-established, and that therefore the lines of communication between the fragments of humankind are continually subject to restoration.

The church's task of Christian education and evangelism must be seen and carried on in the light of the centrality of this deep-seated problem of communication in human life. Indeed, not only the evangelistic task of the church but the very character of the church is involved. Unless we recognize the church as an instrumental factor in God's answer to man's problem of communication, we misrepresent the most obvious meaning of the apostle Paul's symbols for the church, the "body of Christ" and the "community of the Holy Spirit."

Generally speaking, communication occurs in many forms and operates in many dimensions. Human beings share with other living organisms, albeit in a more highly developed form, a marvelous set of physiological and psychological equipment for effective communication. There is the heart and the blood circulatory system, the brain and the nervous system, operating within each living organism. Between us there have developed intricate patterns of sensory perception and cognitive technique in which we make use of visual, tactile, and verbal symbols.

Language, either spoken and heard or written and read, has come to be man's chief instrument of communication, not only of information but of feeling and volition as well. Techniques for increasing the efficiency and range of verbal communication have been improved from the time of the first appearance of Adam to the age of our conquest of the atom. Alphabet and phonetics, vocabulary and grammar, prose and poetry, symbolic logic and dialectic, are all at our disposal. Moreover, a myriad physical and chemical inventions have helped to extend the scope and intensity, the quantity and quality, of interpersonal encounter. Notable have been the printing press, the motion picture, the telephone, the telegraph, the radio, and the television.

However, anything so important to healthy human living is certain to be beset with difficulties and limitations. Differences of language, culture, and religious tradition, as well as those which are rooted in conflicting political ideologies, inevitably make for difficulty in communication. Have you ever been alone in a foreign country, in the social setting of another religious community, or in a cultural group other than your own? Situations of broken communication are often very amusing when seen from a larger perspective, but they are very painful to the person immediately involved.

Take, for example, this ludicrous experience in verbal difficulties in communication which is reported by an American tourist visiting in Germany. A Hollywood cowboy and Indian movie was being shown. The technicians had produced a German soundtrack to take the place of the American conversation. At the crucial point of the story, when the cowboy and the Indian met, you could see the Indian raise his hand and say, "How!" But the German voice said, "*Wie geht's?*"

On some occasions, on the other hand, communication occurs without our being aware of it. A Quaker was attending an auction sale as a spectator, but became carried away by the cross-fire of conversation and nodded his head several times. Suddenly the auctioneer knocked down a parrot to him for $50.00. He was more than a little confused and disturbed. He blurted out, "How can thee be sure this bird can even talk?" Whereupon the parrot looked at him sidewise and said, "Who does thee suppose was bidding against thee, just now?"

A. The Twofold Nature of Communication

These stories underscore the fact that a serious study of human communication must maintain a clear distinction between two different forms or types: (1) transmission through verbal or sensory symbols, and (2) communion through participation in personal encounter. The whole theological climate of today is deeply indebted at this point to a Jewish philosopher and theologian, Martin Buber. In his little classic, *I and Thou,* he traces the roots of this distinction to the twofold nature of the primary words we speak: *I-It* and *I-Thou. I-It* represents our relationships to the world of things which we possess and control and can talk about. The "It" includes also "He," "She," and "They," for all third-person references in human conversation are treated impersonally. *I-Thou* represents the world of personal relationships and is structured by the fact that my "I" is continually being confronted by a "Thou" in an encounter which promises (or threatens) to change me.

Dr. Hendrik Kraemer, in *The Communication of the Christian Faith,* has recently defined the forms of communication which these primary relationships produce as *communication of* and *communication between.*

Communication of applies to ideas, feelings, information, expressed in terms of symbols representing something in which the speaker and perhaps the communicant are interested. This form is best illustrated by the procedures in scientific education and sheds light upon only that part of oneself which is involved in a specific interest.

On the other hand, *communication between* refers to an event which happens when two persons are engaged in a personal encounter. What passes between them is inseparable from each, and more than both. It is best defined as participation or communion. Here one's whole person is involved, for it is oneself who is engaged in the encounter and participates in the common life.

Both forms of communication are important. Neither is to be discredited nor adjudged inadequate to its purpose. By the same token neither can do the job of the other, for each operates in a different sphere of "knowledge." In order to maintain this division of labor, most languages have two different words for the verb "to know." One is for scientific knowledge about our "I-It" world; for example, *savoir* (French) and *Wissen* (German). The other is for acquaintanceship and intimate personal (I-Thou) participation in common life; for example, *connaître* (French) and *kennen* (German).

In actual everyday living, however, these two types of communication refuse to stay as neatly separated as their mutually exclusive definitions might suggest. We must never lose sight of the fact that human life is ambiguous: We are *creatures in the image of God*, a living bipolar tension of *nature and spirit*.[1] Our spiritual gifts and powers open to us the dimension of mystery in which interpersonal communion and community participation occur. But we have these heavenly gifts in earthen vessels. We are organically bound to nature and subject to her limitations. Thus, each actual occasion of interpersonal communion happens in the context of a host of impersonal factors and relationships. It is quite natural for us to use words (for example, I love you!) or actions (a glance, a hand signal, a kiss) to symbolize the deeper dimensions of intimate personal communication. Moreover, we are largely dependent upon verbal, visual, and tactile symbols when we wish to strike up an acquaintance, to recall the occasion of an unrepeatable "encounter," to bridge the gap between "meetings," or to rekindle the simmering flame of love in the soul.

Nonetheless, the most significant moments in our lives defy full

---

[1] The tension between these two orders of communication is rooted in the basic tension within the soul of every man. Our ambiguous situation can be creative if we accept ourselves as we are meant to be in the purpose of God, that is, as stewards of his world and servants of his love and righteousness. This tension leads inevitably to disaster, however, when it becomes the occasion for pretension, for either sensuality or pride. For example, our creatureliness is only a part of life, but it is always subject to the temptation to claim to be the whole of it. Likewise with "the image of God." Although this gift of God's own Spirit is his bestowal of that which makes life whole, it is not itself the whole, to the exclusion of our creatureliness. Rather it is the power to bring our creaturely existence to wholeness.

transmissive communication beyond the community of those who
participated in the event. Words alone fail us in our effort to
report all that has happened. When, however, we recall a common experience in company with other participants, no matter
how disconnectedly or ineptly it is told from a transmissive point
of view, the overtones will carry the meaning and may even become an occasion for "reliving" the event. This, for example, is
exactly what happens at a school or college class reunion or
whenever old friends meet.

B. Communicating in Two Dimensions at Once: Communion and Community

The distinction between "transmission through verbal or sensory symbols" and "communion through participation in personal
encounter" in all human communication is sharpened when one
attempts to understand the life of the Christian church in the
revelation of God.

The Christian church presents a unique situation in human
history, for she belongs to two dimensions of personal encounter
at once. The church is the *community* of those who are bound
to one another in love and righteousness because they are first
engaged in *communion* with God through the Lord Jesus Christ.
She is at every moment sustained and confronted by the justifying grace of God (cf. the vertical arrows on the accompanying
chart). At the same time, she has been endowed with certain
"means of grace" by which to transmit God's revelation from
generation to generation, and through which to prepare all God's
people for participation, as members of families and congregations, in "the nurture and discipline of the Lord" (cf. the horizontal arrows on the chart).

The Life of the Christian Church
in the Revelation of God

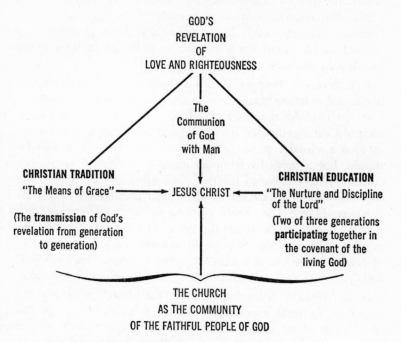

GOD'S
REVELATION
OF
LOVE AND RIGHTEOUSNESS

The
Communion
of God
with Man

CHRISTIAN TRADITION
"The Means of Grace" ——→ JESUS CHRIST ←—— **CHRISTIAN EDUCATION**
"The Nurture and Discipline
of the Lord"

(The **transmission** of God's
revelation from generation
to generation)

(Two of three generations
participating together in
the covenant of the
living God)

THE CHURCH
AS THE COMMUNITY
OF THE FAITHFUL PEOPLE OF GOD

1. THE DIVINE-HUMAN COVENANT TROTH:
COMMUNION

The divine-human covenant troth by which God established
an everlasting bond of love and righteousness between himself
and his people is the primary dimension of Christian communication (cf. the vertical arrows). The divine revelation and the
faithful response of his covenant people meet in Jesus Christ and
define the perfect exemplification of personal communion and
spiritual participation. He is the only-begotten Son of the Father,
full of grace and truth, and he is the first-fruit of a new humanity, the author and perfecter of our faith. (Cf. Part Two, ACT II.)

In New Testament terms this faithful responsive participation of the covenant people is called *koinonia*, that is, commun-

ion with God and community among the people who are the family of God. Fundamentally this double meaning of *koinonia* determines the two dimensions of all Christian communication within the church: vertically, between God and the church (covenant communion); and horizontally, from generation to generation (the community of two or more generations living together in covenant with the living God).

It is precisely because of this two-dimensional, vertical and horizontal relationship in which the church has its existence that the twofold character of all personal communication has such a great significance for us. The above chart is constructed to give a visual representation of our situation. It would be simple, but a gross oversimplification, to declare a one-to-one correspondence between the two dimensions of the church's life and the twofold character of all human communication. That is, we could say: *The church participates in an everlasting troth with God, and she transmits this truth within the covenant community.* Although this is basically correct, we are, as a matter of fact, engaged in a creative tension between "transmission" and "participation" on both dimensions of the church's existence.

In the vertical dimension as such, the church is clearly engaged in spiritual encounter. Just as soon, however, as the church sets about to define the form and content of the divine activity and the scope of her own life and responsibility, she resorts to verbal and sensory symbols. Because we are human beings, living on the horizontal plane, we are even forced to use human symbols to express the divine revelation.

Although the Bible is normative for all our understanding of the vertical dimension of communication, it is not itself "the Word of God." The Bible is "the transmitter" of the Word of God. The form of transmission is unique, however, for the Bible is not a set of philosophical theories about God. God's own self-disclosure is reported and transmitted to later generations in the form of "dramatic recital," that is, by telling the story of "what God has done, is doing, and promises to do."

In so far as we can verbalize the truth of the divine-human

troth in conceptual terms Christian theology is equipped with the basic categories by which to formulate the "doctrine of God." God reveals himself (1) through his Mighty Acts (dramatic encounter), (2) through the gift of his own Spirit (spiritual participation), (3) through his Covenant Word (personal dialogue). Each is a manifestation of the glorious mystery of his own inner life. Thus Christian theology is like the Bible in which it is rooted. Theology's ultimate concern is with the vertical dimension of communication, that is, with God himself, but as a human discipline its major task is human understanding and the horizontal transmission of the truth of God's covenant troth with us from generation to generation.

2. CHRISTIAN TRADITION AND CHRISTIAN EDUCATION: COMMUNITY

Tradition is a very important and honorable aspect of the life of any people that is historically self-conscious. Christian tradition is unique in this respect. Over and above the church's proper regard for passing on her own cultural deposit, she has become the trustee in her very existence of the covenant of the living God and therefore carries in her life "the means of grace." The church is responsible for passing on, from generation to generation, the tradition which she has received, involving her continually in the transmissive communication of the divine Acts, Gift, and Word, and for the corresponding human volitions, emotions, convictions, and personal relationships which flow from a faithful response. For this task the church engages in various practices and rites which have been denoted as "means of grace." Teaching the covenant, celebrating the liturgy, preaching the gospel, and observing the sacraments—each and all together are instruments for reliving the biblical covenant drama and are therefore means of communicating "the justifying grace of God in Jesus Christ."

The traditional "means of grace" and Christian education correspond to each other in the same way that divine revelation and human response are bound together. Moreover, there is the same accent within this tension upon the initiative of the primary pole. Within the life of the Christian community the initiative lies with the older generation, that is, the parents, teachers, and pastors who, as the ministers of God, are entrusted with the means of grace. But the work of Christian education does not really happen until the younger generation, that is, families and congregations, as the children of God, find themselves participating with the older generation in a gracious encounter with the living God. Moreover, the transmission of that which begins and ends in a personal communion with God will be as irrelevant as a set of nonsense syllables if there is lacking a vital personal encounter of love (Christian nurture) and righteousness (Christian discipline) between the generations both in the family and in the congregation. Therefore, we use the traditional means of grace in the divinely established community to the end that a living fellowship may spring up between the children of God and their Lord and between these same children and their parents and their peers of their own generation.

The question is: How can we communicate in terms of transmissive symbols the personal truth of "grace" and "faith"? Again, but from the perspective of our own experience in this dimension of depth, how can we of the older generations be used of the Power in, with, and under the symbols of God's grace and truth, to bring our children and ourselves together into responsible spiritual encounter with the living Christ? Fortunately, we are not left to our own resources. The living Christ himself is present, through the power of the Holy Spirit, whenever the means of grace are faithfully employed and Christian education is responsibly carried on.

C. Special Times for the Nurture and Discipline of the Lord

The people of the covenant who make up the Christian church are the trustees, for the world, of the grace of God in our Lord Jesus Christ. This grace defines her various functions in terms of what have been called "the means of grace"—teaching, healing, preaching, and the sacraments.

In the first chapter we present a "Church and Home" type of Christian education, in which the Mighty Acts of God are recovered as our own covenant story in the daily teaching and studying of the biblical covenant drama.

In the remaining chapters we shall attempt to show how the church has made it possible for her people to encounter the living God again and again, in different forms and in different time spans:

(1) Celebrating and participating in the Lord's Day liturgy once each week.

(2) Preaching and hearing the Word of God according to the structure of the Christian year.

(3) Observing the sacramental pattern of a lifetime.

The church's emphasis upon "times" and "timing" is not accidental or a matter of chance. The Gospel of Mark reports that Jesus opened his ministry in Galilee by saying, *"The time is fulfilled,* and the kingdom of God is at hand; repent, and believe in the gospel"* (Mark 1: 15). The apostle Paul, interpreting the whole significance of Christ's work on our behalf, writes, "While we were yet helpless, *at the right time* Christ died for the ungodly" (Rom. 5: 6).

In the same fashion there are special times when the church celebrates the Mighty Acts of God for the nurture and discipline of her people. The commemoration of the resurrection is the occasion for the celebration of each Lord's Day, making each Sunday a weekly Easter. Over a larger span of time, the Christian calendar commemorates week by week, throughout each year the whole life of Jesus (from the Advent to the Ascension) and his embodiment in the life of the church (from Pentecost to Memorial Sunday). By contrast, the church also takes the crisis points of a human lifetime as the occasion for special sacramental observances, at the beginning (baptism) and for the end of life (the Lord's Supper), and three covenantal observances along the way (confirmation, marriage, and ordination).

ONE

EVANGELISM AND THE TEACHING MINISTRY

Christian education is not just a part of the local congregation's activities; it permeates every phase of her life. Christian education is involved in the total program of the church, educationally conceived, planned, and carried forward.[1]

Over and above formal study and instruction, corporate worship and personal counseling, prophetic preaching and social action, special sacramental celebrations and everyday family life, all bring us face to face with God's nurturing love and righteous discipline. Christian communication takes place whenever and wherever we are involved in a personal encounter with the living God. Every personal relationship in the life of the divine-human covenant community is an occasion for our learning more of the divine will and of our own responsibility thereto.

This position is held by many specialists in Christian education. For example, the late Nevin C. Harner, in his book *The Educational Work of the Church*,[2] declared bluntly, "Nothing which a good pastor can do can possibly fall outside the scope of true Christian education." Elmer F. Ansley, in his study of the teaching ministry in the congregations of the Evangelical and Reformed Church in 1952, acknowledges the basic truth of this view but cautions against its unfortunate implications. If

---

[1] Report of the Workshop on Theological Education in the Practical Field, held at Garrett Biblical Institute, Evanston, Illinois, June 14-17, 1949, p. 35.

[2] Abingdon Press, 1939. See page 19.

everything the church does is conceived to be Christian education, the specific role of the teaching ministry will be lost.[3]

We believe that Christian communication in the broad sense of Christian nurture and discipline does include the total life and activity of the church, but we distinguish here the "teaching ministry" as a special function, among others, of the task of Christian communication. The remaining chapters of this book will explore the educational aspects of each of the church's other "means of grace"—the healing, preaching, and sacramental ministries.

From the earliest times in our spiritual heritage, beginning in ancient Israel and extending throughout the entire history of the Christian church, special accent has been put upon the "teaching" ministry. Teaching the Lord's covenant, his promises and demands, that is, calling forth[4] from our children a grateful obedience and a loyal participation in his blessing and service—this is the primary responsibility of every parent who lives in the spiritual heritage of our father Abraham.

The transmission of the covenant "blessing" from one generation to the next has always been basically a family affair: Abraham to Isaac, Isaac to Jacob, Jacob to his twelve sons, and so on. But with the transmission of the blessing and its corresponding responsibility there developed an historical tradition—the record of the covenant people and an interpretation of its meaning which has been passed on from age to age. Thus the books of the Law and of the prophets of Israel, supplemented and fulfilled by the gospels and epistles written by the apostles of our Lord Jesus Christ, became a permanent deposit of covenant literature, useful in every age to aid and abet parents and other teachers within the church in transmitting the Lord's covenant to their children.

Correspondingly, first Jewish synagogues, then Christian catechetical schools, and, since 1780, Sunday schools have functioned

---

[3] *The Educational Role of Parish Ministers in the Evangelical and Reformed Church*, p. 112. Doctoral Dissertation, Yale University, 1952.

[4] "Education" comes from the Latin *educere* meaning "to lead out" or "to call forth."

in behalf of the whole faith-community to supplement the family in its responsibility for begetting covenant loyalty in each new generation of children. With God's own covenant word as the fundamental curriculum, these schools have been the channel of the church's number one "means of grace."

The family as the covenant unit of life, the Bible as the book of the covenant, the good news of the new covenant as "the Word become flesh" in the man Christ Jesus, the church assembled as a school of covenant responsibility—these are the essential elements in the Christian teaching ministry.

In New Testament terms the teaching ministry is caught up in the task of evangelism, that is, proclaiming the good news of God's gracious renewal of the covenant "once for all" in Jesus Christ our Lord. Although we may properly make a distinction between the teaching ministry and the preaching ministry, it is not to be found primarily in terms of content, for the gospel lies at the heart of each of them. In the New Testament it appears that preaching meant "proclaiming, as a herald," whereas teaching involved personal instruction and moral exhortation. The two are so intimately intertwined, however, that no sharp line of distinction is maintained. One thing is certain. Evangelism is the task of the whole church, with regularly established times for the formal proclamation of the Word of God but with both formal and informal instruction taking place all the time.

In our American culture evangelism has come to be associated in the popular mind with a hortatory style of preaching whereby mature individuals, usually gathered in mass congregations, are urged by the evangelist to "decide for Christ." The effects of such efforts are commonly referred to as a religious revival and have undoubtedly quickened the spiritual life of many people. The general effectiveness of such an appeal, however, rests primarily upon the regular evangelism (teaching and preaching) of Christian families and congregations. The major task of evangelism throughout the history of the church, including our own American heritage, has been carried on by parents and teachers and pastors in the day-by-day nurture and discipline of each new generation into covenant participation and responsibility.

Indeed, in the main line of Reformation churches regular instruction, under the auspices of the church school and the home, is the church's way of bringing her people to decision and commitment. Regular Sunday preaching, which is always evangelical when it is properly done, that is, in accordance with the pattern of the Christian calendar, has the effect of helping God's people who are already committed "to grow in grace" by daily repentance and renewal of faith and to be strengthened with spiritual power for their daily responsibility in the service of God to the world. (Cf. chapter 3, below.)

A. Recovering the Mighty Acts of God as Our Covenant Story

The church functioning as a school is always working on two fronts at once. On the one hand, there is the task of instruction in the story of the Mighty Acts of God. Generation after generation we set about to explain and interpret the meaning of our life in covenant with the living God. On the other hand, there is the communication of God's own Spirit in and through our personal relationships with him and with each other. We are called upon to share within the fellowship of the church what God continually communicates to the fellowship—his healing love and righteous judgments as revealed in Jesus Christ.

In the course of the development of the Christian movement, however, specialized tools of instruction (creeds, catechisms, biblical commentaries, church school curricula) have been constructed, and regularized structures of belief (theologies) and cultic practices (liturgies and sacraments) have been developed.

This has been good and necessary for the sake of propagating the covenant from generation to generation, but it has also brought us difficulties with which to cope. The "Holy Book," the traditional creeds and catechisms, and the teachings of "systematic theology" always threaten to supplant the very existential, personal encounter with God which they are attempting to explain, interpret, and bring to life. Extensive cultic practices and the ritual performances of "organized religion" are a tempting substitute for intensive personal self-discipline and commitment. External obedience to the Law is so much more easily accomplished than the internal exercise of responsible freedom.

Those who shoulder the responsibility for the task of Christian education must therefore be quite clear with regard to the difference between what Christianity has in terms of "tools and structure" and what it is in terms of "purpose and function." *Christianity is a faith, whose purpose is determined by the gospel of "justifying love" and whose function is the nurturing and disciplining of each succeeding generation for responsible freedom.* Not all the words of the Bible are to be identified with the covenant Word. Creeds are not to be mistaken for the gospel. Ritual acts and formal obedience are no substitute for the courage and loyalty of a living faith. External rules of right and wrong are no match for responsible freedom. All of these are, nonetheless, useful means for the propagation of the Word of God and the instruction and disciplining of the young in the nurture of his mighty acts. The basic problem is to apportion them—the tools for the purpose, the structure to the function.

It is essential, therefore, to maintain a fundamental distinction between revelation and the record of revelation, between God's Word and the story of the divine-human encounter in which the Word is spoken, between our faith in God and our beliefs about him. To be sure, most of us have been led to trust and worship the living God by virtue of having been nurtured on the contents of the biblical story. In the long run, however, we believe in the Bible because we trust the God who has chosen to make his self-disclosure in the events which the Bible enshrines. The revelation is not the story, nor is it the book which tells the story. It is God himself who reveals his love and righteousness in personal encounter with people and who enters into covenant with them at points in their lives in which the very meaning and purpose of their existence is being decided. We read or hear the Bible story, therefore, not to get ideas and information about God, but to identify ourselves with his people, that we too may share in their covenant with him and be guided in our life decisions by the same Spirit which led Abraham and Moses, Isaiah and Jonah, Peter and Paul, to become prophets and apostles of God's holy love and sovereign righteousness.

In Part One, chapters 3 and 4, we gathered together a sequence of examples of the biblical covenant drama, drawn from the Hebrew prophets' interpretation of Israel's covenant history with their Lord, and from the apostolic witness to the new covenant in our Lord Jesus Christ. Since the Bible is the record of many generations of people living in a great variety of historical situations, its guidance to our understanding of the meaning of life is broad and inclusive. The drama of the divine-human covenant encounter is repeated in so many different ways that one of them is certain to fit any situation we face. The plot, however, is basically the same, and becomes therefore a living framework for the church's task of interpreting for her people the meaning of human existence.

Having used the ever recurring plot of the divine-human encounter as the outline for "a covenant theology" in Part Two, it is our thesis here that the church's teaching ministry always involves some form of re-enactment of the plot of the biblical story as its ultimate goal.

PROLOGUE—We have been chosen by God to be his servants on the earth, participants in his covenant of love and righteousness.

ACT I—Our humankind persistently rejects this blessing and the responsibility that is bestowed upon us. We are unfaithful to God's trust and insubordinate to his authority. We want "to be like God," that is, to be the center of the world. In consequence, we are estranged and in conflict with God, within ourselves and with the people around us. Moreover, having broken the covenant, there is nothing we can do to mend it and restore our function therein. Left in our hands, the covenant is as dead as a dodo. We are enslaved to the shadow of our own pretension, ridden with guilt and taunted by doubt.

ACT II—Save for the grace of God, revealed in our Lord Jesus Christ, this would be the miserable end of a fruitless venture. But, by the grace of God, the covenant is renewed. We are accepted as we are, not for what we are but for what we are meant to be. We are justified in spite of our insubordination. We are still trusted though manifestly unworthy of any trust. We are reconciled to God and forgiven for our sins. We are delivered from the bondage of our own self-centeredness. Having been accepted, though unworthy, we are enabled to accept the self we were meant to be.

ACT III—By the power of the Holy Spirit we are restored to responsible freedom and meaningful service in God's covenant. Our faith is reborn and our courage is renewed. We are participants in the "new humanity in Christ."

EPILOGUE—We face our destiny with a sure and living hope.

The mature Christian already knows and confesses for himself what the younger generation comes to acknowledge "the hard way" that this story is truly the story of our lives. Although we have not given prominent attention to the fact in either of the previous parts, it is important for us to acknowledge here that, in so far as our human observation goes, not all who are led to the spring of life-renewing waters drink to the health of their souls. To put it another way, the story of individual lives in the covenant encounter does not always have "a happy ending." Notwithstanding the gracious judgment and redemption of ACT II, by which reparation is made for the infidelity of ACT I, ACT III does not inevitably follow.

This was clearly the purpose of the Old Testament prophets and of our Lord Jesus Christ in using contrasting biographical illustrations to teach the covenant story to God's people. For example, the stories of Gomer (cf. p. 23) and of Jonah (cf. p. 41) report the healing work of the same gracious love on God's part, but with unequal effectiveness for the long run in regard to Israel's participation in ACT III. Likewise, Jesus' parable regarding the father and his two sons affirms the full healing and

restoration of the prodigal son and the continued stubborn rebellion of the older brother (Luke 15: 11-32). This contrast is
most irrevocably drawn in the parable of the last judgment
(Matt. 25: 31-46). Our Lord's parable pictures an EPILOGUE of
permanent but isolated self-centeredness for those who persist
in rejecting the responsibility of ACT III (vs. 41-46). It is as if
God were saying, "So be it, not *my* will, but *thine* be done!"

Given the sovereignty of God's will and the graciousness of his
love toward humankind, we are led logically to conclude that
no one would be permitted to exclude himself from God's ultimate blessing. Yet the evidence of human experience, from the
patriarchal incident of the destruction of Sodom and Gomorrah
through our Lord's parables down to the events of our own
time, seems clearly to indicate that the human will to reject
God's blessing and its correlative responsibility often remains
permanently undaunted by either his grace or his righteousness.

Without attempting to bring our theological presuppositions
and our human experience into a forced logical consistency
either way, that is, into a doctrine of "universal salvation" or a
doctrine of "double predestination," we are led to confess that
God's grace is irresistible to those who know that they live by
its power, but is unpredictable to those who presently refuse to
acknowledge its claim.

Parents and teachers whose covenant ministry to children and
to young people involves them directly in this situation, where
grace is rebuffed and responsibility is rejected, may be well
advised to make their own gratitude to Christ an open channel
of grace to those for whom they care, and to pray with John
the Baptist that in all things we may "decrease" and Christ may
"increase" (John 3: 30).

B. Teaching and Studying the Biblical Covenant Drama Daily: The Use of Catechisms and Confessions and Church and Home Curricula

A Reformation-type biblical theology, functioning in the middle of the twentieth century, may well need to look to the
Reformers for help in finding a pedagogy to match. The current

rediscovery of the Bible in the theology of the Reformation heritage certainly portends a corresponding recovery of our biblical heritage in Christian education.[5] Luther, Calvin, and other Reformers formulated catechisms to foster this recovery in the sixteenth century. They used the Bible not just as proof texts, nor yet as illustrations, but *to nurture and discipline the people of God whom they served in the plot of our biblical covenant history.*

Martin Luther is notably first among the authors of catechisms to use the three-act plot of the covenant drama as a means of teaching his parishioners to understand the meaning of their own lives as the people of God. In the preface to *A Short Exposition of the Decalogue, Apostles' Creed and the Lord's Prayer,*[6] published in 1520, Luther observes that there are three essentials that a man should know in order to be saved:

(1) He should know what his duties are, and what they are not.

(2) When at last he comes to understand that, by virtue of his own strength alone, he can neither keep this particular commandment, nor avoid yielding to that particular temptation, he should know where he can seek, and find, and obtain what he needs, so as to achieve the one and withstand the other.

(3) He should know how to set about seeking to obtain what he needs.

The case is similar to that of a sick man: his first requirement is a diagnosis of his illness, as to what he should do and what he should avoid. Next, he requires to know where the medicine is that will help him. In the third place, he must desire that medicine, seek and fetch it, or have it brought.

[5] Cf. *Biblical Theology and Christian Education* (Charles Scribner's Sons, 1956 by Professor Randolph Crump Miller. This Christian educator also uses the "Drama of Redemption" motif and acknowledges Dr. Bernhard Anderson and an *incognito* friend as contributing to its formulation.
[6] English translation by Bertram Lee Woolf. *Reformation Writings of Martin Luther*, pp. 71, 72. Lutterworth Press, London, 1952.

This suggests to Luther the way in which the three parts of a catechism relate to each other and to the story of our life with God.

The Decalogue teaches a man to know what is wrong with himself, until he sees and feels what he should or should not do, what he can or cannot dispense with; and to know himself to be a sinful and unrighteous man.

Then the Creed shows and teaches him where to find the medicine, that is, divine grace, which will help him to become devout and to keep the Commandments; this grace will help him to know God, and also the mercy revealed and offered in Christ.

And the Lord's Prayer teaches him to yearn for this grace, to seek it and take it to heart. This he will do by regular, humble, strengthening prayer. Then he will receive grace, and in this way, by fulfilling God's Commandment, he will be saved.

The outline of the biblical covenant drama is also basic to the pattern of the Heidelberg Catechism (1563), which, although it is a Reformed Church document, was written by men who had felt the influence of Luther's teaching as well as that of Calvin. Back of them all stands the normative work of the apostle Paul's Epistle to the Romans, in which "the drama of man's redemption in Christ" is most extensively worked out. The second question of the Heidelberg Catechism leads into the three-act plot of the covenant drama:

How many things are necessary for thee to know that thou in this comfort, that is, belonging to thy faithful Savior Jesus Christ (ans. to q. 1) mayest live and die happily?

Three things:

(1) The greatness of my sin and misery.
(2) How I am redeemed from all my sins and misery.
(3) How I am to be thankful to God for such redemption.

In the first part, the Heidelberg Catechism treats of the Law of God and of our inability, through perversity, to obey it. This is ACT I of the covenant story (man's infidelity and need of God's saving act—Rom. 1: 18–3: 20) and corresponds to Luther's teaching that the Commandments are for "the diagnosis" of sin.

In the second, the Creed and the sacraments are interpreted as witnessing to the grace of our Lord Jesus Christ, by whom we have been forgiven and are being renewed through faith. This is ACT II of the covenant drama (the saving Act: justification by faith—Rom. 3: 21–4: 25) and concurs with Luther's prescription of "the medicine."

In the third, the Law of God and the Lord's Prayer are taught as guideposts to the new Man in Christ in fulfilling his calling as a servant of God. This is ACT III of the divine-human covenant (the new life into which this justifying Act admits the believer—Rom. 5: 1–8: 39). It corresponds to Luther's "desiring the medicine."

To be sure, sheer memorization of the questions and answers of the catechism has very questionable pedagogical merit. When, however, the skillful teacher helps the adolescent or young adult to examine himself and ask himself the basic questions concerning the meaning of his existence, to which the biblical story offers not just answers but living examples, the nurture and discipline of the Lord are taking place. Such questions will prepare him to acknowledge God's authority and to accept responsibility for his own freedom (PROLOGUE), to face up to his own disobedience and God's gracious judgment (ACT I), to confess his own guilt and be healed by God's forgiveness (ACT II), to give expression to his own gratitude by accepting God's mission for him (ACT III), and to confess that, in life and in death, he belongs to his faithful Savior Jesus Christ (EPILOGUE).

Our purpose here is not to declare Luther's catechetical works[7] or the Heidelberg Catechism as the ultimate word in Christian education. It is simply to recognize them as historic and still normative examples of instructional tools for explaining and

---

[7] Luther's *Small* and *Large Catechism* were first published in 1529, nine years after his first venture quoted above in note 6. The 19th-century fathers of the Evangelical Synod of North America had both *Luther's* and the *Heidelberg Catechism* in hand when they produced *The Evangelical Catechism.*

interpreting the meaning of our life in the divine-human covenant. In similar fashion former Congregational Christian Churches look with the Presbyterian Churches to the Westminster Confession (1647) as their historic landmark in the Reformation affirmations of faith. In America these churches have established their own doctrinal standards, from the Cambridge Platform (1648) to the Kansas City Statement of 1913.

Even so, the former Evangelical and Reformed Church found it necessary to recommend a supplementary study guide for the instruction of her young people for confirmation, called *My Confirmation* (1942, rev. 1954). This book arose out of recognizing the need to include in our instruction both more information about the Bible and a more existential picture of life in the church today. This book was not meant, however, to be a substitute for the catechism but rather a supplement to it.

For much the same reason, our boards of Christian education have worked ceaselessly in the production of a more adequate curriculum for the church school. The United Church of Christ, following nine years of experimentation in the Congregational Christian Churches through the Pilgrim Series, and in the Evangelical and Reformed Church through the Church and Home Series, is working with a family-oriented curriculum. This program takes each member of the family at his or her level of interest and comprehension through a week-by-week schedule of teaching and study (day by day in the home).

In the first year of this curriculum the unifying themes for the whole family will be:

(1) Growing as a Christian
(2) Exploring Our Christian Heritage
(3) Christian Living with One Another

Since the classes are planned to cover two-year spans of interest, there will be a second-year course with these unifying themes:

(4) Responding to God's Love
(5) Belonging to the Christian Fellowship
(6) Living in God's World

In order to insure that the church will be able to fulfill her teaching ministry, she will be ever alert to the training of her teachers. Most broadly this means every parent, more intensively it means those who are called to minister the Word of God at each level of the church school's curriculum.

What is being done in confirmation classes to prepare each new church member for his responsibility in the covenant community is just a beginning. It belongs to the age of grade school and junior high. The public schools have long since made senior high mandatory for responsible citizenship in the world. Moreover, nowadays college training is essential for nearly every business or profession one wishes to enter. By the same token, continued theological education for all, at least to the age of maturity, and leadership training for those who accept leadership responsibility is clearly a "must" for every Christian congregation that takes its stewardship of the gospel seriously.

The pastor of the church has many roles. One of the most significant is his position as the teacher of the Word of God. This he will be doing in many different ways. Perhaps the most effective, in the long run, is his regular class of church school teachers and leaders, who look to him for training in biblical studies, theology, and church responsibility. Every congregation should have a layman's theological seminary[3] at its heart—the pastor with his teachers and leaders engaged in a study of the biblical and theological background and content of the church school curriculum.

C. The Church as the School of Courageous Faith: Learning "to Have Faith" and "to Be Faithful"

The church is a school. The curriculum is the story of our covenant relationship with the living God. The church as a school has but one goal—to bring up each generation of the people of God in the nurture and discipline of the Lord.

As we have emphasized earlier, Christian education is not

---

[3] Seminary means "seed bed," or the place where the life of the church is renewed.

primarily concerned with the transmission of information—not even of Christian information. Our teaching ministry becomes the occasion for "the nurture and discipline of the Lord," in and through the transmission of Christian wisdom, when the learner is confronted with "the Mighty Acts of God" and decides to accept himself as an actor in the covenant drama. Then the Word becomes flesh in him and he can say, "This is the story of my life."

The primary product of Christian education is faith. Thus the primary job of Christian education is to help each person in the covenant community to acknowledge the faithfulness of God and to confess his faith in response. Otherwise stated, the central task of the church's teaching ministry is to inculcate covenant loyalty, that is, trust and trustworthiness, in each generation of God's people.

Faith in God is a grace and cannot be "taught." Indeed, it is not just one characteristic among others. It is the matrix of personal character out of which all that is worthy in human life ultimately comes. Patriotism and family loyalty are variant forms but limited expressions of the same response.

A contemporary psychiatrist defines faith in terms of life-affirmation. Faith is "the wish to be born, to leave the certain and to enter into the uncertain." In these terms, life is a constant process of being born, and faith is the courage to be delivered from the past into the future.

We live by faith. The question is not whether one shall live by faith or not. The question is: In what or in whom is our trust to be placed? All human beings live by faith. We live by faith or die for the lack of it. The peril of human life, however, is much more insidious than the simple alternative—faith vs. no faith. Our greatest peril is idolatry, the misplacing of our faith.

Misplacing our faith means not merely that we are like a ship without a rudder, or a mariner without a compass, but that we have substituted an anchor for the rudder, a mirage for the pole star, "cisterns that can hold no water" for "the fountain of living waters" (Jer. 2: 13; cf. Part Two, page 94). The greatest enemy of the work of Christian parents and teachers, continually threatening their efforts to channel the promise and demands of God's covenant, is the welter of idols—the golden calves—that we make and admire.

Take, for example, this parody called "The Materialist's Twenty-third Psalm":

Science is my shepherd; I shall not want.

He maketh me to lie down on foam rubber mattresses;
he leadeth me beside the four-lane highways.

He rejuvenateth my thyroid gland;
he leadeth me in the paths of psychoanalysis for peace
of mind's sake.

Yea, though I walk through the valley of the shadow
of the iron curtain, I shall fear no communists, for thou
art with me; thy radar screen and thy hydrogen
bomb they comfort me.

Thou preparest a banquet before me in the presence
of the world's billion hungry people; thou anointest
my head with home permanents; my alcoholic glass
foameth over.

Surely prosperity and pleasure shall follow me
all the days of my life, and I shall dwell in
Shangri-la forever.

—Edward K. Ziegler. Used by permission.

We have no dearth of faith in our time. Our difficulty is rather to direct our "trusting" toward trustworthy ends. Even Christian faith has been woefully misunderstood in popular terms. People have sometimes been heard to say, either seriously or facetiously, "Faith is believing what you know isn't so." Faith is believing what cannot be proved, I suppose, is the more judicious way of saying the same thing. Now, to be sure, the scientific and philosophic use of reason cannot establish what is revealed to us and to which we respond in faith. But we ought never give the impression to people, either inside or outside the church, that faith is a kind of second-best tool which we use when we run out of reasons, that faith is something we fall back upon when we have no real foundation for what we believe. Faith has its foundations. As the philosopher Pascal has put it, "The heart has its reasons, whereof the head knoweth not." Faith has its reasons, that is, its foundations in the experience of divine-human encounter with God's self-revelation in, with, and to his covenant people.

Our Christian faith in God means two things: "having faith" and "being faithful," trusting and being trustworthy. Both aspects are determined by God's own faithfulness, and they give expression to our human need, respectively, for security and significance.

The story of the Bible, however, like the story of our life, is a dramatic account of our covenant situation, in which fear rather than faith, and infidelity rather than trustworthiness, are the predominant marks of human life. This is why Christian education is such a central part of the church's work. We are continually subject to the infection of unfaith and need ever to be renewed at the source of our being in the divine faithfulness. The church's teaching ministry gives her people guidance and help in both respects: (1) in their search for a dependable center of trust (the living God), (2) in channeling an endless source of renewal (a life-giving faith). By the steadfastness of God's covenant faithfulness, his people are given courage to face life in spite of fear and the threat of death. By the same grace, revealed in our Lord Jesus Christ, we are reborn into a new life of loyal obedience, in spite of infidelity which in itself would merit our moral condemnation.

Thus, participating in our Lord's own covenant faithfulness, at whatever stage of life one is confronted by his nurturing love and sovereign righteousness, is the fullest fruit of the church's teaching ministry. There is, however, no way to predict precisely how this "means of grace" is being channeled to us. Surely, it comes through regular formal instruction in the Word of God. Equally as surely, it is found in informal personal encounter in family and congregational life. In the complex of many channels there is, nevertheless, a very well-established pattern within which the drama of our participation unfolds.

Although we are all continually in the process of becoming Christian and are never entirely able to affirm with confidence that we have arrived, there are still definite stages that can be distinguished in the process. These stages are not to be mistaken for levels of achievement which may be climbed like a ladder. They are the stages by which we are led to acknowledge the threefold form of human freedom in the purpose of God: aesthetic (freedom as self-enjoyment), ethical (freedom as social responsibility), and religious (freedom as suffering service to God). (Compare Kierkegaard: *Stages on Life's Way*.)

The Christian life involves us in two "leaps of faith," that is, in two conversions. These two opportunities arise when, in times of personal crisis, we are given the courage to make relevant life-determining decisions:

(1) In the midst of conflict between two or more persons, each of whom is bent upon irresponsible self-enjoyment, we face the need to accept the "courage to be as a part," the power to move into the stage of social responsibility.

(2) In the despair which results from the conflict between the consequences of lawless self-enjoyment and our acknowledged moral obligations, we face the need to accept "the courage to be as oneself," the power to transcend the claim of social responsibility with suffering service.

Both decisions are born of human conflict and the power of the Holy Spirit and become the occasion for a "leap of faith" to a higher stage of life, from the aesthetic to the ethical, and from the ethical to the religious. The leap of faith amounts to "giving oneself away." On the ethical stage this means "giving oneself away to another," that is, to love and be loved. On the religious stage this means "giving oneself away for another," to love the unlovely and to make them lovable.

The main characters in T. S. Eliot's play, "The Cocktail Party," represent these stages and the conversion from one to another in a very striking fashion.

In the first act, Edward and Lavinia (husband and wife) entertain at a cocktail party as an occasion for escaping from the boredom of living together without loving each other. Each is involved in an affair with a paramour, but without finding the satisfaction for which the diversion was sought. The encounter of each with an Unidentified Stranger who came to the party is the only instance of real personal communication in the whole situation. In soliloquy each indicates the shallowness of their common life, but with little awareness of the reason for its emptiness. Edward's friend, Celia, is disillusioned first. She is burdened with guilt at her moral duplicity. She breaks off the relationship she has had with Edward but with no satisfaction for her moral consciousness.

In the second act, both Edward and Lavinia find their way to the office of the Unidentified Stranger (a psychiatrist), and discover by his careful manipulation of their interviews (each is permitted to eavesdrop upon the other) that each accuses the other of being responsible for their marital failure. She accuses him of being unable to love anyone but himself, and he declares her to be incapable of being loved by anyone. This much, at least, they have in common, the counselor observes, "the same isolation." For this reason he discourages them when they suggest going to "the sanatorium."

> You are no case for my sanatorium:
> You are much too ill!

They finally decide between themselves that there is nothing to do but to go home and try to find each other.

Celia also comes, but alone, to the counselor. She unburdens her deep sense of guilt and need for atonement. She has no prescription to offer, but pleads, "I want to be cured of a craving for something I cannot find and of the shame of never finding it." With courage born of despair she decides to accept a new life which, the counselor warns, "You will journey blind. But the way leads toward possession of what you have sought for in the wrong place." Once Celia has made her decision she is asked to be ready to go to the sanatorium at 9 P. M. that same evening. The reader discovers in the final act that "the sanatorium" to which Celia is sent, but for which Edward and Lavinia were "too ill," is a school for the training of Christian missionaries.

The third act sees the preparation for another cocktail party two years later. The affair is surrounded with quite a different spirit. Edward and Lavinia are clearly very much in love with each other. They have reached the second stage on life's way. A new crisis arises for them, however, and the horizon of their social responsibility is suddenly broadened. A friend brings word that Celia was the victim of a cannibalistic attack upon the mission station where she was serving. Both Edward and Lavinia acknowledge a sense of guilt and show that they are beginning to accept responsibility not only to each other but for someone else.

The counselor, representing the divine acceptance, offers Edward and Lavinia "the courage to be as a part," in their case freedom to accept the responsibility of married life. To Celia, on the other hand, he offers "the courage to be as oneself," in her case the freedom to decide for a life of suffering service for the Lord. In biblical terms the first decision was to forsake lawlessness for a new life under the Law; the second was to acknowledge the Gospel as the fulfillment of the Law.

The truth of a first and a second conversion in the stages of the Christian life has tremendous significance for the church's educational ministry. It helps us avoid mere moralism and legalism as the full purpose of Christian education and at the same time it helps us to avoid a spiritual emotionalism that lacks fundamental moral fiber. In other words, we can no more prepare our people to jump from stage 1 to stage 3 without their struggling over the demands of stage 2 than we can permit them to be satisfied with a do-it-yourself moralism in stage 2. Justification by grace cannot be experienced apart from the judgment of sin, and the judgment of sin cannot be experienced apart from submission to the demands of the Law.

A word of caution is in order here, lest we misrepresent the status of those who accept the demand of stage 3. We tried to protect the reader when we warned against interpreting the stages as levels to be climbed. Granted that the Gospel fulfills the Law and it does not eliminate it. In Christ we are not set free from the Law, but from the curse of the Law, from despair at not being strong enough to keep it. Christian freedom is not a new irresponsibility; it is a renewal of the power to be responsible.

The works of John Calvin and the Heidelberg Catechism are both clearly emphatic about this peculiar implication of the Christian doctrine of grace for Christian education. Specifically, the Heidelbergers, Ursinus and Olevianus, took seriously Luther's formula:

the Law for the conviction of sin,
the Creed for the assurance of justifying grace,
the Lord's Prayer for the new life in Christian freedom.

Their catechism teaches the Law, however, both as the judge of human sin and as the base lines for the game of life in which the redeemed are more than ever responsible to play. The Lord's Prayer and the Ten Commandments are taught by the Heidelberg Catechism for the structuring of our new life in Christ. Participating in stage 3 (Christian love) both gives us the power and underscores the responsibility for living in stage 2 (social justice and community participation).

Carrying on Christian education for "two conversions" places a high value upon the teachers' sensitivity to the existential facts of life. For example, the same human situation has a very different meaning to each of the parties in a personal relationship. A father may have his first real encounter with grace-inspired suffering service at precisely the point at which he is attempting to help his son to face his first responsible decision regarding social vs. self-centered freedom. Obviously, the church's educational ministry needs not only to help a family in such a situation, but it should be wise enough to help each member to recognize the stage of life in which he is involved.

Many a son never really acknowledges the righteousness of filial responsibility until he becomes a father and is suddenly cast in the role of paternal authority. Happy is the man to whom this revelation comes and who can, on this account, be gracious to the new young "offender" and at the same time begin for himself a new life of fidelity in the role of one who is "vested with authority from on high."

The whole implication of a family whose members are currently living at different "stages on life's way" can be spelled out clearly and with striking relevance in a "church and home" type of curriculum. For example, our Lord's own parable of the father and his two sons (Luke 15: 11-32) becomes good covenant education when we are helped to identify ourselves with the relevant role and at the crucial spot at which the encounter fits our life. The parable not only teaches young people that steadfast faithfulness is the mark of covenant parenthood, but that by this means young rebels may be redeemed—one from the futile attempt to run away from paternal authority (the prodigal), the other from pretending that he can buy special favor by servile but loveless obedience. By the same token, it teaches parents to acknowledge these two contrasting types of rebellion in their children and their own continuing responsibility to manifest divinely blended redeeming love and righteous judgment toward each child.

TWO

CELEBRATING AND PARTICIPATING IN THE LORD'S DAY LITURGY

The Lord's Day liturgy, as the name for our regular weekly service of divine worship, gives us a somewhat unfamiliar but historically well-established definition of what we experience as "the innermost sanctuary of the whole Christian life." The liturgy is that "means of grace" through which we glorify God in his service and are renewed in our being through personal encounter with his life-giving Spirit.

When Christian people engage in divine worship, three fundamental actions occur together—worship, celebration, and liturgy:

(1) *Worship*—We locate and acknowledge as our ultimate concern the Ground of our being and the Source of all worth, the One who manifests sovereign "worth-ship." The ultimate significance of all worship is the glorification of God.

(2) *Celebration*—The Lord's Day liturgy is the church's celebration of her Lord's glorious victory on Easter. This means that we are celebrating the victory of God, through our Lord Jesus Christ, both over our human weakness and over the powers of death, sin, and Satan, which estrange us from him, from each other, and from our own essential being. In fact, the whole drama of divine-human encounter is relived in an hour's time in this weekly alternation of divine worship with daily work.

(3) *Liturgy*—In the course of the celebration we are confronted by God's gracious promise and demand, and a grateful acceptance and renewed commitment is called forth. When our celebration of what God has done is fulfilled in us, we submit

ourselves to Christ, participate in his power, and enter into his service. Liturgy means, literally, "the work of the people," that is, the people of God renewing their covenant of suffering service through the grace of our Lord Jesus Christ.

A. Reliving Isaiah's Spiritual Encounter with God as the Pattern of Regular Re-examination and Renewal of Our Life

The historical Christian church has established a pattern for its life in worship which varies in many details, from group to group and from age to age, but is normatively defined in its movement by the experience recorded in Isaiah 6. As we have already noted in Part One (pp. 24-27), a crisis moment in this one man's life epitomizes the entire plot of Israel's covenant encounter. What is all the more amazing is that Isaiah's temple experience is still being recapitulated, 2700 years later, in every celebration of the Lord's Day liturgy in our churches.

Our encounter in Christian worship, however, is not bounded by the experience of the prophet Isaiah, for we have been and are being renewed in our being by our participation in the life, death, and resurrection of the man Christ Jesus. Although the plot of the drama of our encounter is the same, our worship is Christo-centric and therefore trinitarian in total perspective.

The form of the liturgy has been the subject of wide variation in Christian practice, often leading to controversy between those who use a fixed form and those who would allow more freedom to the Spirit and more room for the ingenuity of the worship leader. The ecumenical movement of the twentieth century has made possible a remarkable amount of conversation leading to mutual and fruitful influence between these two points of view. Note, for example, the Lund report on "Ways of Worship."[1] On the one hand there is a growing awareness in this generation that the essentials of Christian worship are fixed by the divine revelation in which we participate and are not a matter of preference or of psychological mood. On the other hand it is

---

[1] The Third World Conference on Faith and Order, World Council of Churches, Lund, Sweden, August, 1952.

acknowledged that traditional forms serve us best when they become the channel of creative variety of worship practice from time to time and from place to place.

The truth of the matter is that human beings are basically creatures of habit and therefore tend toward fixed patterns in all phases of life. The so-called free-church worship is usually just as bound by fixed forms as is the case where the traditional forms are used. It is ultimately not a question of formal vs. free worship but of which form best sets us free to the leading of God's Holy Spirit.

The following pattern, suggested by the movement of Isaiah's encounter and transfigured by the life story of Jesus Christ, is generally recognized as a minimal outline for the divine service of the people of God. Functionally, it presents us with an opportunity for the regular, periodic re-examination and renewal of our spiritual life. In the relationship between our common biblical covenant and the various liturgical traditions of the church, this pattern represents what in mathematics is called the highest common factor.

ISAIAH'S ENCOUNTER WITH GOD IN THE TEMPLE (ISAIAH 6)	THE LORD'S DAY LITURGY
	The People of God Renewing Their Covenant By the Grace of Our Lord Jesus Christ
PROLOGUE —Isaiah's Vision of the Lord and The Seraphic Hymn of Praise	Our Meeting with the Living God
ACT I —Isaiah's Confession of Sin	The Confession of Sin
ACT II —The Seraphim's Healing Work and Declaration	Acknowledging the Justifying Grace of God in Jesus Christ
ACT III —God's Call to Service and Isaiah's Loyal Commitment	The Renewal of the Covenant of Suffering Service
EPILOGUE —God's Mysterious Promise	The Glorification of God

Worship, thus understood as the regular celebration and participation in the divine-human covenant drama, centers in what God has done and is doing, and issues in what his people are called upon to do in his name and by his power. The Lord's Day liturgy is therefore the central instrument of "the nurture and discipline of the Lord" in the life of the church.

There follows an order of worship for the Lord's Day liturgy which represents the combined heritage of our Lutheran and Reformed background in the United Church of Christ, but is familiar in outline, if not in every detail, to all the major traditions of the church.

THE CELEBRATION OF THE LORD'S DAY LITURGY
THE PEOPLE'S DIVINE SERVICE

FOR PROLOGUE
OUR MEETING WITH THE LIVING GOD
- The Trinitarian Invocation[1]
- The Introit for the Day[2]
- Hymn of Adoration (Processional)[2]

ACT I
THE CONFESSION OF SIN
- The Prayer of General Confession[2]
- Kyrie Eleison[2]
- Assurance of Forgiveness[1]
- Gloria in Excelsis[2]

ACT II
ACKNOWLEDGING THE JUSTIFYING GRACE OF GOD IN JESUS CHRIST
- The Collect for the Day[2]
- The Scripture Lesson[1]
- Gloria Patri[2]
- The Confession of Faith[2]
- Hymn or Anthem[2]

ACT III
THE RENEWAL OF THE COVENANT OF SUFFERING SERVICE
- The Word of God
  - Proclaimed (Scriptural Text)[1]
  - Interpreted (The Sermon)[1]
- The Response of His Faithful People
  - Consecration to Service (Prayers and Hymns)[2]
  - Dedication of Gifts[2]

EPILOGUE
THE GLORIFICATION OF GOD
- The Sacrament of the Lord's Supper
  - Eucharist and Sanctus[2]
  - Words of Institution[1]
  - The Intercession[2]
  - The Communion[1]
  - Nunc Dimittis or Te Deum Laudamus[2]
- The Benediction[1]
- Doxology (Recessional)[2]

[1] Minister for God to the People (celebrant and preacher)
[2] Minister for and with the People to God (liturgist)

The drama of the people's encounter with the living God in worship is a dialogue of revelation and response, revelation from God to man (cf. parts marked 1 in the outline of the liturgy), and response from man to God (cf. parts marked 2 in the outline of the liturgy). Both God and the people participate in every Act. The center of attention is steadily upon God and the power of his grace, and yet the whole event is traditionally called "the work of the people," the liturgy.

The minister occupies a dual role in the service of worship. He is both the leader of the people and the spokesman of God. As God's spokesman he properly but humbly adopts the perspective of God and, guided by his Word, speaks to the people face to face. As the leader of the flock in prayer and praise, he joins them in their perspective and faces with them toward the Lord. This dual function of the minister in relation to the whole congregation's dialogue with God is most strikingly expressed in the versicle:

> *Minister:* The Lord be with you.
> *Congregation:* And with thy spirit.
> *Minister:* Let us pray . . .
> *Congregation:* Amen.

The minister bespeaks God's blessing upon the people, and they confirm it to each other. The minister calls the congregation to follow his lead in prayer, and they affirm "so be it" in the response "Amen." In the course of Christian history it has come to be general practice for the congregation to bow or kneel for prayer, to stand for praise, and to sit while listening to the Word of God.

PROLOGUE—*Our Meeting with the Living God*

Through the trinitarian invocation, "In the name of the Father, and of the Son, and the Holy Spirit," the minister presents the living God to his people, and through the introit for the day he calls the people to God. In the processional hymn, the choir and the congregation respond by approaching the altar, the place where God and man meet. This is symbolically enacted where it is customary for the minister to open the service from the rear of the sanctuary. As the choir and minister move toward the altar, the people join in the processional hymn and begin to participate in the divine-human encounter.

ACT I—*The Confession of Sin*

Now that they are face to face with the living God, the people's first responsible act, led by the minister and the choir, is the corporate confession of sin. An ancient tradition, arising in the Greek tongue, allows the minister and people to make their confession in antiphonal form. The *Kyrie Eleison,*

> Lord, have mercy upon us,
> *Lord, have mercy upon us, . . .*

is so old that it continues in both Latin and English-speaking churches to bear its original name. The same purpose is filled in some churches by the responsive reading of a penitential psalm. In this act, all who are in the house of God are facing the Lord, whose presence is symbolized by the altar. In anticipation of ACT II, in which we know that the judgment of God will come to us as the justifying grace of our Lord Jesus Christ, the minister announces the assurance of forgiveness in his name, and the grateful congregation sings the *Gloria in Excelsis*.

ACT II—*Acknowledging the Justifying Grace of God in Jesus Christ*

The gracious Word of God is read and heard from the Scriptues, both Old and New Testaments, but always including the Gospel lesson as the central act of the divine revelation. The response of the people manifests their thanksgiving and finds joyful expression in various types of "confession of faith." The most universal forms of confession are the *Gloria Patri,* our trinitarian theology of history, and the Apostles' and the Nicene Creeds. A congregational hymn or an anthem by the choir may voice the same response.

Act III—*The Renewal of the Covenant of Suffering Service*

Once the covenant is renewed through the people's response in faith, they are called to responsible participation in the divine service. The Word of God is proclaimed from a scriptural text, and is interpreted, for this day, in the sermon. This is the primary prophetic act of the minister and is at once his most creative and most dangerous role in the whole liturgy. As a preacher he is free, under God, to declare the relevance of God's Word to this day's concern and to demand the relevance of our actions to God's command. The response of God's faithful people, upon hearing the Word of God, involves both their acts of consecration of themselves to his service and the dedication of their gifts to his glorious kingdom. At this point there is a maximum of participation by the people. This is the climax of "the liturgy."

Epilogue—*The Glorification of God*

The final glorification of God is at once the fulfillment of the covenant and the anticipation of what shall only be fulfilled in the final consummation of his kingdom. The liturgy is incomplete without the celebration of the mystery of God's fulfilled, and yet to-be-fulfilled, victory through the sacrament of the Lord's Supper. As celebration it is the commemoration of the central act of the gospel in its eschatological setting. As liturgy it is the Eucharist, a thanksgiving for what God has already done in the life, death, and resurrection of our Lord Jesus.

The minister again bears two roles: he is the celebrant of Christ's redemptive work, the spokesman for the Host at this heavenly banquet, and he is the representative of the people, giving thanks for the whole drama of salvation and our privilege of participation in our Lord's gracious fellowship and service.

The liturgy of the Lord's Supper includes the *Sursum Corda*, "we lift up our hearts," the Eucharistic and intercessory prayers before the altar. At this point, however, at which our Lord's own words of institution, "This is my body, . . . this is my blood, . . ." are spoken, and his invitation, "Come to me, . . ."

is given, the minister as the divine spokesman should most properly speak from behind the altar, which thereby becomes the communion table. This raises the question of church appointments in relation to the liturgy and the covenant encounter it represents. In order to restore the New Testament meaning of the Lord's Supper, our Protestant Reformers declared the primacy and the once-for-allness of the sacrifice of God on our behalf and the secondary and responsive character of our sacrifice to God. More radically, on the Reformed side they emphasized the once-for-allness by removing the altar entirely from the sanctuary and erecting a communion table in its place. Although Protestant history has produced many variations on this theme, the fundamental genius of Reformation theology can best be expressed when the altar is placed away from the wall, making it possible at this crucial point in the service for the place of "divine-human encounter" to be what ultimately it always is for our Christian faith—the Lord's communion table. Clearly, this is what is happening when the celebrant takes the bread and wine, during the words of institution, and offers them directly to the people.

Where the sacrament of the Lord's Supper is not celebrated every Lord's Day, the final act of the glorification of God includes prayers of thanksgiving and intercession, silence for communion, the benediction and doxology. Like the processional which leads to God, the recessional symbolizes our obedience to the apostolic command of our Lord to go forth in his name and service.

B. The Church as the Fellowship of Healing Love: Corporate Worship and Pastoral Counseling

The healing ministry of the Christian church, like the teaching ministry, is direct heir to the work of our Lord Jesus. "[Jesus] went about all Galilee, teaching in their synagogues and preaching the gospel of the kingdom and healing every disease and every infirmity among the people" (Matt. 4: 23). "And he called the twelve together and gave them power and authority over all demons and to cure diseases, and he sent them out to preach the kingdom of God and to heal" (Luke 9: 1-2).

The breadth of our Lord's activity in the healing ministry alone obviously covers a wide scope of services. In our present-day society many of these have achieved specialized professional status, more or less independent of the church, such as medicine, social service, psychiatry, and so on. Nonetheless, much of the deepest motivation for engaging in these services still roots in the Christian faith and warrants our referring to them broadly as forms of the "healing ministry."

By virtue of the growing concern for the healing ministry within the church in this generation, two important developments are taking place: on the one hand, a deepening acquaintance between representatives of the healing profession and the ministry of the church,[2] and on the other hand, a revitalization of interest in the doctrine of "Christian vocation," that is, finding in Christian love the motivation for every form of service activity.

Except for a fringe of so-called faith-healing, expressions of the church as a "fellowship of healing love" have traditionally been limited to incidents of corporate worship on Sunday morning and the pastor's activity as a personal counselor whenever the occasion presented itself. To be sure, much of what has been claimed in the past as faith-healing was most likely a form of charlatanism. Nonetheless, there is today an increasing awareness of a *bona fide* form of healing activity which should properly be called "healing by the spiritual power of sacrificial love." This has always marked the church at its best.

It is very important to clear up several popular misconceptions on this point. Most important of all, perhaps, is the fact that the healing power is not our "faith." Our mere human capacity for "faith" is so easily subject to idolatrous attachment that it is extremely misleading to claim for it such "magical" powers. Moreover, on the other side of this same coin is the disturbing fact that for many persons evincing stellar faith a specific healing

---

[2] Medical students and theological students, and pastors and psychiatrists, meet regularly in the St. Louis area under the auspices of the Metropolitan Church Federation.

has not been forthcoming. Christian healing is, in the best non-magical sense of the word, a miracle. It cannot be predicted with scientific accuracy, nor can it be controlled or manipulated. Ultimately we must trace the agency of Christian healing to the power of God's love, that is, the Holy Spirit. To the point it is possible to add, however, that the love of a faithful community of Christian people and of consecrated persons within their fellowship often becomes the channel for the divine grace. But when healing power is confessed, it is clearly the activity of grace and not the work of our "faith" or of individual "healers."

The Protestant Reformation doctrine of the "priesthood of all believers" roots precisely here. Often mistaken as a justification for the claims of rugged individualism in spiritual matters, the "universal priesthood" dramatizes what a living community of faithful Christian people actually is—a fellowship of love intent upon mediating the grace of God for, to, and by each participating member.

Corporate worship and pastoral counseling, therefore, remain the major expressions of the church's healing ministry. Even though these activities may appear to be quite unlike each other on the surface—one a community experience, the other limited to a single person or at most several persons, the one public and corporate, the other private and individual—there is a common factor which binds them together. The norm for a healing experience in each case is the plot of Isaiah 6.

PROLOGUE—Isaiah went into the temple.

The patient, prompted by his awareness of the need for help, goes to the church worship service and/or to the pastor's study.

ACT I—"Woe is me."

Through confession the patient is encouraged "to get it off his chest." To a greater or lesser degree, he acknowledges his enslavement by the powers of evil: loneliness, conflicts, infidelity, guilt, and his inability to help himself.

ACT II—"Your guilt is taken away, and your sin is forgiven."

The patient is assured that he is accepted as he is, despite his sin and guilt. Through being forgiven he is enabled to begin to accept himself. At least, he is free from having to pretend that he is not what he is!

ACT III—"Who will go for us?" "Here I am. Send me."

The patient begins the road to recovery by being given and accepting responsibility for another in the "community of concern."

EPILOGUE—"How long, O Lord?"

Together the therapist and the patient acknowledge the grace of God, whereby they participate in a universal fellowship of healing and being healed.

Pastoral counseling is thus a very specialized form of "the nurture and discipline of the Lord," in which the minister, as the servant of the Lord and the representative of the covenant community, mediates the healing power of God's holy love to those patients who come, usually one by one, to seek for help. The divine help they receive, however, involves the supporting activity of the entire congregation as a "fellowship of acceptance."

Corporate worship becomes the occasion for "the nurture and discipline of the Lord," in and through the cultic ritual by which the church recapitulates Isaiah's encounter with God in the temple, when the worshiper encounters the healing power of God's love and gratefully prepares to make every crisis of life in the week to come redound to the glory of God. Indeed, it may fairly be said that corporate worship is an example of group therapy on the spiritual dimension of life, in the same way that personal counseling is aimed at helping an individual to work through from stage to stage the steps of Isaiah's life-giving encounter.

THREE

THE CHRISTIAN YEAR OF PREACHING AND HEARING THE WORD OF GOD

Much of Protestantism tends to equate the whole of the church's ministry with preaching. The minister is popularly called "preacher," probably because he manages to give the impression that his sermon on Sunday morning is the most important thing he does. In our multiple conception of the church's ministry we want to place each one of her "means of grace" in its proper perspective without allowing any one of them to be underrated or overplayed.

Both the teaching and the healing ministries deal directly with people, either as individual persons or as members of a socially related community. Preaching, on the other hand, sets the stage of the divine-human encounter in cosmic focus. In Christ we have not merely "the author and perfecter of our faith" and the gracious love whereby we are bound into a new community of the Holy Spirit. In Christ we have "the hope of the world." He is proclaimed as "the Word become flesh." In him we bear witness to the man in whom God has acted "once for all" as the Judge and Redeemer of our whole human situation. His saving work involves not only individuals and social groups, but the entire drama of human history in which we participate as individuals and groups. The preacher, like the prophets of old, is God's mouthpiece and, therefore, proclaims the divine truth to all who will hear.

The Word of God is the covenant formula: "You shall be my people, and I will be your God." The new covenant affirms that in Jesus Christ the Word has become flesh and dwells among us full of grace and truth.

The proclamation of the Incarnate Word of God at the heart of the church's life fulfills a threefold function:

(1) Wherever the Word of God is proclaimed the ultimate meaningfulness of life is affirmed. The sovereignty of God's love gives a framework within which to understand and interpret the meaning of our human existence. In biblical terms the dimensions of our life in covenant with the living God are recognized to be election, suffering service, and spiritual participation.

(2) To the covenant people the Incarnation of the Word of God stands as a continual reminder of the covenant faithfulness of God. It says, in effect, God's Word is good. The church lives and moves and has its being in the gospel, the good news of God's faithfulness.

(3) To the world, marked by natural contingency and human finiteness and inclined to blow alternately hot and cold between arrogant self-assurance and utter despair, the hearing of the Word of God offers hope and confident assurance. Jesus Christ is "the hope of the world." "The kingdoms of this world have become the kingdom of our Lord and of his Christ, and he shall reign forever and ever."

In much popular thinking, the role of teaching and preaching is easily confused. This is because, in actual fact, their functioning is intertwined. *The gospel is at once the meaning of what God has done in our behalf and the actual relationship with him in which we stand right now*. The one aspect occasions the church's preaching, the other the need for teaching. The preaching of a good sermon should be broadly concerned with the meaning of our whole divine-human situation, but should ultimately teach us how to participate in it where we now are. We really preach "theology," that is, the meaning of our covenant relationship with

God, but when we preach *to people*, we must teach them how to live with God and with themselves as his creatures and servants. The use of illustrations in a sermon is a proper resort to the teaching technique. When people say that they remember the illustration better than the sermon, it means that the preacher is an effective teacher. People remember better what affects their lives than what answers their questions!

Obviously there can be no wall of partition between these two forms of the church's ministry. Indeed, they are both dealing with the same truth, God's troth with his servant people. The one is the proclamation of the whole truth, that is, the truth in its whole import; the other is the actual nurturing and disciplining of our lives for fuller participation in the troth we have been given and have been rejecting.

In a fundamental sense the sermonic form and the pattern of the Christian year for the proclamation of the gospel offer the large and inclusive framework within which the teaching ministry does its intensive, daily work of evangelism. In chapter 1, on "Evangelism and the Teaching Ministry," we have discussed at length this process of intimate personal participation from day to day in spiritual nurture and discipline. Here we are concerned with the broad and deep affirmations of the eternal gospel and with the instrumentalities by which the church has both "timed" the edification of her own members, year by year, and embodied in her activity of social revolution and reconciliation "the hope of the world."

A. Reaffirming the Eternal Gospel of Our Lord and Savior Jesus Christ Through a Yearly Commemoration of His Life

The pattern of the Christian year, like the Lord's Day liturgy (Isaiah 6) and the outline of the Heidelberg Catechism (Law, Gospel, and Lord's Prayer), is a recapitulation of the whole drama of our salvation. It is, however, more thoroughly transfigured by the life, death, and resurrection of our Lord Jesus than is the case in either of the other two "means of grace." Following the form of the earliest Christian preaching and confessions of faith,[1] the church relives the whole life of Jesus in the first half of each year, and publicly announces her role as his servant people in the second half. The two halves complement each other, in the way indicated by the apostle Paul in 2 Corinthians 5: 19: God was in Christ (1) reconciling the world to himself; (2) entrusting to us the ministry of reconciliation.

In order that we may clearly trace the development of the gospel and the yearly pattern of its commemoration, we shall set up a comparative chart indicating the parallels between (1) the universal biblical covenant drama, (2) the new covenant story of Jesus, (3) the New Testament proclamation of Jesus as the Christ, and (4) the days and seasons of the year.

The earliest Christian records include both "reports of what Jesus did" and "interpretation of the meaning of his life for us." The distinction is roughly the same as that between the gospel writings and the epistles, but this is by no means a complete dichotomy. Whereas there is no attempt at reporting as such outside the written Gospels, interpretations are found in many forms in the various New Testament writings, in the Gospels as well as in the Epistles. Our Lord's birth, healing ministry, death, and resurrection are at once *historical* events and *theological* truths. It is nonetheless important, precisely from the point of view of our human participation in this drama, that we be able to distinguish the one from the other.

The insights that this kind of study brings to light are three:

(1) *The obvious influence of the prophetic theology of history upon the form of New Testament writing and the equally obvious transfiguration of the story in the life of Jesus.*

In the new covenant setting, ACT I of the covenant drama is no longer "sin," the people's estrangement from God and enslavement to the shadows of their own pretensions. It is rather the struggle of the New Man against the powers of evil. This is the gospel, not only that God will redeem his people but that

---

[1] Cf. Philippians 2: 5-11; Acts 2: 22 ff.; 10: 34-43, and the dramatic plot of Luke-Acts, Part One, chapter 4, pp. 44-46.

The Universal Biblical Covenant Drama	The New Covenant Story of Jesus	The New Testament Proclamation of Jesus as the Christ	The Days and Seasons of the Christian Year
(The Prophetic Theology of History)	(The Luke-Acts Report of What Jesus Did and What Happened to Him)	(The Interpretation of the Meaning of What God Has Done in His Life for Ours)	(The Way in Which We Communicate the Gospel Story in a Year's Time)
THE PROLOGUE— God's Election of a Servant People	**THE CHOSEN ONE—** Promised by Prophets Born of Mary Baptized by John	**THE INCARNATION OF THE WORD OF GOD—** God's Word Good (Faithfulness) God's Word Embodied in Man (Love) God's Word the Light of the World (Hope)	Advent Season Christmas Day and Season Epiphany Day and Season
ACT I— The People's Estrangement and Enslavement (The Divine Judgment)	**MINISTRY OF MIGHTY WORKS—** Temptations Regarding His Mission Encounter with Demonic Powers Conflict with the World	**GOD'S FULL IDENTIFICATION WITH MAN—** Identification with Sin Identification with the Sinner Active Opposition to Powers of Evil	The Lenten Season
ACT II— God's Gracious Deliverance: Redemption and Reconciliation	**THE SUFFERING SERVANT—** Crucifixion—Rejected and Put to Death by Men Resurrection—God's Triumphant Servant	**GOD'S SAVING ACT—** The Expiation of Sin (Atonement) The Forgiveness of Sinners (At-onement) The Victory of Love and Righteousness over Powers of Evil	Good Friday and Easter
ACT III— The Renewal and Responsible Service of the Covenant People	**THE ESTABLISHMENT OF THE CHURCH—** Resurrection Appearances Empowerment of Disciples with the Spirit	**THE NEW MAN AND THE FAITHFUL COMMUNITY—** The Gift of Newness of Life in Christ Participation in the Fellowship of the Holy Spirit	Easter Season and Pentecost
THE EPILOGUE— Anticipation of the Glorious Kingdom of God	**HIS EXALTATION—** Ascension into Heaven	**THE LORDSHIP OF CHRIST OVER THE CHURCH AND THE WORLD**	Ascension Day and the Trinity Season

in Christ humanity has a champion who has fought and vanquished the foe.

This new perspective gives the pattern of the Christian year its unique character. It is first of all the recapitulation of God's identification with man at the point of his historical debacle in ACT I, and at the same time a call to man to identify with Christ in the same act, that is, in the struggle against the powers of evil. Lent is the occasion in the Christian calendar year where we take seriously the suffering of the Suffering Servant and identify, as it were, with him in his identification with humanity's sin and misery.

(2) *The thoroughness with which the New Testament writings both record and interpret the role of the God-man in his identification with the sons of Adam.*

Jesus Christ is at once the hinge of the divine triunity of God and the head of the covenant community of God's people. In him God's Word has become flesh; in him God's mighty acts have brought judgment and redemption to his people; in him God's Spirit has been given to his redeemed people that they may be prophets (the mouth of God) to the world.

Our Lord Jesus is the permanent mediator of God's grace and truth and of man's courage and trust. He is the only-begotten Son of God and the teacher, prophet, priest, and king both of the church and of the world.

(3) *The completeness with which the whole of Jesus' life and mission is covered in the celebration of the Christian year.*

It is not surprising that the regular preaching of the gospel of our Lord Jesus should suggest the commemoration of the major events in his life. One is actually surprised to discover how slow and sporadic has been the development of the festival celebrations. In our time, however, the Christian calendar offers a perfect outline, both for preaching the meaning of God's mighty acts in his Son our Lord and for teaching his people to participate in the life which God has prepared for us through him.

The earliest Christian celebration, as we noted earlier in connection with our discussion of the liturgy, was the Lord's Day, that is, the weekly Easter. This observance appears to have been begun almost at once by the apostolic church. Since their Hebrew heritage had already structured their life with the keeping of the weekly sabbath, it was not difficult to develop a weekly Lord's Day. Our Christian observance is different, however, not only because it falls on the first day of the week as against the seventh day, but more basically because it is primarily a celebration and not a sabbath.

The Christian Sunday is not substituted for the Jewish sabbath, the day for cessation from work and for sacrifice to God. In truth, the sabbath day is actually abolished, there no longer being any need for its sacrificial service. God having fully revealed his gracious forgiveness in Jesus Christ, the analogous Christian day of worship becomes a time for the celebration of our Lord's glorious resurrection. By the same token that the Lord's Day abolishes the sabbath day, however, *every* day becomes a sabbath. By virtue of the sacrifice of our Lord Jesus on our behalf, the Christian's whole life is to be hallowed, as a sabbath, in the sacrificial service of God.

Our liturgical year, likewise, arose out of the celebration of Easter, that is, around the yearly Easter. Good Friday and Easter, Ascension and Pentecost, Christmas and Epiphany are the three centers of interest in the slowly developing Christian calendar. They arose in pairs as indicated and in this order of priority.[2]

Already the Jewish lunar calendar had identified certain historical events as the occasion for the commemoration of the covenant drama of Israel. The Passover recalled the liberation from Egypt; Pentecost the law-giving on Mount Sinai; and harvest home the forty years of wandering in the wilderness.[3] Since, according to the Scriptures, the time of Passover and

---

[2] The historical information in the following pages can be greatly embellished by reading A. Allan McArthur's *The Evolution of the Christian Year*, Seabury Press, 1953.

[3] Cf. Part One, pp. 29-30.

Pentecost became the occasions of our Lord's death and resurrection and the birth of the Christian church, respectively, the development of a Christian calendar year actually stems out in both directions from these two foci.

Luke, the Evangelist, reports that at the time of Jesus' Transfiguration Jesus spoke of his "departure, which he was to accomplish at Jerusalem" (Luke 9: 31). As in the old covenant, divine deliverance from human bondage is the central event (ACT II) in the new covenant account of our life with God through Christ. From the first the crucifixion and resurrection were one event theologically, seen as the divine triumph in spite of human defeat. Thus, in retrospect, even the day of crucifixion is called Good Friday. Dom Gregory Dix, one of the greatest liturgical scholars of our time, writes: "There is no idea anywhere in Christendom, before the fourth century, of a separate commemoration of the Passion on Good Friday and the resurrection on Easter Sunday, the one a day of mourning and the other of joy in our fashion."[4] From the first, our Lord's redemptive work was viewed as a single act.

The later separation of Good Friday from Easter, the observance of Holy Week and the development of Lent, are parts of the same process—the establishment by the church of periods of fasting, penitent self-examination, and so on, as preparation for the great central event of the resurrection. The historian reports that the church in Jerusalem, sometime in the fourth century, played a key role in the development of the Holy Week celebration, hallowing thereby both the locations and the events of our Lord's Passion story, from the paean of palms along the Jericho road to the cries of condemnation on the *Via Dolorosa*. The later development of the period of preparation into a full Lenten season involved the extension of the six days of Holy Week into six weeks of commemoration of our Lord's struggle with the powers of evil. In contemporary practice precisely forty days of fasting and penitence are counted by starting with Ash Wednesday before the first Sunday of Lent and excepting the

---

[4] Cf. *The Shape of the Liturgy*, Dacre Press, Westminster, 1945.

Sundays. Sundays are unalterably days of celebration, no matter where they fall in the yearly pattern.

The celebration of Christmas and Epiphany is also a part of the process of reading the events of our Lord's life backward from its center (ACT II), in this event to the beginning (the PRO- LOGUE). It appears that here too there was at first a single festival of the Beginning of the Divine Manifestation (Epiphany) and that the earliest celebration fell upon January 6. Specifically em- phasized was the manifestation of the Christ to the world, com- memorating at once the birth (Matt. 1–2; Luke 1–2), the bap- tism (Mark 1), and "the light [that] shines in the darkness" (John 1).

When, however, the celebration of the coming of the divine Love into our human life is traced back to the most definitive historical event, it comes to rest upon the birth of our Lord (Christmas) as the primary festival of the Incarnation. Ulti- mately this became a separate festival and is celebrated by the Western church on December 25. The Epiphany remains as a correlative commemoration of our Lord's baptism and is still celebrated on January 6.

The practice of observing Christmas as the festival of the Incarnation on December 25 has not been found earlier than the fourth century. Scholars believe that this day was chosen by the church in Rome to strengthen its position in the struggle against pagan sun worship, whose festival fell upon the winter solstice. Thus Christmas became the occasion for proclaiming the birth of the Son of Righteousness as the true Light of the World.

Just as in the case of Easter, the Western church developed a period of preparation for Christmas. Advent, like Lent, was at one time a six-week period of anticipation of the fulfillment of the prophetic promises regarding the Savior's coming. Our con- temporary practice observes but four Sundays. Celebrating the Advent season as our "Christian New Year" offers an excellent opportunity for preachers and teachers to explain the biblical doctrine of God's election and his covenant faithfulness. This is the ground of our Christian hope and the framework of the drama which is about to be unfolded once again in the year ahead. This will stand in the sharpest contrast to the weak resolutions and uncertain predictions which abound in our secular celebration on January 1.

One can take heart regarding the fact that the celebration of Christmas and the rounding out of the Christian calendar awaited the fourth century of the Christian church's activity, for it was in that century that the great creedal formulations of the faith were also produced. The Nicene Creed was adopted in 325 A.D. The Apostles' Creed has roots, of course, in the scriptural confessions but becomes the pattern of the church's "rule of faith" in the third and fourth centuries. Our thesis concerning the variety of means and the unity of purpose in communicating the faith is supported by history as well as by the contemporary experience of the church, for from the beginning the church bore witness to the resurrection of our Lord in teaching (the rule of faith), liturgical celebration (Sunday), preaching according to the Christian year, and sacramental practice (baptism and the Lord's Supper).

Moving forward from Easter, on the other hand, the church was on familiar ground although living in a new spiritual climate. Pentecost, like Passover, was another traditional Jewish festival which underwent a radical transformation. Pentecost, commonly called Whitsunday in Christian history, is the church's own birthday. It is very unlikely that a Christian calendar year would ever have developed had there not been both a Christian Pentecost and a Christian Easter. Easter is "the spiritual transformer" of history, but Pentecost is the event in which the power of God electrified a small group of the followers of Jesus and transformed them from disciples into apostles. This is the point in history where the meaning of our Lord's words in his high priestly prayer become quite clear: "As thou didst send me into the world, so I have sent them into the world" (John 17: 18). Reliving Pentecost, year by year, gives the assurance not only that we are sent but that we are empowered by the gift of God's Holy Spirit to carry his mission of hope to the world.

Just as in each of the other cases, pairs of festivals arose out of what was at first a single celebration, so Pentecost was originally the commemoration of our Lord's ascension to heaven as well as of his authoritative gift of power to his people. The church's separation of Ascension Day (40 days after Easter) and Pentecost (50 days after Easter) indicates the recognition that the Christian year is really not just one drama but two overlapping ones—the second (the life of the church) growing out of the completion of the first (the life of her Lord).

Proclaiming the whole story of the new covenant in the life, death, and resurrection of our Lord Jesus Christ, in accordance with the pattern of the Christian year, is the means whereby the church commemorates his victorious mission to the world. Preaching becomes the occasion for "the nurture and discipline of the Lord" in and through the recapitulation of the gospel, when the "hearer" confesses with the apostle Paul: "I have been crucified with Christ; it is no longer I who live, but Christ who lives in me" (Gal. 2: 20). Through year-round participation in the life and work of our Lord Jesus, the hearer is helped to grow in grace and in responsible service to the world.

B. The Church as the Embodiment of Living Hope: Prophetic Preaching and Christian Social Action

The second half of the Christian calendar year, following Pentecost, is quite properly called Kingdomtide. In this period the church faces the world and proclaims "the acceptable year of the Lord."

Each year's celebration of our Lord's gracious gifts culminates in an accent upon the grace of "hope," that is, of "what shall be" by virtue of God's faithfulness to us as revealed in the resurrection of our Lord Jesus. At no point in the church's life is it so important that we be clear about the ultimate (eschatological and cosmic) and the immediate (personal and social) significance of her witness as in the preaching of hope and the coming of the kingdom of God.

In popular thinking hope is the most distorted of our spiritual gifts. In some times and places the eschatological dimension of hope is so strongly emphasized that its relevance to the here and now is nearly obliterated. The charge of social philosophers that Christianity tends to offer the world nothing for now but "pie in the sky by and by" cannot be shrugged off as mere misrepresentation. Too often the proclamation of the hope of life after death has become an excuse for the church's social irresponsibility in allowing people to continue to live in hopeless destitution in this world.

Largely because of this woeful distortion of the real hope that the resurrection offers in ultimate terms, the immediate form of "the hope which springs eternal in the human breast" is reduced to a naïve kind of humanistic optimism: "Everything will come out all right," or more realistically, "Hope for the best, even though you expect the worst." Christian hope for the immediate and every day is the farthest removed from what we may naturally expect from good fortune, the law of averages, or the cliché, "Where there is life there is hope."

In truth, it is only when the immediate and the ultimate hope are seen together in the purpose of God, as revealed in our Lord's resurrection, that the right perspective can be had on either. Christian hope is the fulfillment of the promise inherent in the covenant of the living God. It is the destiny implied in our election as the servants of God. Christian hope does not seal us off from failure, defeat, pain and suffering, disaster, or death. It is rather the assurance of victory over any and all eventualities by the power of God's own Holy (healing) Spirit. *All authentic human hope rests upon the miracle of renewal.* Christian faith localizes the source of the victorious renewal of history and of our human existence in Easter. Recall the central thrust of the first-century apostolic witness: "Blessed be the God and Father of our Lord Jesus Christ! By his great mercy we have been *born anew to a living hope* through the resurrection of Jesus Christ" (1 Peter 1: 3).

The miracle of renewal, however, is not without its divinely initiated human conditions. Just as Easter **is paradoxically in-**

separable from Good Friday, so the miracle of renewal is inseparable from the power of vicarious sacrifice!

Those who die can come alive again, because in the man Christ Jesus, God has taken death into his own life and has overcome it.

That which is wrong in human life can be righted, because in our Lord Jesus, God has taken our human guilt into his own life and has healed it.

Those for whom life has lost its meaning and whose lives have lost integrity can be restored to responsible participation in the purpose of God because, through Christ, God has taken Satan's cynical doubt and spiritual disintegration into his own life and has destroyed it.

These three dimensions of renewal are all both ultimate and immediate in their implications. In ultimate terms the church bears witness to the cosmic victory "already achieved" and yet "to be consummated at the end of history." The faithful celebration of the liturgical year serves this end. In immediate terms, however, the church is the embodiment, corporately and in her members individually, of the power of renewal through vicarious sacrifice and suffering service. Ours is the responsibility that the world's social and personal ills be overcome in the course of history, day by day and year by year.

The proclamation of "the acceptable year of the Lord," along with the actual personal and social transformations for which this symbol stands in our biblical heritage, is the occasion for what must in every age and temper be acknowledged as "the social gospel" and the mandate it carries for Christian social action.

Our Lord Jesus announced his own ministry on earth in precisely these social and personal terms:

> "The Spirit of the Lord is upon me,
> because he has anointed me
>   to preach good news to the poor.

He has sent me to proclaim release to the captives
    and recovering of sight to the blind,
to set at liberty those that are oppressed,
to proclaim the acceptable year of the Lord."

(Luke 4: 18-19; cf. Isaiah 61: 1-2)

In presenting himself as the fulfillment of this ancient prophecy, Jesus committed himself to a ministry of three R's: the
ministry of revelation, the ministry of reconciliation, and the
ministry of revolution.

Jesus' ministry of revelation is implied in the words: "The
Spirit of the Lord is upon me, because he has anointed me."
Anointment, that is, messiahship, to the Hebrews was an indication of special divine election. Specifically, Jesus announces that
he has been anointed to proclaim the good news of God's love
and faithfulness to all his people. The content of the divine
revelation is the ministry of reconciliation. The news is good to
all who are estranged: the poor, the bodily disabled, and the
brokenhearted. The news is good to all who are captives: the
enslaved, the exploited, and the dispossessed.

But the ministry of our Lord Jesus—a ministry of revelation
which unveils God as the one who is, through him, reconciling
the world to himself—was announced in three R's. The third is
the ministry of revolution. "To proclaim the acceptable year of
the Lord" may not sound particularly revolutionary to modern
ears, but it was to those who heard it in ancient Nazareth. If
there had not been something revolutionary about what Jesus
said, the response of his fellow townspeople would have been
unintelligible. It is reported that they "were filled with wrath."
They tried to ride him out of town on a rail.

Nine chances out of ten, those who were filled with wrath
were not the poor, the blinded, and the enslaved. It was those
for whom a change of status for the poor, the blinded, and the
enslaved would be disturbing, would upset their plans, their
source of wealth, their superior social position.

The "acceptable year of the Lord" was the jubilee year, explained in Leviticus 25: 8-19 as a fifty-year deadline for the restoration of communal justice in the Hebrew community. This commandment was an attempt to restore to the descendants of all the original tillers of the land the opportunity to make their living upon it too, despite the fact that in the meantime a crafty monopoly landowner (a Baal) had reduced them to serfdom. Again, this commandment was an attempt to restore the descendants of those whose forefathers had bartered away their liberty, or had had it taken from them involuntarily, to the freedom which is the God-given right of every man—whatever his race, nationality, or economic fortune.

There were few devotees of such revolutionary doctrines in Israel's history. Indeed, the true prophets of the Lord were few in number. Yet there was one at work during every crucial political showdown, engineering a revolution in behalf of the poor and enslaved: Ahijah with Jeroboam against Rehoboam, the intolerant son of the imperial Solomon; Elijah with Jehu against the House of Ahab, the land-grabber; and Jesus proclaiming the revolution of the kingdom of God against the kingdom of Caesar (whether Caesar lives in the first or the twentieth century). Indeed, it is only by virtue of the action of this revolutionary Spirit of love and righteousness continually challenging the status of the social, political, and economic patterns of our human life in every age that good news for the poor, the blinded, and the enslaved ever becomes a reality. It is the ministry of revolution which makes possible the ministry of reconciliation, which is the divine revelation that Jesus Christ unfolded.

The major long-run result of the total ministry of Jesus has been the coming into being of the Christian church. The apostle Paul has given us the normative conception of the relationship between our Savior and the church. He speaks of the church as "the body of Christ," thereby suggesting that the first R of our ministry is to embody the sacrificial spirit by which our Savior revealed the will and character of God. But, being the body of

Christ in the midst of the world's infidelity and self-estrangement lays upon the church two very difficult demands:

(1) The church must hold the world together!

(2) The church must turn the world upside down!

The first is the church's ministry of reconciliation. The second is her ministry of revolution.

Already in the second century of the Christian era, Christians acknowledged that it was their duty and within their power "to hold the world together." In an ancient letter, addressed to Diognetos, an unknown writer says: "What the soul is to the body, this the Christians are in the world . . . they hold the world together." At the end of the paragraph the following imperative is appended: "So great is the office for which God has appointed them, that it is not right for them to decline."

To most of his contemporaries this prophet's words were undoubtedly absurd. However, within two centuries the world found in Christianity a bulwark of community in the midst of a tottering and decadent empire. In our day such a word may not appear to be quite so absurd, but in point of fact it still remains an unredeemed promise. Withal it is notable that the year 1938, which saw the final collapse of the League of Nations as a political instrument for the maintenance of international order, witnessed the conception of the World Council of Churches. To be sure we can be grateful that the following decade, largely occupied with the international debacle called World War II, saw the birth not only of the World Council of Churches in 1948, but in 1945 the new United Nations dedicated to the maintenance of the peace of the world. Nonetheless, who knows to what extent the world-wide Christian fellowship whose fundamental nature allows it to ignore the boundaries of race and nation may yet be called upon to "hold the world together" in the tense days of international and interracial power politics which loom ahead?

Wherever there is disharmony, disunity, distress, or distrust; wherever there is pain and suffering, imprisonment and starvation; wherever there is exploitation of the poor and the helpless; wherever war and the threat of war bring their indiscriminate vengefulness upon the innocent and guilty alike—there is the field of the church's ministry of reconciliation. Where the children of God are at enmity with one another, be it between neighbors, within families, between races, or within the family of nations—there the healing work of the ministry of Jesus Christ is the light that shines in the darkness.

All the church's ministry of reconciliation is futile and surface-scratching, however, unless it is undergirded by the ministry of revolution. Paradoxical as it may be, it is clear that unless the church can turn the world upside down she cannot hold it together. The world must be brought to repentance, that is, be turned right side up, before there is any possibility of holding it together.

When, however, the prophetic voices within the church do attempt to get the world to remove the rotten timbers of arrogant nationalism and blind devotion to power politics, along with the filth and stench of racial arrogance and the myriad forms of human exploitation, vested interests in these manifestations of the *status quo* arise to cry "treason."

The apostle Paul was properly accused of being a "treasonous" revolutionary when the complacent citizenry of Thessalonica charged: "These men who have turned the world upside down have come here also" (Acts 17: 6). Paul lived in a world which was like ours in at least this respect: its civilization was in danger of being buried alive in the moldy tomb of a past that lingered too long. The greatest danger which confronted it was not change but stagnation. The specific charge against the apostle and his companions was that they were "all acting against the decree of Caesar, saying that there is another king, Jesus." That was revolutionary! It was seditious to idolatry, but radical in its loyalty to the dynamic whereby mankind may move over from decadence to renewal, from death to new life.

Nineteen centuries later, this same revolutionary spirit drove our American nation to set a generation of Negro people free from their bondage to chattel slavery. Pursued, as it were, by the "Hound of Heaven," to which this persistent Spirit has been likened, twentieth-century America finds that it must in good conscience, but with considerable sacrifice of pretension, emancipate their children's children from the status of "citizens second-class."

The Christian church, moreover, has not always and in all places been dominated by this Spirit of communal love and equalitarian justice. She has often numbered among her members the staunchest defenders of the institutions of Baal and the vested interests of the proud and the mighty. Indeed, the story of the New Testament, received by a soldier of occupation in India during the days of British imperial rule, marked "not dangerous" by the censor, is ominous. It indicates the extent to which the New Testament may be judged by the supine attitudes and acts of the church, instead of judging the church by the Spirit of the New Testament.

When it comes to stimulating fundamental changes in our social life with regard to racial relations, economic systems, and international organizations, the total effect of the revolutionary spirit within our churches is often no greater than that which resulted from the decision of certain Irish town fathers to build a new jail. This revolutionary change was to be made within the following stipulations: (1) the builders shall use the materials salvaged from the old jail in constructing the new one, (2) the new building shall stand on the site of the old one, and (3) the old jail shall be in use until the new one is constructed. Most of us are such tame revolutionaries!

The ministry of revolution as the way to reconciliation requires that the church be downright serious about identifying herself, in full obedience, with the Spirit of love and righteousness revealed in our Lord Jesus. Then and only then can we be hopeful for fundamental improvements in our social institutions. A divided and crumbling world must be held together; a sick and dying world must be given new life. It is the imperative duty and within the power promised to that ongoing embodiment of the Spirit of Christ known as the Christian church to minister to the world at the point of its two most fundamental needs: reconciliation and revolution.

We are confronted in this generation with one of the most serious social issues that has ever faced the church in more than 1900 years of history. The issue is the use and abuse of atomic energy. Throughout the ages the church and the human society to which she has ministered have had to face many revolutions which they did not foster but which the Spirit of love and righteousness has been more or less instrumental in directing or transforming toward the welfare of mankind. For example, modern times have seen the rise of bourgeois capitalism, the industrial revolution, the development of technology and automation, the rise of Marxist communism, and now the atomic age.

To make this new source of power help and not hurt us is the joint responsibility of scientists, government officials, educators, and community leaders. In this as in all other human affairs it is the function of the Christian conscience, inspired by the preaching of the gospel and its interpretation of the meaning of human life, to beget a responsible stewardship of the conditions of personal health and social peace, and thereby of "hope" for the future of humankind here on earth.

One cannot help but be appalled, however, at the widespread indifference and general irresponsibility that presently manifest themselves among us regarding the testing and use of atom bombs. We are being confronted by a double threat to all human life. On the one hand, there is the possibility of a large-scale atomic war that no nation wants but which all the major nations are feverishly preparing to implement. On the other hand, there is already the serious threat of disastrous effects to the health of all human life on this planet resulting from the extensive program of atom-bomb testing.

Even though we were to adopt the dubious ethical position that the making and testing of thermonuclear weapons is a positive factor in the maintenance of peace in our world of intensive power politics, there is a further question crying to be asked. How seriously do we judge the hazards, to unborn generations as well as to those of us who are now living, which are resulting from the increase in our atmosphere and on the earth's whole life-sustaining surface of the deadly radioactive element known as strontium-90? This is the newly discovered chemical element which associates itself with calcium, and tends to supplant it, thus threatening to weaken and disease our human bone structure.

In this regard, as in many other matters where technical knowledge is not readily available to everyone, Christian churchmen and women are at the mercy of the experts. Moreover, when the experts disagree, we are forced to judge their testimony rather more in terms of the vested interests they represent than upon the evidence they present. Frankly, one tends to discount the demurrers of those scientists who speak for the Pentagon and the Atomic Energy Commission on this matter, when they tell us that there is nothing to worry about.

In truth, when we deal with the issue of the life and death of innocent generations still unborn, we cannot lightly judge what our own nation has done and is currently responsible for doing to the destiny of humanity as a calculably justifiable risk, on the ground that we face the threat of what another nation might possibly do sometime in the future. Fear of Russian communism must not be permitted to drive us into becoming the Frankenstein of the twentieth century on the arrogant and mistaken assumption that we are its military messiah. At no time in human history have a few men been in a stronger position to "play God" to all mankind, and incarnate Satan in so doing, than now appears to be the case.

The church of the prophets must stand with Dr. Albert Schweitzer[5] and with many laymen within the church and outside her community who have both sufficient technical information and the moral courage to warn us of the grave dangers in the course we are taking. Can the church which proclaims Jesus

---

[5] Cf. "A Declaration of Conscience," *Saturday Review of Literature*, May 18, 1957: "We are committing a folly in thoughtlessness. . . . We must muster the insight, the seriousness and the courage to leave folly and to face reality."

Christ as "the hope of the world" sit idly by and permit a new form of satanic destruction steal away from humanity the physical conditions of ever being able to share in this hope?

It is heartening to know that the Executive Committee of the World Council of Churches meeting in New Haven, Connecticut, on August 5, 1957, called upon Christians to urge their governments to abolish war, to control armaments, to establish the conditions for peace, and to forego the testing of atomic bombs.

This message, available from the World Council of Churches office at 297 Fourth Avenue, New York 10, New York, says in part:

We are bound to ask whether any nation is justified in continuing the testing of nuclear weapons while the magnitude of the dangers is so little known and while effective means of protection against these dangers are lacking. We must ask further whether any nation is justified in deciding on its own responsibility to conduct such tests, when the people of other nations in all parts of the world who have not agreed may have to bear the consequences. Therefore, we call upon each nation conducting such tests to give full recognition to this moral responsibility as well as to considerations of national defense and international security. . . .

We know that a comprehensive program for disarmament must proceed by stages, and we realize how much depends upon a deepening of confidence between the nations. But we urge that as a first step governments conducting tests should forego them, at least for a trial period, either together or individually, in the hope that the others will do the same, a new confidence be born, and foundations be laid for reliable agreements.

We therefore appeal to all our brethren to act with Christian courage, and to pray to Almighty God to guide the peoples and their governments aright.

FOUR

OBSERVING THE SACRAMENTAL
PATTERN OF A LIFETIME

No form of the Christian church's ministry has been so open to partisan expression or denial as the holy sacraments. The "Catholic" type of church—Eastern Orthodox, Roman Catholic, and Anglo-Catholic—is usually classified as "sacramental" and contrasted with the Reformed and Lutheran churches in which the preaching of the Word has been placed in the central position. This classification is accurate, however, only on a scale of emphasis and not as an indication of mutually exclusive forms of ministry. Granted that a sacramental type of church will not be pulpit-centered, it does not follow that the Word of God is thereby excluded from the life of that congregation. By the same token, save for the extreme sectarian expressions of Protestantism, the Reformation-type emphasis upon the centrality of the Word of God does not imply a denial of the sacramental pattern of divine-human communication. In fact, both the Word and the sacraments bespeak the gospel of our "justification by grace through faith." Moreover, the central mystery—the love and righteousness of God revealed in the death and resurrection of the Lord Jesus Christ—which lies at the heart of the catechism, the liturgy, and the Christian calendar, is also the foundation of the holy sacraments.

Martin Luther and John Calvin were much more careful to conserve the whole heritage of Christian communication through the sacramental "means of grace" than some of their heirs have been in the traditions which bear their names. For example, the celebration of the sacrament of the Lord's Supper is "reformed" by the Word of God to bear witness to the central fact of our Lord's crucifixion as a "once for all" atoning sacrifice. This reform was a protest against the medieval "miracle of the mass" which had become a priestly ceremonial wherein it was declared that Christ's self-sacrifice was being re-enacted in his name in each service. Nonetheless, this reforming of the church's ritual practices in accordance with the New Testament teaching, thereby more correctly focusing the Lord's Day service upon the celebration of the one sacrifice of our Lord rather than upon the church's continuing need to make sacrifice, is no warrant for casual practice in its observance. Whereas many congregations have substituted the pattern of the fiscal year for the Christian calendar, observing the Supper on a "quarterly" basis, both of the reformers considered the celebration of this sacrament as essential to the worship of each Lord's Day.

Latter day Protestantism has a similar difficulty with the practice of the other major rites of the church. Either by radical reduction or by perfunctory and inept practice, the sacramental ministry has generally suffered detraction at the hands of Protestant influence. To some extent this has been due to anti-Roman bias which has tended to result in "throwing out the baby with the bath." In truth, however, it has never been the real genius of the Reformation heritage to be anti-Roman, and much less to be anti-Catholic. Historically understood, the proper name for the non-Roman churches which have arisen out of the Protestant Reformation is "the church Catholic, Reformed according to the Word of God." To use a word popularized in our generation by Dr. Walter M. Horton of Oberlin, we are the *Evangelical* Catholic Church.

The ecumenical movement in the life of the churches of the twentieth century is an overt affirmation of our awareness of our common belonging to the one Universal Church of Jesus Christ in all times and in all places. Furthermore, it represents our zeal to recover and find our own place in the universal heritage of faith and practice which flows from the revelation of God in Christ.

Members of the United Church of Christ will represent a variety of specific traditions in regard to the sacraments and rites of the church. Variety is a major factor in this venture of faith into which we have entered. Moreover, our variety is not to be merely tolerated while it is secretly despised. From the beginning the church has enjoyed varieties of gifts, while she has owned the same Spirit. "And there are varieties of service, but the same Lord; and there are varieties of working, but it is the same God who inspires them all in every one" (1 Cor. 12: 5-6). What, from the apostolic times, has proved to be the greatest misfortune for the church, is the tendency for her diversities to harden into divisions and manifest themselves as divisiveness and the occasion for quarreling and dissension (cf. 1 Corinthians 1).

In this final chapter we shall seek to uncover the wholeness of purpose which undergirds the church's sacramental ministry, just as we have already attempted to do in the case of her teaching, healing, and preaching ministries. This requires that we study the sacramental observances of the church in the context of her responsibility for "the nurture and discipline" of God's people from womb to tomb and beyond, that is, from the beginning of life to its end, not just as the first and last steps, but as the *initiation* and *consummation* of life's purpose.

The traditional "seven sacraments" of the Catholic churches are not all of equal import. Specific rites arose in the course of church history to meet different needs, and they have different forms of biblical sanction. Some are once for a lifetime: baptism, confirmation, marriage, ordination, and extreme unction. Two are to be repeated regularly: confession and the Holy Eucharist. Only five of these are essential to everyone in the church. The remaining two, marriage and/or ordination, are sacramental only for those who choose to make the specific vows entailed. Roman priests take vows of chastity; Greek orthodox priests may marry. Of the seven, however, two alone have *direct* theological ties with the central mystery of the new covenant faithfulness of God revealed in the death and resurrection of our Lord Jesus Christ— baptism and the Eucharist (Lord's Supper).

The Protestant reformers were profoundly wise in understanding this latter truth, claiming that two sacraments alone have been instituted by Christ himself as essential for our salvation. The actual Reformation movement, however, was sparked in the recognition by Martin Luther that the very important rite of "penance" had become the occasion for radical perversion and distortion in its practice. The practice of private confession of sin and of priestly assurance of forgiveness was then and is today as much a necessary part of the church's pastoral ministry as is its counterpart in the corporate service of worship on the Lord's Day. The sale of indulgences, however, had made the whole practice a ludicrous mockery in Luther's time and had to be reformed. Reformation does not mean abolition, however, but restoration.

A. Recapitulating the Covenant Drama at the Crisis Points in Life

Churches of the Reformation heritage generally celebrate two sacraments only: baptism and the Lord's Supper. Each of the other traditional rites remains, however, in some fashion as an instrument of the church's nurture and discipline of her people through the stages of life's pilgrimage, and to help them meet the crisis points along the way. It is our thesis that the plot of the covenant drama appears here again in the church's life, this time giving us the sacramental pattern for a lifetime of covenant troth with the living God.

There is a fundamental difference, however, in the way in which our experience of "time" is recapitulated in the sacramental pattern as compared with the church's other means of grace. There are two different Greek words for "time"—*kairos,* denoting "the right time" or "God's appointed time," and *chronos,* denoting "a period of time" without reference to its quality or significance. Our chronology is made up of hours, days, years, and a lifetime. Certain moments, events, and experiences, on the other hand, participate in the divine dimension of time, in which "eternity" breaks through to reveal God's purpose for our lives. The church uses the biblical covenant drama to give us as many *kairoi* opportunities as our *chrono*-logical days and years can carry.

As we have already seen, the church encourages us to engage in *daily* Bible study for regular instruction in the faith, *weekly* celebrations of the Lord's Day liturgy, and *yearly* celebrations of our Lord's entire life and ministry. In this manner our individual lives are structured by regular "times" set aside for us to recover, relive, and reaffirm the good news of God's covenant purpose. In the sacraments, however, the perspective of "the times" is reversed. Our human chronology—a lifetime—is taken as the framework for the drama, and the crisis points in our life's pilgrimage become the occasion of our participation in the Mighty Acts of God.

Each of the major stages on life's pilgrimage involves humankind in times of crisis. Actually it is probably more accurate to say that the transitions from stage to stage are the occasions of crisis.

One of the most significant books in Christian education that has appeared in our time is L. J. Sherrill's *The Struggle of the Soul*.[1] In the light of the biblical revelation we discern that the Christian life is "a pilgrimage of faith." Dr. Sherrill's thesis is that this understanding of the Christian faith gives us the perspective to overcome two antithetical and equally distorted views of life (1) the saga, (2) the treadmill. The first philosophy enthralls many of us in our youth, especially in the American cultural climate. It calls us to heroic fulfillment in self-propelled achievement. The failure of most of us to come anywhere near these heroic proportions, indeed, the actual fate of humdrum existence and the meaningless struggles of every day, are more accurately pictured in terms of enslavement to an endless treadmill.

Christian faith is realistic enough to reckon with our human weakness and the disappointments which flow from our pretensions, but it knows that life has a glorious destiny in the purpose of God, because it is rooted in the gospel of God's *Gabe* (gra-

---

[1] Published by Macmillan, 1951.

cious gift) and motivated by his correlative *Aufgabe* (demand for sacrificial service).

Dr. Sherrill's "a lifetime of pilgrimage" takes one through each of the critical stages of divine-human encounter which we have called the plot of the covenant drama. A careful study of the purpose of the sacraments and rites of the historic Christian church reveals the same pattern of covenant drama, apparently designed to offer a lifetime of spiritual resources for directing and carrying the pilgrim on his way. When placed side by side, the stages and the sacramental pattern lay out for us the church's most complete prospectus for the task of Christian education.

STAGES ON LIFE'S WAY	THE SACRAMENTAL PATTERN OF A LIFETIME
	BAPTISM
PROLOGUE —Birth and Infancy	Baptismal Vows
ACT I —Childhood and Early Adolescence	Parental Nurture and Discipline
	Confirmation and
ACT II —Adolescence and Young Maturity	First Communion
ACT III —Maturity and the Middle Years	Christian Marriage and Christian Vocation
EPILOGUE —Old Age and Death	Visitation of the Sick and Burial of the Dead
	THE LORD'S SUPPER

Sacramentally speaking, the Christian life falls into two parts, roughly distinguished by the generation to which one belongs at the time. In the first half, one belongs to the younger generation, marked by childhood dependence and growth. Here we live under personal nurture and discipline. The second half finds us in the reverse situation with regard to the relationship of the generations. We are adults, in a position of responsibility and vested with authority to bring up our children in the nurture and discipline of the Lord. Accordingly, the Christian faith celebrates two sacraments, whereby we are betrothed for the entire span of our life to the holy love and sovereign righteousness of God. Both draw their symbolic meaning from the death and resurrection of our Lord Jesus Christ, but they are directed to meet the needs, respectively, of the two generations which make up the perspective of a lifetime.

Baptism marks our initiation into the mystery of the new covenant and carries us through the age of dependence to the threshold of adult responsibility. The Lord's Supper reveals the mystery of our destiny, that is, that God's love is steadfast and that his covenant is fulfilled in eternal life. Baptism is the sacrament of divine election, announcing the promise that from the beginning we are included in God's covenant love and shall be delivered from the powers of evil. The Holy Communion marks the regular participation of the faithful and responsible servants of God in the redemptive work and re-creative power of his own Holy Spirit, through the broken body and the shed blood of our Lord and Savior Jesus Christ.

Within the broad sacramental framework of our election (baptism) and destiny (Holy Communion) in Jesus Christ, the church practices a sequence of specific rites. These rites are designed to declare the active presence of God in every critical stage of our human growth and personal involvement.

In the plan of God's holy love for his people, the baptismal sacrament incorporates three steps of responsive covenant activity:

(1) The vows that are made by parents and sponsors in behalf of the child in infancy.[2]

Do you sincerely desire that this child be baptized into the faith which the church confesses (The Apostles' Creed)?

Answer: I do.

---

[2] Cf. *The Book of Worship*, "The Order for Baptism of Infants."

Do you promise to instruct this child in the Word of God, and by precept and example to bring him up in the nurture and admonition of the Lord?

Answer: I do.

Do you promise to bring this child to the House of God, and to see to it that in due time he be instructed and prepared for Confirmation and the Holy Communion?

Answer: I do.

(2) The carrying forward of these vows in the course of their parental nurture and discipline during the stages of childhood and adolescence, looking to the time of the young person's own public confession of Christ and confirmation.

(3) The actual rite of confirmation,[3] in which the minister says:

Dearly Beloved: Following the example of the apostles of our Lord, the church bestows upon those who have been baptized, and have been properly instructed, the blessing of confirmation by prayer and the laying on of hands.

In this sacred ordinance you, on your part, renew and ratify the promise and vow made in your baptism; whilst the church, in God's stead, claims you publicly for his service, blesses you in his name, confirms you in his covenant, and invokes upon you in larger measure the Holy Spirit by whose help alone you are able to fulfill your vows by leading holy and obedient lives.

Do you now, in the presence of God and this congregation, renounce the vain pomp and glory of the world, the lusts of the flesh, and all evil works and ways?

Answer: I do.

Do you confess Jesus Christ as your Lord and Savior?
Answer: I do.

---

[3] Cf. *The Book of Worship,* "The Order for Confirmation."

Do you promise according to the grace given you, to live a Christian life, and always to remain a faithful member of the church of our Lord Jesus Christ?

Answer: I do.

Confirmation stands in the middle of the sacramental pattern. On the one hand, it marks the completion of the baptismal covenant. On the other, it is immediately preparatory to the first communion. Most significant of all is the fact that the confession of Jesus Christ as Lord and Savior is the central event to which our baptism is directing us and from which we embark upon a "new life." This event brings the first half of life (PROLOGUE to ACT II) to a close by unfolding the vision of life's goal in the diligent service of the Lord (ACT II to EPILOGUE).

The second half of life likewise incorporates a sequence of rites by which we acknowledge the covenant faithfulness of God-with-us in every crisis we face. The sacrament of the altar begins with the first communion. This marks the adolescent's first privilege of participation in the sacrificial body of Christ and his first call to responsible participation in the Lord's service. The two major events of the mature period of human life—the choice of one's life partner in Christian marriage and the choice of one's lifework as a Christian vocation—are celebrated by the church with special observances. In this fashion we not only acknowledge the continuing need that we have for God's blessing in every enterprise we undertake, but we confess that, in fact, these decisions of ours are meaningful only because their basic structures are rooted in God's everlasting covenant. It is not that we have chosen God; he has chosen us!

Thus our marriage vows, like our professional and vocational commitments to one another, are first of all and ultimately vows and commitments to the Lord. He is always "the party of the first part." By his grace he has endowed us with the mysterious powers of his own creative love and wisdom. Christian marriage is quite literally the occasion of fulfilling the sacred trust of procreation and is therefore "a holy order." The covenant family is the basic unit of the historical drama of human life. Here the pulse of life flows on from generation to generation, and the generations are continually brought into intimate personal encounter with each other and with the Creator of life himself.

The rite of ordination is customarily practiced in the church for the setting apart of men and women for the ministry. Since by "the ministry" is usually meant the professional leadership of the church, ordinations are a rather rare and exceptional occasion in any given congregation. This is not as it ought to be on two counts: (1) Each congregation, in order to assure its own reproduction, ought to produce at least a half dozen young men and women in each generation who will give full and professional service to the church for the teaching, preaching, or pastoral ministry; (2) our Reformation heritage properly motivates us to recover the New Testament concept of the "universal priesthood of believers" (cf. 1 Peter 2).

It is one of the misfortunes of Protestant history that undue emphasis has been placed upon the negative criticisms of the function of the priesthood. When rugged individualism and the priestly privilege of every man are confused, the major import of the Reformers' challenge is siphoned off into secularism. Quite properly, our acknowledgment of the sole and sufficient priesthood of Jesus Christ repulses the claims of others to presume to mediate between God and man. We miss the point of the biblical teaching, however, if we neglect the fact that the covenant people is defined as one corporate personality—an organism of many members and not an aggregate of individuals. In the fullness of time this one corporate personality is revealed in the man Christ Jesus! Thus the injunction to the universal priesthood in the apostolic age is a call to each member of the body of Christ to fulfill his role, in and through the corporate ministry of the whole people of God, to the world of broken humanity roundabout.

The recovery of the responsibility of each member of the church to make his lifework a Christian vocation in and through the body of Christ will throw a new light upon the rite of ordination. In effect, it will mean that confirmation is the ordination of every layman to a Christian calling. What is commonly called "ordination" is the setting apart of particular persons to posts of special responsibility—not only of preachers, priests, and pastors, but of teachers, healers, and elders, deacons and deaconesses—all who are trustees of the divine stewardship of love and righteousness. When ordained ministers are called not only to minister *to* a congregation, but *through* a congregation of ministers, the promise of the universal priesthood will be coming into realization.

Throughout the mature years of our life our spirits continue to need to be fed and our wills to be strengthened. Regularly we accept the invitation of our Lord:

> "Come to me, all who labor and are heavy-laden,
>   and I will give you rest.
>
> Take my yoke upon you, . . . For my yoke is easy,
>   and my burden is light."
>
> (Matthew 11: 28-30)

The Lord's Supper, as the sacrament of the altar, has three different meanings, depending upon our perspective in the covenant drama:

(1) the Eucharist—our remembering to give thanks for the boundless grace of God in Jesus Christ (ACT II),

(2) the presence of God's Holy Spirit in the Holy Communion, empowering us to keep our covenant responsibility (ACT III),

(3) a growing anticipation of the glorious community which shall be in the final consummation of the kingdom of God (EPILOGUE).

Not only does the sacrament of the Lord's Supper give us the perspective of eternal life in the midst of time, it sustains a pair of rites within the church that are clearly eschatological in import. The services of the church for "the visitation of the sick" and "the burial of the dead" underscore the fact of our finiteness and temporal limitations by confronting us with the fact that the drama of life has an end as well as a beginning and a middle.

Certainly no one ministering in the name of Christ would ever underestimate the importance of the church's healing ministry for those who, in the course of life's pilgrimage, fall into affliction in body, soul, or spirit. We have emphasized its significance in Part Three, chapter 2. In this context an equally important but distinctly different function is being fulfilled by the church's sacramental ministry. This is our responsibility to help God's people to face the reality of death and accept it.

Christian faith looks death in the face without wincing, because our Lord Jesus, by his death and resurrection, has taken the sting out of dying and given us the assurance of a living hope. Thus, in the perspective of faith, we rejoice with those pilgrims who rest from their labors, because they have died in the Lord.

The sacramental pattern is the church's way of announcing God's providential government over us and his identification with each individual through the whole of a lifetime, and continuously with the generations as they relate to each other. The sacrament of baptism, the rites of confession and confirmation, the sacrament of the Lord's Supper, and the rites of marriage, ordination, and Christian burial, are timed to witness to the grace of God's new covenant in Jesus Christ at each stage of life's pilgrimage.

Observing the sacraments becomes the occasion for "the nurture and discipline of the Lord" in and through the traditional rites of the church whenever two or three generations join together in acknowledging the immediate activity of the grace of God at some one of the stages on life's way from birth to death and eternal life.

B. The Church as the Pilgrimage of the Generations: The Sacramental Pattern and Family Life

The family is the basic unit of the Christian life. It is a reflection of the divine life, rooted in the order of creation, and, through the grace of our Lord Jesus Christ, becomes the sacramental carrier of the divine purpose—that human beings should live in a community of faith and love and glorify his holy name.

The Christian family is rooted in the order of creation and is consecrated by Christian marriage. As human beings we are bi-sexual: male and female.

> God created man in his own image, . . .
> male and female he created them.
>
> (Genesis 1: 27)

This basic polarity of function is not merely biological. It is also psychological and sociological, and gives tone and quality to the whole of life, accounting for such polar personal traits and characteristics as initiative and receptivity, virility and creativity, courage and fidelity.

Although individuals are predominantly male (man) or female (woman), there are recessive characteristics of the female in man and of the male in woman. By virtue of this bisexuality within individuals, a relatively stable, but incomplete, unity of existence is achievable in each person. The normal tendency, however, is to seek and find the unity of our existence in the polar community which results from the love of a man and a woman for each other.

The consecration of this new unity of a man and a woman in marriage constitutes the covenantal foundation of the family. Jesus said:

> "From the beginning of creation,
> 'God made them male and female.'
>
> 'For this reason
> a man shall leave his father and mother
> and be joined to his wife,
> and the two shall become one.'
>
> So they are no longer two but one.
> What therefore God has joined together,
> let not man put asunder."
>
> (Mark 10: 6-9; cf. Genesis 2: 24)

The Christian church recognizes the marriage troth as a much deeper kind of personal relationship than a legal contract. A contract is usually put in such terms that, if one person fails to fulfill the agreement, the other is released. A covenant is "for better for worse, for richer for poorer, in sickness and in health, to love and to cherish, till death us do part."

The promise of our Lord that by marriage "the two shall become one" is not automatic, however. The unity which we cannot find in our individuality is not achieved by multiplying individuality by two. Thereby we simply multiply the difficulty. Indeed, married love is the subject of the most rigorous test, and offers the most certain proof of the truth of the paradox of "saving and losing." He who would save his individuality in marriage shall lose it. There, more than anywhere else, one sees the self-defeating character and the devastating consequences of selfishness. The broken home is often tragic, for the loss is suffered by the innocent and the guilty alike.

The blessed unity for which Christians are wed is found neither in the husband nor in the wife, nor yet in the family which is formed by their marriage. It is found in the Lord, who covenants with each and both to love them with an everlasting love.

The apostle Paul exhorts us:

"Be subject to one another out of reverence for Christ.
Wives, be subject to your husbands, as to the Lord. . . .
Husbands, love your wives, as Christ loved the church
    and gave himself up for her. . . .
Be kind to one another, tenderhearted, forgiving one
    another, as God in Christ forgave you."

(Ephesians 5: 21, 25; 4: 32)

Much of our human love (*eros*) is begotten of desire for the lovely, attraction to the attractive. Christian love (*agape*) is not limited by the fickle character of temporal loveliness and attractiveness. In Christ the love of a man and a woman for each other will be transfigured into a common bond of self-sacrifice and creative power. Christian love is infinitely more than mutual, because it comes from him who so loved the world that he gave his only Son for our reconciliation. There is a well-known parable which expresses this truth:

> The closer the spokes of a wheel approach the hub,
>   the closer they are brought to each other.

The real union which the marriage covenant consecrates is a gift of God's grace. It is accepted in the only way that the essence of a gift can be accepted, by participation in the spirit of the giver.

The family as the community of a man and a woman in love is incomplete without children.

> And God blessed them, and God said to them,
>   "Be fruitful and multiply,
>   and fill the earth."
>
>   (Genesis 1: 28)

Married love, functioning through the basic human bisexuality, is normally consummated in procreation. The birth of children into a Christian family is not only a seal of God's promise, but also the price of the family's participation in God's covenant purpose. For covenanted parents, the gift of a child is the symbol of family fulfillment, defining for the husband his central role as "father," and for the wife her central role as "mother." Fatherhood, motherhood, and childhood constitute together the inner spiritual situation in which the meaning of existence may be uncovered.

In our acknowledgment of the occasion for the writing of this book (cf. the Introduction) we noted that a revolution is currently occurring in the way in which the church is going about the task of Christian education. The major feature of what is happening in many different communions is symbolically expressed in the name of the curriculum which the Evangelical and Reformed Church has been using since 1950—"The Church and Home Series." This is a deliberate effort to implement the truth that the family is the basic unit of the Christian life and that Christian education is the communication of the gospel to and through at least two generations at once. The home is not only the sole life setting in which the generations are naturally in communication; it is the one in which participation as well as transmissive communication can and does take place during the formative years of childhood and adolescence.

Our biblical heritage of Christian education hinges upon two formulations of the divine imperative for parents in regard to the upbringing of their children.

From the early days of Israel's life, the words of the great commandment,

> And you shall love the Lord your God
>   with all your heart,
>   and with all your soul,
>   and with all your might,

define her existence as the people of God. More specifically, God's words are to constitute the warp and woof of covenant family life.

> You shall teach them diligently to your children,
>   and shall talk of them
> when you sit in your house,
>   and when you walk by the way,
>   and when you lie down,
>   and when you rise.
>
> (Deuteronomy 6: 7)

This prophetic injunction is matched by the apostolic reminder to Christian parents and their children that the ancient covenant responsibility still holds.

> "Children, obey your parents in the Lord,
>   for this is right.
> 'Honor your father and mother, . . .
>   that it may be well with you
>   and that you may live long on the earth.'
> Fathers, do not provoke your children to anger,
>   but bring them up in the [nurture and discipline]
>   of the Lord."
>
> (Ephesians 6: 1-4)

There is additional assurance that parents who are "in Christ" have the power of his grace and the authority of his righteousness for the task.

The task of communication between the generations is never easy. In part this is conditioned by our human finitude, but it is disastrously augmented by our own self-estrangement as parents. We are at best only clay vessels through which to channel God's precious gift. Our own mixed motives in regard both to discipline and to nurture confuse the child and corrupt the communication. There is more than mere childish whimsy in the report of the ten-year-old who was in discussion with her peers about the problem of parent-child relationships. She said: "The trouble is that we get our parents so late that there isn't much we can do about them anymore." To which one Pennsylvania Dutchman is constrained to confess:

> Ain't it the truth!
> Old ve get too soon,
> Schmart ve get too late.
> If only ve could have von child
> before the first von
> to learn on!

The larger truth is that parents and children are undergoing the discipline and nurture of the Lord together. Each of us is the occasion for what the Lord is doing for the other. Parents are learning that discipline must be consistent if children are to enjoy the freedom which they so desperately want and need, and children are learning that they also want and need limits within which to bear the burden of freedom. The father of an adolescent boy reports that his son wanted to go out "for a ride" with a group of his friends after the close of a school dance. When permission was refused in the presence of his friends, he ranted and raved, but a few moments later when he was back home with his family, he thanked his father for being firm.

Another group of adolescent boys and girls wanted to go to a nearby drugstore for sodas after a school concert. The store had a bad reputation and had been declared off-bounds by most of their parents. On this occasion the mother of one girl weakened and let her go, thinking that it would give her a chance to see for herself. Anyway, she would follow and wait for her outside. What a surprise she had coming to her! When her daughter returned home that evening she exclaimed: "You let me down, Mother. I didn't want to go to the awful place, but I couldn't tell my friends that. You let me down. I wanted you to say no!"

Our children are caught in the same ambiguity that we find so difficult to live with and within which to keep our balance—the common need for security and for significance, to belong and be accepted and to be one's true self and stand for the right no matter how often wrong appears to be on the throne. Children unconsciously mimic their parents in their earliest attempts at balancing their lives. In this stage and in adolescence when they are beginning to experiment for themselves, they need from us our very best in terms of depth of love and strength of self-discipline.

We used to sing, "Two loves have I." Every child has, or, shall we say, needs "two loves." In principle God has arranged for this eventuality by giving each child a mother and a father. In his book, *The Art of Loving*, Dr. Erich Fromm has recovered for our time something of the fundamental genius of the biblical view of the family when he points up the fundamentally different and yet correlative function of "mother love" and "father love."

Mother love by its very nature is unconditional. . . . There is nothing I have to do in order to be loved . . . *I am loved because I am.* . . . Unconditional love corresponds to one of the deepest longings, not only of the child but of every human being. . . . Mother has the function of making him secure in life.

Fatherly love is conditional love. Its principle is "I love you because you fulfill my expectations, because you do your duty, because you are like me." . . . He represents the other pole of human existence: the world of thought, of man-made things, of law and order, of discipline, of travel and adventure. Father is the one who teaches the child, who shows him the road into the world.[4]

In each family where Christ is Lord and Savior, "fatherhood," "motherhood," and "childhood" become sacramental symbols of the divine life in human terms:

To "father," because of his call to initiative, virility, and courage in the direction of the family's destiny, belongs the symbol of divine authority and discipline (God the Father).

To "mother," because of her calling to bear, nurture, and care for her children through the long years of their infancy and growth, belongs the symbol of the divine creativity and steadfast love (the Holy Spirit).

To "the child," because of his correlative "awakening to power" and "call to growing responsibility," belongs the symbol of *human* faith, obedience, and willing service (the Sonship of God, incarnate in Jesus Christ).

Failure, on the part of any one or combination of family members faithfully to fulfill the God-given role entrusted to them, breaks covenant in two dimensions at once: (1) within human families, where individual roles vary according to calling; and (2) within the universal family of God, where all appear as unfaithful children, needing to be re-created by God's gracious forgiveness.

Cognizant of our human weakness, the apostle admonishes us: "Children, obey your parents in the Lord. . . . Fathers, do not provoke your children to anger, but bring them up in the [nurture and discipline] of the Lord."

Because life is understood to be a *pilgrimage of faith,* Christian education does not prescribe the same "pink pill" for everyone at the same time nor for the same person at different stages of life. We recognize (1) that each one of us is on the pilgrimage and that *we are where we are* and not somewhere else, and (2) that our relationship to each other, our peers, our parents

---

[4] Harper & Brothers, pp. 39-43. Copyright, 1956, by Erich Fromm. Used by permission.

and/or our children, is essential to determining precisely who we are at any point along the way. The sacramental pattern of a lifetime, when played within the family setting, offers a common framework for all to participate in the love and righteousness of God together. The divine-human encounter is the constant factor for us all, but it has a variable content—varying according to the form that our needs for creative individuality and community participation take from time to time. That is to say, our "personal existence" needs disciplining in proportion as our "religious faith" receives nurturing.

PROLOGUE—Birth and Infancy: *Becoming an Individual Person*
  Nurture — Being given the security of belonging to one's family.
  Discipline — Learning to distinguish persons from things.

In the normal course of affairs, we are all born individually. Individuality is in the first instance no achievement; it is rather a given biological fact of life. The event of our separation, the cutting of the umbilical cord, becomes the occasion, however, for an immediate and serious hurdle, for once we are born we stand in need of being rescued from the threat of isolation and death by being accepted into the status of a "person." In so far as the biological family becomes a social family, that is, a community of mother, father, and child with or without brothers and sisters, the little bit of individuality is en route to becoming a person.

It is a fundamental part, although not the most important aspect, of the baptism of an infant that he is given a name by his parents. This act bears a twofold significance. The parents choose from the names of faithful family forebears one that they wish to mark the child's individuality for the rest of his life. In baptism this name defines one's Christian existence, and is first used by the pastor in declaring the child's divine election by bestowing upon him the sign and the seal of the triune name— the Father, the Son, and the Holy Spirit. At the same time the parents acknowledge that they are a Christian family and bequeath to their child the personal status of permanent social participation in their little, and the congregation's larger, faith community.

Infancy and childhood are the occasions in which an individual discovers that he is a person, because persons roundabout him distinguish between him and things and incorporate him into their love. Without knowing it, children born into Christian homes and baptized into covenant with Christ are well on their way to becoming Christian persons in their own right.

Act I—Childhood and Adolescence: *Becoming Oneself*

Nurture — Being loved for one's self by parents and teachers.

Discipline — Being helped by them to come to one's self.

This is the age in which the status of parenthood undergoes the most radical change. The little child's parents are not only, to all intents and purposes, "gods" to him, but they are actually God's dedicated servants committed by their vows at the child's baptism to bring him up in the nurture and the discipline of the Lord. At the conclusion of this period, parents who have done their work well will find themselves completely relieved of their halos but having the satisfaction of participating in "authentic" parenthood.

For parents to be able to absorb adolescent rebellion without falling prey to compulsive authoritarianism or agonizing despair is possible only by the grace of God. They learn thereby, however, what is meant in the Scriptures by the idea that "the people of God" must become his "suffering servants." This is the age for which the apostolic injunction to parents regarding the nurture and discipline of their children receives its most formidable test and its most obvious validation.

The child, for his part, is faced with the herculean task of "cutting off the psychological umbilical cord" without shattering the image of his parents in his own soul. Fundamentally, this is a token of Everyman's inevitable failure to actualize his own individuality in the face of the authority of God without falling prey to pretension and infidelity.

Christian parents will need all the grace that God can and does bestow (1) to love the child for himself and for what he chooses to become and not for what they want him to be: (2) not to "play God" in his life but to be the servants of God's love and righteousness to him; and (3) to accept and forgive him when he mars and disfigures not only the image of his parents but actually the image of God within him. Most important is it to help and not to hinder him in his effort to wean himself from parental dependency, by internalizing the discipline which was once the responsibility of parents to exercise over him. Equally important will it be for him to throw off external parental discipline, by helping him to internalize the nurturing love which was once the parents' joy to shower upon him.

The adolescent must be played like a Stradivarius and not like an instrument of mass production. There are no professional rules of thumb that can be learned and applied to our family relationships. We all begin, it seems, by playing by ear. Parents, not having been parents before, and the child, being a child for the first time, are amateurs and, by the grace of God, learn from each other's mistakes as well as each other's achievements.

One thing becomes more and more certain: that Christian nurture and discipline in childhood are not designed to produce Christians without conversion. The truth is, rather, that parental love and discipline help, by the grace of God, to establish the conditions within which it is possible for our children to come to themselves and acknowledge their need for our Savior's forgiveness.

Fundamentally, the adolescent has to accept for himself, voluntarily and directly from the Lord, the nurture and discipline which his parents and teachers have mediated to him through his baptism and upbringing. He is called upon to become himself and no other (responsible individuality) and to have one self (a unified person) as against the many selves he is continually being tempted to be—one self with the fellows and another with the girls, one self with his parents and another with the gang, one self in public and another in private life, and so on.

Our adolescent life is often like the man in Jesus' parable who was beset by a legion of demons, that is, of conflicting selves.

Serious self-examination, at this stage of life, will push back the blinds and let the sunlight in, thereby revealing how desperately we are incapacitated by infidelity to those who love us, through pretending to be what we are not. The insidious character of pretension is its demonic "possession." It is like quicksand. Once we fall into its grasp, and we all do, we become enslaved to the pretension that we must live up to our pretension. Every effort to escape serves only to mire us more deeply. The awareness that our parents and teachers, acting as the servants of God, love us for ourselves, neither rejecting us for our infidelity nor accepting our pretension, becomes for many an adolescent the occasion for "coming to himself" as did the prodigal son in the far country. One despairs of one self, actually of many false selves, in becoming one's self. The transition from ACT I to ACT II in the life of God's covenant people is always fundamentally rooted in the act of confession which marks the beginning of the prodigal's return: "I will arise and go to my Father, and I will say to him, 'Father, I have sinned against heaven and before you; I am no longer worthy to be called your son; treat me as one of your hired servants'" (Luke 15: 18-19).

ACT II—Adolescence and Young Maturity—*Becoming Someone: Making Basic Identifications*

Nurture — Being accepted by Christ and within his church.

Discipline — Accepting acceptance and committing oneself to covenant service.

Negatively, confirmation involves what is popularly called "eating crow." On one level this means that I confess that I have been wrong and need to be forgiven. On another level, however, I am led to acknowledge that I am not only wrong but helpless. I can do nothing to get straightened away, either with myself or with anyone else. I not only need to be forgiven—I need a Savior. Our human pilgrimage goes through the valley of the shadow of death and reaches the heights of the renewal of life

by no other means than through entering into the vicarious sacrifice of another, who has identified himself with me in my suffering.

When parents and teachers and the pastor, working together,
bring a young person to face up to and ask the question, "Who
am I?" he is ready to make a "confession of sin." When, however, they help him find the meaning of his existence in the general confessional terms of the answer to Question 1 of the Heidelberg Catechism, he has made his basic identification for life and
is ready to be confirmed—

That I, with body and soul, both in life and in death, am not
my own, but belong to my faithful Savior Jesus Christ, who
with his precious blood has fully satisfied for all my sins, and
redeemed me from all the power of the Devil; and so preserves
me, that without the will of my Father in heaven not a hair
can fall from my head; yes, that all things must work together
for my salvation. Wherefore, by the Holy Spirit, he also assures me of eternal life, and makes me heartily willing and
ready henceforth to live unto him.

Knowing, from hearing the gospel proclaimed, that I am accepted, and confessing that I am accepted, thereby "accepting
acceptance,"[5] are two very different states of affairs. Moreover, it
is the confession which serves as the key to the door of maturity
in our human pilgrimage. No matter how old we might be
chronologically, without it we are still wallowing in adolescent
defiance and pretension and threatened by every new decision
we face. With it we are prepared to enter into the demands of
life with full obedience and into its gifts with joy.

Our basic identification with Christ is marked by membership
in his church. The members of the fellowship of love and righteousness by which we have been nurtured and disciplined become our spiritual family, and the fellowship becomes our home.
Here we make our two major lifetime decisions: the choice of a
life partner in marriage and the choice of a life work. These become the main channels for our Christian vocation, our "calling"

---

[5] Cf. Dr. Paul Tillich's *The Courage to Be.*

to covenant service. Parenthood and useful work in sustaining, guiding, and guarding our common life become warp and woof throughout the middle years of life's pilgrimage.

ACT III—Maturity and the Middle Years—*Accepting Responsibility and Exercising Authority*

Nurture — Life of devotion: "Come to me."

Discipline — Life of courage: "Take my yoke."

At this point the pilgrim family comes full circle. The second generation has reached ACT III. Parents are now moving into the upper middle years, and their children are supplanting them on the front line of family activity. Suddenly the children find themselves no longer simply responsible to someone (their parents) but responsible for someone (their children). Under authority vested by the Creator and by their responsibility, a new generation enters the drama of life, and the PROLOGUE and ACT I begin to be lived all over again.

I am quite sure I did not understand my own childhood when living in it as now I have come to understand its significance in the life of my own children. Each of us lives a childhood twice. Of course we do not mean what is commonly called "second childhood"; we mean that each of us lives his life a second time through his children or through those young people who are close to us in our mature years. When we recognize this to be true we come to see all human life as a dialogue in two dimensions at once: (1) between the two generations of parents and children, and (2) between both together, as children under God, and our heavenly Father.

Not until children become parents, however, do they realize the responsibilities that are theirs as children of God. Our eyes are not fully opened, it seems, to see the purpose of God until we have brought forth a new generation which is as blind and irresponsible as we were before them. And so it goes, generation after generation. The old adage about each new generation standing on the shoulders of the former is at best only a half-truth. The more difficult half of this truth is the persistent tendency on the part of each new generation "to kick the props out from under the old folks" so that it is easier to climb over them in pursuit of its own selfish satisfactions.

Exercising parental authority and responsibility is not only a difficult role for erstwhile rebellious children to perform—it is the nearest thing in the world to the biblical pattern of the suffering servant. As with the children of Israel of old (cf. the parable of Jonah) we generally have to be backed into our responsibility and accept its demands quite involuntarily. The authority of parenthood and responsible leadership in the world of affairs hangs like a millstone about the neck of many who are not prepared to carry "the yoke of the Lord."

Spiritual resources to meet the heavy demand for strength and courage in bearing our responsibility, and for knowledge and wisdom to exercise the authority vested in us, are open to us for the taking. Daily feeding on the Word of God in study and contemplation, the weekly fellowship of the Holy Spirit in worship, the yearly cycle of Gospel celebrations, and the regular participation in the Holy Communion are the church's major "means of grace" for the mature and middle years of life. Maturity is marked by a rhythmic pattern of alternating accent upon the Lord's nurture *and* discipline, respectively. Only those who regularly respond to the Lord's call, "Come to me, all who labor and are heavy-laden, and I will give you rest," can know that "my yoke is easy, and my burden is light" (Matt. 11: 28-30).

The great hope of Christian education is not only that we can produce better children under the nurture and discipline of Christian parents, but that the responsibility of parenthood may be accepted by Christian people with deeper insight into the divine demand for obedience from all his children, no matter what their stage on life's pilgrimage. The church is not fulfilling her covenant responsibility unless she calls her people as families to suffering service, one on behalf of another. Christianity is a mission which begins but does not end at home.

EPILOGUE—Old Age and Death: *Achieving the Simplification of Life in the Vision of Its Wholeness*

Nurture — Becoming "as a little child"—confident assurance of the faithfulness of God.

Discipline — Becoming "an elder"—retiring from heavy responsibility without losing authority, facing death with the assurance of victory.

The end of the drama of life, like its beginning, is anchored in the mystery of God's election in our Lord Jesus Christ. Our destiny is in his gracious love and sovereign righteousness.

"None of us lives to himself,
　and none of us dies to himself.
If we live, we live to the Lord,
　and if we die, we die to the Lord;
so then, whether we live or whether we die,
　we are the Lord's.
For to this end Christ died and lived again,
　that he might be the Lord both of the dead
　　and of the living."

(Romans 14: 7-9)

The church has always shown at once a deep respect for the wisdom of age and a tender concern for the aged. Thus the ambiguity of our human situation is determinative for the church's ministry of righteous discipline and nurturing love to this as to each of the other stages of life. We are all endowed with creative individuality and marked by creaturely dependence; from beginning to end our basic needs are for the opportunity to love and the assurance of being loved.

It is an expression of the church's gratitude to Christ her Lord that she cares and continues to plan for the security and welfare of her senior members. When older people cannot be in the love of their families any longer, there is great comfort in knowing that homes and hospitals are available to meet their needs.

Properly understood, the responsibility of the strong to bear the burdens of the weak, always a mark of the church's mandate in serving the world, is no respecter of generations. Every generation, however, when it comes to what we call the middle years, finds itself standing "in the middle." In the pilgrimage of life our children are following after and our parents have gone on before, and yet as we go along together it is the middle generation which is called upon to undergird the last days of the third generation even as it nurtures and sustains the new generation from birth.

On the other hand, the church from the New Testament time onward has ordained "elders" to a position of unusual authority in her life. In practice this has often had more to do with maturity of wisdom and good counsel than with age. Nonetheless, it does represent the opportunity for continuing authority and creative participation for those who are no longer able to carry full responsibility in the heavy work of every day.

Becoming an elder, full of wisdom as well as of years, is a blessing to be enjoyed and a trust to be guarded, both in the church and in the family. Just as college freshmen look to seniors rather than to sophomores for encouragement and inspiration, so many children look beyond their parents to their grandparents for the mediation of God's love and righteousness in their lives. It is a great loss to Christian family life when the influence of the third generation is lacking. Much of the rootlessness of our times can be measurably healed by diligent effort to maintain family and congregational continuity, despite the hazards of time and space.

Over and above these evidences of family love and church fellowship, pilgrims of the oldest generation will find more and more comfort for their souls in the covenant promises of our Lord Jesus himself:

"This cup is the new covenant in my blood. Do this, as often as you drink it, in remembrance of me. For as often as you eat this bread and drink the cup, you proclaim the Lord's death until he comes" (1 Cor. 11: 25-26).

Christian theology begins in wonder, and when theological thought and Christian nurture and discipline have done their best the mystery still remains. This is why the Christian church always confesses the faithfulness of the Eternal God as both the Alpha and the Omega of her life, and sings her faith in the risen Christ as a glorious "hallelujah."

Glory be to God the Father, and to the Son, and to the Holy Ghost.

As it was in the beginning, is now and ever shall be, world without end. Amen.

In the meantime, some questions have been answered, some new and more serious questions may have been raised, but above all, life itself has taken on a new luster. The creative Spirit of love and righteousness, incarnate in human history at its center in the man Christ Jesus, has been bequeathed to us who live in his church, as both gift and command. Members of the Christian community, in each day and year, through every lifetime and from generation to generation, participate together in a glorious pilgrimage—the pilgrimage of steadfast love.

Our *invitation to theology*, as we noted at the outset, comes from the Word of the living God himself, calling us to love him with all our heart, and with all our soul, and with all our mind. In the perspective of life in his covenant, as a dramatic encounter of heart and soul and mind, we can now reaffirm this invitation and address it to each new generation of children and their teachers: The call of the Christian faith is *an invitation to pilgrimage!*

Almighty God, Father of all mercies, we, thine unworthy servants, do give thee most humble and hearty thanks for all thy goodness and loving-kindness to us and to all men. We praise thee for our creation, preservation, and all the blessings of this life; but above all for thine inestimable love in the redemption of the world by our Lord Jesus Christ; for the means of grace, and for the hope of glory. And, we beseech thee, give us that due sense of all thy mercies, that our hearts may be unfeignedly thankful, and that we show forth thy praise, not only with our lips, but in our lives, by giving up ourselves to thy service, and by walking before thee in righteousness all our days; through Jesus Christ our Lord, to whom, with thee and the Holy Spirit, be all honor and glory, world without end. Amen.

INDEXES

Index and Dictionary of Theological Terms

We have combined with the Index that follows a dictionary of the theological terms used in this book. An effort has been made to produce a combination that will be helpful as a teaching and study guide for those who accept our *invitation to theology*. For valuable assistance in preparing the Index and Dictionary, and the two other indexes also, the author gratefully acknowledges his indebtedness to the Rev. Ernest A. Rueter.

The extensive amount of cross-referencing is meant at once to indicate that theological terms come in families and belong to each other and to assist the reader in tracing their lineage. The plot of the drama of our Covenant with the Living God, represented in the chart on page 66 of the text, is the trunk of the theological family tree.

The book references that occur in connection with certain key words of our theological vocabulary indicate the author's desire to share with his readers his own most treasured resources.

ABRAHAM—the father of the covenant people of God, 32 f., 165, 169

ACCEPTANCE—the Gospel in existential language, 109, 181 f., 195, 239 f.

    being accepted—Cf. GRACE
    accepting acceptance—Cf. FAITH (being justified)
    accepting oneself—Cf. FORGIVENESS and REPENTANCE

ACTS OF GOD, MIGHTY—dramatic symbols of the Living God's activity in human history, e.g., in the Exodus of Israel and in the Resurrection of Jesus for the Church, xxi f., 2, 12, 19 f., 49, 66 ff., 161, 163, 177, 221

    Cf. COVENANT THEOLOGY; COVENANT DRAMA, PLOT OF THE:
    PROLOGUE: Creating the Order of the World and Man, 67-79
    ACT I—Sustaining and Judging with Righteousness, 80-96
    ACT II—Judging and Redeeming Through the Grace of Jesus the Christ, 97-111
    ACT III—Recreating and Sanctifying by the Gift of His Holy Spirit, 112-131
    EPILOGUE: Consummating His Kingdom of Peace, 132-149

    Cf. Gustaf Aulén: *The Faith of the Christian Church*, Muhlenberg, 1948.

    Cf. G. Ernest Wright: *God Who Acts*, SCM, 1952.

ADAM—the truth about Everyman; the marks of our humanity, 33 f., 45, 62, 72, 84, 155, 201

Cf. COVENANT DRAMA, PLOT OF THE:

PROLOGUE: Creatures in God's Own Image

ACT I—Beguiled and Enslaved by Pretension

ACT II—Justified by the Grace of Jesus Christ

ACT III—A New Man in the Body of Christ

EPILOGUE: Heavenly Son of Man

(Cf. separate references.)

Cf. Reinhold Niebuhr: *The Nature and Destiny of Man*, Scribners, 1941.

ADOLESCENCE—growing up, becoming adult, becoming "oneself," 237-241

AGED, THE—achieving the simplification of life in the vision of its wholeness, 243 f.

ALCOHOLICS ANONYMOUS—a fellowship of acceptance, 113 f.

ALPHA AND OMEGA—the framework of our human existence; the divine initiative (election) and the divine fulfillment (destiny), 19, 48, 66, 71, 133 f., 140 f., 245

Beginning and End of life

Ground and Goal of existence

Source and Consummation of history

AMBIGUITY—human awareness of an equivocal responsibility to the bipolar factors in our divine-human situation, 59, 73 f., 77 f., 90 f., 115, 127 f., 157, 234

Cf. BIPOLARITY.

ANTITHESES—terms which we use to express the ultimate conflict between what is given in the purpose of God and its perversion. They are mutually exclusive alternatives. Choosing the one is to reject the other.

Christ (grace) vs. Satan (demonic power of pretension), 100 f.

Heaven (eternal life) vs. Hell (spiritual death), 138

faith vs. unfaith, 90

freedom vs. slavery, 110

hope vs. despair, 214

peace vs. broken community, 125 ff.

ANXIETY—the insecurity of faith continually tempted to unfaith, 75 explanation for "the fall," 88 f.

Cf. SPRINGS OF OUR HUMAN ACTION.

APOSTLES—followers of our Lord Jesus who were "sent out" upon a mission of love and righteousness; interpreters of the New Covenant drama, xxiii, 9, 12, 19, 48, 52, 78

ASCENSION OF OUR LORD—the exaltation of Jesus as the Christ; his Lordship over the church and the world, 44, 135, 200-206

ATOMIC ENERGY—use and abuse, 214 ff.
atom bomb, 82, 91

ATONEMENT—at-one-ment with God; reconciliation by redemptive healing; the expiation of human guilt and deliverance from the bondage of sin, 19, 23 f., 25 f., 27, 32, 34 f., 42, 44 f., 49, 62 ff., 97, 102-107, 138, 170, 173, 200, 239
Cf. RECONCILIATION; CRUCIFIXION AND RESURRECTION OF JESUS.
Cf. D. M. Baillie: *God Was in Christ*, Scribners, 1948.

AUTHORITY—power, either God's or from God, by which righteousness is sustained and freedom is disciplined, 52, 53 f., 98, 241 ff.
rebellion against, 94, 184, 237 f.
and freedom, 138 f., 293 ff.

BAALISM—idolatrous pretension by which man claims "to play God"; a religious cult symbolized by sexual prowess and the fertility of the soil; economic exploitation by the "landlord," 24, 31, 38, 59, 92, 210
Cf. IDOLATRY.

BAPTISM—the Christian sacrament of divine election; initiation into the mystery of the New Covenant, 144, 163, 168, 174, 220
Infant, Order for, xix, 223 ff., 236
of John, 42

BEGUILED AND ENSLAVED BY PRETENSION—an existential confession regarding the status of "fallen" man; the "image of God" perverted but not destroyed, 84-87, 89 ff.
Cf. ADAM; EVIL, POWERS OF.

BIBLICAL HERITAGE, OUR—reliving the drama of the divine-human covenant of the biblical history as the story of our life, 11, 64 f., 67, 104, 160
Cf. COVENANT DRAMA, PLOT OF THE.

BIPOLARITY—the name we use to express the axis-like, inner unity-in-tension which defines what is given in our knowledge of God, of ourselves and our relationship to him, 35, 55 f., 73 f., 77 f., 115, 129, 157
the love and righteousness of God, 77 f.
Jesus Christ as our Lord and Savior, 223 f.
revelation and response, 7 f., 159 f.
the nurture and discipline of the Lord, xx
creatureliness and the image of God, 73 f.
religious faith and existential freedom, 55 f.
communion and community, 61 f., 158 ff.
tradition and education, 161 f.
male and female, joined in marriage, 229

251

BLESSING, GOD'S—the love and righteousness of God as transmitted from generation to generation in the covenant, 77, 165, 171

CATECHISMS—formulations, coming out of the Reformation heritage, for teaching the meaning of our biblical covenant with the living God, 167, 172
Evangelical Catechism, 174
Heidelberg Catechism, 173, 183, 198, 240
Luther's Small and Large Catechisms, 174
My Confirmation, 175
Westminster Confession and Catechism, 175

CELEBRATION—the spontaneous response of gratitude and joy which wells up out of the church's memory of her Lord's glorious victory on Easter, thereby accounting for her regular liturgical and sacramental observances, 185 ff.
Cf. LITURGY FOR THE LORD'S DAY; SACRAMENTAL PATTERN OF A LIFETIME.

CHRISTIAN, BECOMING A—the central theme of Sören Kierkegaard's philosophical and religious writings, 7, 180-184
Cf. CONVERSION; STAGES ON LIFE'S WAY.
Cf. Kierkegaard: *Purity of Heart*, Harper's, 1956.

CHRISTIAN COMMUNICATION—twofold nature: *transmission* through verbal or sensory symbols (the Word of God), *participation* in personal encounter (the Holy Spirit), 6, 153-161, 223
Cf. COMMUNION AND COMMUNITY.
Cf. L. J. Sherrill: *The Gift of Power*, Macmillan, 1955.

CHRISTIAN EDUCATION—communicating the Gospel of Jesus as the Christ to and through two generations at one and the same time, "calling forth" covenant responsibility, xxi f., 151 ff., 161, 164 ff., 231 f., 242
and progressive education, xx f.
Cf. EVANGELISM AND THE TEACHING MINISTRY.
Cf. Randolph Crump Miller: *The Clue to Christian Education*, Scribner's, 1950.

CHRISTIAN FAMILY—the basic unit of Christian life; a reflection of the divine life, rooted in the order of creation, and, through the grace of our Lord Jesus Christ, the sacramental carrier of the divine purpose—that human beings should live in a community of faith and love, and glorify his holy name, xviii f., 11, 51 f., 65, 141, 175, 184, 228-245

CHRISTIAN FREEDOM—in Christ we are set free from the slavery of pretension and fear; faithful acceptance of the service of God, 8, 19, 51, 97 ff., 110, 168, 170, 174, 180

CHRISTIAN MINISTRY—"Ministers of Christ are set in the world to be the representatives of his authority and the ambassadors of his grace," 189 ff.

Fourfold office of the ministry: teaching, priestly, prophetic, and pastoral, 162 f., 164-245

CHRISTIAN MORALITY—an acknowledgment that human freedom involves responsibility to and for each other, 8, 76

CHRISTIAN NURTURE AND DISCIPLINE—

"The Nurture and Discipline of the Lord"—being brought up to know and enjoy the love of God and learning to accept and use the freedom which this love affords, responsibly, xx, 78, 150, 158 f., 206, 219, 233, 235-245

The Church's Task of Nurture and Discipline—the awesome task of communicating the love and righteousness of God from one generation to another, xviii ff., xxiii f., 8, 59, 150, 159, 162 f., 165, 168, 172, 188, 195, 222, 228, 235-245

through the teaching ministry—a school of courageous faith, 176 ff.
the priestly ministry—a fellowship of healing love, 192 ff.
the prophetic ministry—the embodiment of living hope, 206 ff.
the pastoral ministry—the pilgrimage of the generations, 228 ff.
Cf. LOVE AND RIGHTEOUSNESS OF GOD.

CHRISTIAN THEOLOGY—loving God "with our whole mind"; a confession of what God has done, of what he is doing, and of what he promises to do, through the New Covenant in Jesus as the Christ, xxiii, 3 ff., 8, 161

Cf. INVITATION TO THEOLOGY; COVENANT THEOLOGY.

CHRISTIAN TRADITION—the responsibility of the church for the transmission of "the Mighty Acts" and the Covenant "Word of God" from generation to generation, 161 ff.

Cf. MEANS OF GRACE.

CHRISTIAN VOCATION—being called to the service of humankind in the name of Jesus Christ, 46, 58 f., 111 ff., 117 f., 126 f., 193, 207, 225 f., 240

Cf. SUFFERING SERVANT.

Cf., John Oliver Nelson (editor): *Work and Vocation*, Harper, 1954.

CHRISTIAN YEAR OF PREACHING—the plan whereby we communicate the whole Gospel story of Christ and the church in a year's time, xxiii, 118, 135, 198 f.

Cf. Chart, 200.

Life of Jesus—Advent to Ascension Day, 201-206

Life of the Church—Pentecost to Memorial Sunday, 206-216

Cf. MEANS OF GRACE.

CHURCH—the people of God who belong to the new Covenant in Jesus as the Christ, 14, 158, 161, 210

New Testament Symbols:
Body of Christ, 46, 123, 125 f., 210 f.
Chosen People of God, 18, 54, 59 f., 122, 133
Community of the Holy Spirit, 64, 107, 118 ff., 123, 125, 131, 159 f.

Other synonyms:
Servant People of the Lord, 54
Community of the Faithful, 61
Community of forgiven sinners, 114

CHURCH AND HOME—partners in Christian education, where the home is the family church all week long and the church is the weekly family reunion of the people of God, xviii ff., 8, 163, 175, 184, 231
Cf. CHRISTIAN FAMILY.

CHURCH AND STATE—the divine strategy for community in our fallen world:
State—a community of the world intent upon the security of its members; ordained under the sovereignty of the divine righteousness to keep order and to establish justice by law
Church—the covenanted community, glorifying God; ordained under the holiness of the divine love to maintain fellowship and to proclaim the freedom of the Gospel, 125-131

CHURCHMANSHIP AND CITIZENSHIP—participating at one and the same time in both communities, 61 f., 77, 127-131
Establishing community on "love" *and* maintaining order with "justice"
Peace-making (reconciling evil-doers) *and* police-action (restraining evil)

COLONY OF HEAVEN—the church as a beach-head of the eternal kingdom, witnessing to the lordship of Christ on earth, 134-138

COMMUNION AND COMMUNITY—complementary poles of the life of God's covenant people, 60 f., 118 ff., 158 ff.
Communion—participating in the divine resources of love and righteousness, 158
Community—bringing the love and righteousness of God into the life of the world, revolutionizing the world's social structures and reconciling the world's people to each other and to their God, 24, 120 ff., 130, 147, 195
Cf. STATUS OF OUR LIFE IN COVENANT ENCOUNTER.

COMMUNISM—a Christian "heresy" regarding community, 120, 214 f.

CONCERN—the will to "suffering service," the motive to love another for himself, accepting responsibility *for* someone, 113 f., 182 ff., 192-195, 238
Cf. SPRINGS OF OUR HUMAN ACTION.

CONFESSION OF FAITH—acknowledging our covenant troth with God; proclaiming the faithfulness of God in Jesus as the Christ, 57, 108, 139, 190

CONFESSION OF SIN—acknowledging our infidelity in our covenant troth with God, 26, 57, 108, 187 f., 190, 194, 239 f.
Cf. SIN.

CONFIRMATION—a rite of the church marking the completion of the baptismal covenant and preparation for the first communion, 225 f., 239

CONVERSION—the renewal of the center of one's being, 181 ff.
and revivalism, xix
and evangelism, 166 f.
double conversion, 181 ff.
Cf. CHRISTIAN, BECOMING A.

COURAGE—the motive power, begotten of our divine acceptance in Jesus Christ, to have the heart to be faithful and obedient to our trust. Courage is "faith in action," 54, 58, 96, 113, 170, 179 f., 216, 229, 240 ff.
Cf. SPRINGS OF OUR HUMAN ACTION.
Cf. Paul Tillich: *The Courage to Be*, Yale University, 1952.

COVENANT, THE—a key term in the biblical understanding of God and Man, defined by God's Word: "You shall be my people, and I will be your God."
Cf. the Covenant terms which follow.

COVENANT DRAMA, PLOT OF THE—a sequence of five episodes of covenant relationship between God and man, bounded by a prologue and an epilogue which affirm the divine origin and consummation of human life, and between which occur three acts of interpersonal encounter:
PROLOGUE: Divine Creation and Human Existence
ACT I—Our Human Sin and the Divine Judgment
ACT II—Jesus Christ and Our Christian Freedom
ACT III—The Church and Our Christian Vocation
EPILOGUE: The Kingdom of God and Our Human Destiny
    xv, 10, 19-46, 62-65, 66-149, summarized, 97 f., 133, 143, 200
in Christian education, 161, 169, 172 f., 188 ff., 200, 222 ff., 235-244

The Christian theologian views the plot of the covenant drama from the following perspectives:

ACTS OF GOD, MIGHTY
ADAM: THE TRUTH ABOUT EVERYMAN
DECISIONS WHICH WE MAKE (Acceptance vs. Rejection)
LIFE'S CENTER OF GRAVITY (God or Nothing)
LIFE'S POLAR TENSIONS (Religion and Existence)
SPRINGS OF OUR HUMAN ACTION (Faith vs. Unfaith)
STATUS OF OUR LIFE IN COVENANT ENCOUNTER
(Cf. separate references.)

Cf. Bernhard W. Anderson: *The Unfolding Drama of the Bible*, Association Press, 1953.

COVENANT ENCOUNTER, DIVINE-HUMAN—the dramatic dialogue through which there is unfolded at once the character and purpose of God and the meaning of our human existence, 8, 9 ff., 12, 19-46, 47, 56, 62 f., 66, 81, 112, 133, 150, 159 ff., 168 ff., 179, 185-192, 196 ff., 222

Cf. Emil Brunner: *The Divine-Human Encounter*, Westminster, 1943.

COVENANT THEOLOGY—the recording, in existential terms, of the church's New Covenant dialogue with the Living God through Jesus as the Christ, xxiii, 8, 21, 34, 39, 47-65, 66-149, 169

Cf. Emil Brunner: *The Christian Doctrine of Creation and Redemption*, Westminster, 1952.

COVENANT TROTH, THE—the "Word of God"; God's *pledge* of everlasting faithfulness to and corresponding *demand* for undivided fidelity and loyalty from his people. The *truth* about our human situation is the *troth* with which God has *entrusted* us—to be stewards of his creation and servants of peace and justice in his world, xxii, 9 f., 12, 15 ff., 48, 51, 55, 63, 65, 71, 78, 96, 143, 159 ff., 176 ff., 198, 200, 229

Cf. Norman H. Snaith: *The Distinctive Ideas of the Old Testament*, Westminster, 1946.

CREATURES IN GOD'S OWN IMAGE—the ambiguous state of all human existence, marked by the umbilical cord (symbol of dependence) and the breath of life (symbol of our creative freedom) respectively

IMAGE OF GOD—man's kinship with God; the ability to respond to the love of God; the source of human responsibility; the creativity of human freedom; the authenticity of human existence, 55, 59, 72-77, 157

Cf. ADAM.

256

DESTINY—the biblical symbols of "destiny" and "election" complement each other as Omega complements Alpha. Destiny marks the
consummation of what in election is divinely purposed—the covenant
troth between the living God and the people he has chosen to create,
19, 28, 30, 34, 36, 170, 207
Our destiny (the epilogue of the covenant drama) is defined as:
Participating in God's Kingdom of Peace and Righteousness, 28,
60 f.
Living under the Lordship of Christ in History, 136 f., 143
A Colony of Heaven, 134-138
Sharing in Christ's Victory over the Powers of Evil, in the Lord's
Supper, 144 f., 223, 227 f.
Life Everlasting, 138
Cf. STATUS OF OUR LIFE IN COVENANT ENCOUNTER.

ECUMENICAL MOVEMENT—church movement in the twentieth
century in response to the prayer of our Lord "that they all may be
one," 61, 123, 218
Cf. Paul S. Minear: *The Nature of the Unity We Seek*, Bethany,
1958.
Cf. Walter M. Horton: *Christian Theology: An Ecumenical Approach*, Harper & Bros., 1955.

ELECTION—the symbol which the Bible uses to declare the divine
initiative in establishing the everlasting covenant, in which, genera-
tion after generation, we live and move and have our being, 48, 51,
66, 136
Our election (the prologue of the covenant drama) is defined as:
Being created in the image of God, 19
Having freedom with responsibility, 27
Who we are meant to be, 19, 207
The basis for infant baptism, xix, 144, 223
Cf. STATUS OF OUR LIFE IN COVENANT ENCOUNTER.

ESCHATOLOGY—the meaning and fulfillment of our human destiny
in the purpose of God
Covenant troth in Jeremiah, 39
Church's anticipation, 64, 206-216
in the Lord's Supper, 148, 191

ESTRANGEMENT AND ENSLAVEMENT—the awful consequences
of Man's rejection of his rightful status as a servant of God and
steward of his creation. We are estranged from the love of God and
of each other, and from authentic selfhood, being enslaved to the
shadows of our own pretension, 19, 29, 31, 45, 62 f., 69, 94 f., 97,
103, 194, 199 f.
Cf. STATUS OF OUR LIFE IN COVENANT ENCOUNTER; SIN;
RECONCILIATION.

ETERNAL GOD, THE—the Lord who declares: "I am who I am" and "I am the Alpha and the Omega," 50, 136, 140-143
Cf. LORD OF HISTORY, THE; IDENTITY.

EVANGELISM AND THE TEACHING MINISTRY—a "church and home" type of Christian education, in which the Mighty Acts of God are recovered as our own covenant story in the daily teaching and studying of the biblical covenant drama, xiii, 60, 161 ff., 164-184, 179, 198
Cf. MEANS OF GRACE; CHRISTIAN EDUCATION.

EVIL, POWERS OF—symbols for all that threatens to undo and destroy humankind, 45, 138, 194, 199, 224
Sin—the distortion of life which puts some form of human pretension in the place of God
Satan—the power which enslaves us to our own pretensions
Death—the threat of individual extinction
Hell—the permanent separation (estrangement) of man from God
(Cf. separate references.)
Christ, the Victor over the Powers of Evil, is the Gospel of reconciliation and atonement. 45, 64, 134, 137 f.
Cf. FALL OF MAN; ATONEMENT; RECONCILITION.

EXISTENCE—a basic category for understanding our human situation; symbolizes a person's being "put out here on one's own" (exsistere) and, at the same time, "over-against" the Ground of one's being, and other persons; raises the questions of: freedom, responsibility, decision, encounter, authenticity, pretension, acceptance, rejection, courage, et al., xxii, 3, 8, 56 ff., 67, 72, 76 f., 231
Cf. LIFE'S POLAR TENSIONS; RELIGION.

EXISTENTIAL PHILOSOPHY—asking questions about the meaning of human existence; a helpful tool for Covenant Theology, xviii, 3, 67, 80, 87, 97, 112, 132

EXODUS, THE—God's deliverance of Israel from enslavement in Egypt by the hand of his servant, Moses; the symbol in Israel of God's covenant faithfulness, 20, 69
Resurrection of Jesus as "new exodus," 45, 50
Cf. CRUCIFIXION AND RESURRECTION OF JESUS.

FAITH—the authentic spring of human action, 228; a loyal response to the love and righteousness of God, 3, 96; accepting acceptance, 7, 56 ff., 107 f., 221; the courage to be delivered from the past, 177
Faith vs. unfaith, 8, 108, 110
Faith and belief, 7
Faith vs. doubt, 7, 208
Faith and healing, 108, 193
"product" of Christian education, 177 ff.
Cf. SPRINGS OF OUR HUMAN ACTION; COURAGE.

FAITH, HOPE, AND LOVE—a trilogy of personal qualities which mark the Christian life in its fulness (cf. 1 Corinthians 13), 6, 140 f.

FALL OF MAN—the symbol for the mysterious origin of evil in human life; human pretension, 35, 81-91
Cf. EVIL, POWERS OF.

FORGIVENESS AND REPENTANCE—forgiven-ness and repentance are both responses to the gracious activity of God in forgiveness and appropriated by faith, 181 ff., 239 ff.
Forgiveness is the unconditional acceptance of the unacceptable, 195
Forgiven-ness is the acknowledgment that our righteousness depends upon the divine acceptance, 109
Repentance is the act of self-acceptance which accompanies forgive-ness; man's rejection of himself as a pretender; the resolve to be responsible, to be responsive to the divine intention, 105, 108, 167, 174, 181 ff., 239 ff.
Cf. ACCEPTANCE; GRACE OF GOD.

GENERATION AFTER GENERATION—a biblical figure for the continuity of God's covenant purpose in human history, and the responsibility of the generations to and for each other within the covenant, xvii, xix, xxii, 19, 32, 62, 63 ff., 160 f., 167, 222 f., 226, 232 f., 241

GIFT AND TASK (Gabe und Aufgabe)—a play upon words in the German language which expresses the polar unity of God's covenant "promise and demand," 56, 147, 221 f.

GLORIA PATRI—a liturgical form of trinitarian confession of faith, 142, 190

GLORY OF GOD—God's victorious consummation of his covenant purpose—the holy communion as the anticipation of the community of the kingdom of God, 40, 43, 46, 64, 135, 145-148, 200
Man's glorification of God, 188, 191, 243
Cf. LIFE'S CENTER OF GRAVITY.

GOD—the Subject of our worship, the Ground and Power of our being, the Meaning of our existence, the Goal of our living, 4 ff., 9-18, 47-55, 71, 139-143
Biblical names:
  The Living God
  The Lord of History (Yahweh)
  The Eternal "I am"
  The Spirit of Holy Love and Sovereign Righteousness
Revelation:
  The Mighty Acts of God
  The Word of God

Qualities of Character:
  Grace, Glory, Holiness, Law, Love, Love and Righteousness
Triune Name:
  Father, Son, and Holy Spirit
              (Cf. separate references.)
  Cf. Emil Brunner: *The Christian Doctrine of God,* Westminster,
  1950.
  Cf. Paul Tillich: *Systematic Theology,* Vol. 1, University of Chicago,
  1950.

GOSPEL, THE—the good-news of God's New Covenant with humankind in the man Christ Jesus; the Act of God whereby Man is
  justified by grace through faith, 6, 15, 18, 51, 97, 102, 107, 197, 199 f.,
  221
  Cf. JUSTIFIED BY THE GRACE OF JESUS CHRIST.

GRACE OF GOD—unmerited and unexpected love of God, bringing
  healing and peace to humankind from the time of Abraham to the
  present moment, symbolized in the Old Testament by the Ark of the
  Covenant and in the New Testament by the person of Jesus Christ;
  the love of God in action, forgiving our sin and delivering us from
  bondage, 3, 12, 15 f., 19, 30, 48, 51, 159, 161 f., 170 f., 173, 188, 190,
  195, 200 f., 231, 237 f.
  Cf. LIFE'S CENTER OF GRAVITY.

GRATITUDE—our living response to the grace of God, motivating us
  to give ourselves in sacrificial service; the mainspring of the distinctively Christian life, 113, 144 ff., 174, 243
  Cf. SPRINGS OF OUR HUMAN ACTION; LORD'S SUPPER.

GUILT—the power of sin to immobilize us at the center of our being;
  man's unconscious and/or conscious despair of his own pretensions;
  awareness of being responsible for irresponsible activity, 181 f., 194 f.,
  208
  Cf. SPRINGS OF OUR HUMAN ACTION.

HEAVENLY SON OF MAN—by the grace of our Lord Jesus Christ,
  we are a "colony of heaven," anticipating what we shall become in
  the fulness of time, 134-138
  Cf. ADAM.

HELL—symbol for the permanent separation of man from God; a
  possibility at the point at which God may say to a man: "So be it!
  Not my will but thine be done!" 93, 95, 154
  Cf. EVIL, POWERS OF.

HOLINESS OF GOD—the unapproachable mystery of God's being,
  the deity of God, 10, 54, 79, 195, 223

HOPE—the power to anticipate the fulfillment of our destiny in the resurrection of the Lord Jesus, 24, 37, 121, 132 f., 137, 170, 196, 206 ff., 214, 216, 243
Cf. SPRINGS OF OUR HUMAN ACTION.

IDENTITY AND IDENTIFICATION—the mystery of life
Identity: God's affirmation regarding himself—"I am who I am," 50, 137
Lost Identity: Man's search for himself—"Who am I?" 3
Identification: God's incarnation in Jesus as the Christ—"My Chosen One," 44 f., 90-101, 108 ff., 200 f.

IDOLATRY—religious prostitution, the perversion of natural and human creativity into the position of ultimate concern, 57, 75, 84, 91 ff., 177, 210, 212 f.
Symbols:
Baal—sexual prowess and natural fertility, 84, et al.
Mammon—economic wealth and power, 84
Mars—military power, 84
Provincial nationalism and racial purism, 41, 130
Equation of wants and needs, 85 ff.
Cf. BAALISM; SIN, EVIL, POWERS OF.

"IN SPITE OF"—a term of Paul Tillich's, derived from Martin Luther, underscoring the *unwarranted* characted of God's forgiving love, 109, 179

INCARNATION—the Gospel of "the Word become Flesh" in Jesus as the Christ; God's covenant troth with humankind fulfilled, 45, 97, 100, 154, 196-200, 204
Cf. WORD OF GOD, THE.

INDIVIDUALISM, in nineteenth-century America, xix, 122, 226

INFIDELITY—failure of faithful response to God's covenant love, with consequent impotence to be oneself, 23, 26, 89 f., 144, 194, 237 ff.
Cf. SPRINGS OF OUR HUMAN ACTION.

"INVITATION TO THEOLOGY"—the search for the meaning of our human existence in the mystery of God's love and righteousness, xv, xviii, xxiii f., 3, 66-149, 167, 197 f., 244-245
Cf. CHRISTIAN THEOLOGY; COVENANT THEOLOGY.
Cf. John Baillie: *Invitation to Pilgrimage*, Scribners, 1942.

ISLAM—Semitic religious movement taking its name from the prophet Mohammed's teaching, 13

ISRAEL—the Old Covenant "people of God," the heirs of Abraham chosen to be the Lord's servant to the world, 14 f., 19, 30, 37, 59, 210

262

JESUS AS THE CHRIST (MESSIAH)—the Man anointed by the Spirit of God to mediate the New Covenant, 14, 44 f., 97-111, 200 ff.
Paradoxical Union of God and Man:
Authentic Humanity *and* Grace of God, 45, 137
Man of God's Own Choosing *and* the Living Lord, 18, 41, 44, 99-101
Remnant of One in Israel *and* Only Begotten Son, 41, 64, 201
Suffering Servant of God *and* Christus Victor, 17, 40 f., 44 f., 54 f., 99, 142, 208 f.
What God Means by Man *and* What Man Means by God, 77, 99 f., 103
Polar Unity of God's Purpose:
Author *and* Perfecter of our faith, 107 f., 196
Crucified *and* risen from the dead, 102 ff.
Judge *and* Redeemer, 137
Lord *and* Savior, 99, 223 ff., 235
Word of God *and* Mightiest Act of God, 64
Life of, in Christian preaching according to the Church Year, 200 ff.
Cf. John Knox: *Jesus: Lord and Christ*, Harpers, 1958.

JUDAISM—the religious tradition of the Mosaic Covenant, 13 ff.
Cf. ISRAEL; OLD AND NEW COVENANTS.

JUSTIFIED BY THE GRACE OF JESUS CHRIST—the renewal of our broken covenant in the man Christ Jesus, 102-111, 174
Grace—the divine acceptance of man as he is, i.e., a pretender, estranged, enslaved, thereby setting him free to the truth that he is the servant of God
Being "justified by faith"—Man's acceptance of the divine acceptance; acknowledging the truth that God is God—and the self-confidence which results therefrom
Cf. JESUS AS THE CHRIST; ADAM; ACCEPTANCE; ATONEMENT.

KAIROS AND CHRONOS—a distinction in the Greek language between two meanings of time:
Kairos means a qualitatively "opportune time."
Chronos means a quantitative "period of time." 163, 220 f.
Cf. TIMES.

LAITY—the covenant people of God; a term used to emphasize the "corporate" character of the church, and servant role of each of her members
lay-theologians, xxiii f.
layman's theological seminary, 176
Cf. CHURCH AS CHOSEN PEOPLE OF GOD.

LORD'S PRAYER—the model, given by our Lord Jesus, for divine-human dialogue, 173 f., 183

LORD'S SUPPPER—the Christian sacrament of divine fulfillment; participation in the mystery of the New Covenant; variously referred to as the Eucharist (thanksgiving), Holy Communion, the *Agape* (love) Feast, our Lord's Victory Banquet, 16, 46, 144-148, 163, 167, 174 f., 218, 220, 223, 227, 230

Cf. SACRAMENTS OF HOLY COMMUNION AND BAPTISM.

LOVE OF GOD, THE—along with Holiness, the most basic biblical term for the character and action of God:

election love—an expression of God's freedom and motive power (Hebrew, *ahabhah;* Greek, *agape*), 49, 61, 234 f.

covenant love—the way God's love orders his life and activity manward (Hebrew, *chesed*, faithfulness, steadfastness; Greek, *charis;* Latin, *gratia*, grace, favor), 51, 101, 113, 144

Source of the church's healing ministry, 192-195

God's love vs. man's love, 230

Cf. COVENANT TROTH, THE.

LOVE AND RIGHTEOUSNESS OF GOD, THE—biblical terms for the inner character of God's being, representing at once his manward movement in acceptance and his holy demands for right personal relationships as our proper response, xxiv, 8 f., 45, 56, 60, 65, 71, 77 ff., 83, 96, 104, 134, 137, 143, 150, 158 f.

The Spirit of love and righteousness defines the church's task of "Christian Nurture and Discipline," 167, 169

Cf. CHRISTIAN NURTURE AND DISCIPLINE.

Cf. Emil Brunner: *The Christian Doctrine of God*, Westminster, 1950.

MARRIAGE—a rite of the church acknowledging the divine covenantal foundation of the family, 65, 225, 229 ff.

Cf. CHRISTIAN FAMILY.

MATURITY—becoming "someone"; making basic identifications, 239 ff.

MEANS OF GRACE—the church's means of passing on from generation to generation what God has *given* us all—the renewal of our being in and through Jesus as the Christ, xxiii, 158, 166, 179, 196

EVANGELISM AND THE TEACHING MINISTRY

LITURGY FOR THE LORD'S DAY

CHRISTIAN YEAR OF PREACHING

SACRAMENTAL PATTERN OF A LIFETIME

(Cf. separate references.)

Cf. TRADITION.

MESSIANIC HOPE IN ISRAEL—the anticipation, in every generation, that God will fulfill his covenant promise to his people; the figures of Noah, Joseph, Moses, the judges, presage the kings who were "anointed" to mark the role of "deliverer" sent from the Lord; of this line Jesus is "the One" who is not only a Messiah, but the Servant of God in whom is established the New Covenant, 14, 37, 41, 64
Cf. JESUS AS THE CHRIST.

MIDDLE—"the middle" of life, of history, 20, 22, 68, 204, 244
Cf. TIMES.

MINISTRY OF RECONCILIATION—the church's priestly and pastoral functions; mediating the Gospel of God's acceptance to the poor, bringing healing into broken lives, release to captives, recovery of sight to the blind, setting at liberty those who are oppressed; "holding the world together," 60, 107, 115 f., 123, 193 ff., 199, 209 ff.
Cf. CHRISTIAN MINISTRY.

MINISTRY OF REVOLUTION—the church's prophetic function; the conscience of human existence, in individuals and in social groups, speaking from a position vertical to man's broken communities, initiating and supporting movements aimed at protecting freedom and restoring equality; "turning the world upside down," 60, 124, 191, 196 ff., 206
Cf. CHRISTIAN MINISTRY.

MISERY AND JUDGMENT—Cf. SIN.

MOSES—the man through whom God delivered Israel from her bondage in Egypt and by whom the Old Covenant Torah was made known, 12 ff., 20 ff., 29, 37, 48, 50, 64, 169
and Jesus, 16 ff.

MYSTERY OF GOD AND MAN—Mystery belongs to that dimension of personal life which involves "the hidden and the revealed," 5 f., 8, 19, 48 ff., 66, 71, 108, 139, 144
basis of the sacraments (*mysterion* in Greek), 217 ff.
Cf. WONDER.

MYTH—technical term for what is commonly known as "parable," the "story" of divine action in human history, 33 f.

"NEW MAN" IN THE BODY OF CHRIST (CHURCH)—accepting oneself as a servant of God, becoming a responsible person, growing in grace, 39, 62, 112, 115-118, in communion with God and in community with one's fellowmen, 118-124, faithful in broken community, still "sinner" though "justified," 124-131
Cf. ADAM.

OLD AND NEW COVENANT—the covenant of God, made and renewed again and again in Israel and in the Church, xxiii, 12-18, 34 f., 37-46

New Covenant in Jesus, "once for all," 18, 134

Cf. MOSES; JESUS AS THE CHRIST.

ORAL TRADITION IN THE BIBLE—prophets and apostles telling the story, time after time, of the divine-human covenant drama, 19 ff.

Cf. CHRISTIAN TRADITION; CHRISTIAN EDUCATION.

ORDINATION—a rite of the church for the setting apart of men and women for the Christian ministry, 226 f.

Cf. CHRISTIAN MINISTRY; PRIESTHOOD OF BELIEVERS, UNIVERSAL.

PACIFISM VS. MILITARISM—contradictory political philosophies, each making pretentious claims concerning one or the other of the two poles of our ambiguous social situation; *love* as the basis of community and the *restraint of evil* as the condition of social order, 128 ff.

Cf. CHURCHMANSHIP AND CITIZENSHIP.

PARADOXICAL—a technical term used in Christian theology to express the prevailing human attitude toward the Gospel "event." "It couldn't happen!" "The appearance of the New Being in Christ under the conditions of human existence, yet judging and conquering them, is the paradox of the Christian message. . . . It is an offense against man's unshaken reliance upon himself, his self-saving attempts, and his resignation to despair" (Tillich, *Systematic Theology,* Vol. 2, p. 92).

Cf. JESUS AS THE CHRIST (PARADOXICAL UNION OF GOD AND MAN).

PARENTHOOD, CHRISTIAN—the stage on life's way where we are cast in the role of mediating "the nurture and discipline of the Lord," 238, 242

PASSOVER—Jewish festival of deliverance, forerunner of our Lord's Supper, 16, 30

PATRIARCHS—men of an older generation who exercise the authority of a living example in Israel's covenant heritage, Abraham, Jacob, Joseph, et al., 29, 32 ff.

PERSONAL RELATIONS—"I—Thou" encounter, the stuff of which the covenant is made and through which it operates and is fulfilled the heart of theology, 8, 162

in community, 61, 119 ff.

in communication, 163-162

in "The Cocktail Party," 180 ff.

in the family, 231-244

Cf. Martin Buber: *I and Thou*, Clark, 1952.

PERSONALITY, CORPORATE—biblical understanding of the corporate solidarity of humankind, in covenant, in sin, and in the purpose of redemption, 5, 48, 59 f., 61 f., 226

PHILOSOPHIES—competing views of our human situation and of what it means; pragmatic, xviii; *laissez-faire* individualism, xix; existential, xviii, 3, 179-182

PLOT OF THE COVENANT DRAMA—Cf. COVENANT DRAMA, PLOT OF THE.

PRETENSION—Cf. SIN.

PRIDE AND SENSUALITY—Cf. SIN.

PRIESTHOOD OF BELIEVERS, UNIVERSAL—not that everyman is to be his own priest, but that each man is called to be a priest (servant of God's forgiving grace) to every other, xxiv, 123, 194, 226 f.
Cf. CHRISTIAN MINISTRY.

PROPHETS—the "mouth of God," 21, 201; spokesmen for the Lord in Israel, xxiii, 9, 18, 20 f., 25, 48, 52, 67, 78
teaching prophets, 19 f., 29 f., 68-70, 170, 199 f.
preaching prophets, 12, 21, 37
and Jesus, 17, 210

RECONCILIATION—the central Act in our covenant drama and the crucial turning point in our life, through our participation in the death and resurrection of Jesus, involves a miraculous re-newal of our being. It begins in our reconciliation through redemptive healing, leading to our re-creation. Note the number of *re-* words in our Christian vocabulary.
Cf. STATUS OF OUR LIFE IN COVENANT ENCOUNTER; ATONEMENT.
Cf. Paul Tillich: *The New Being*, Scribners, 1955.
Cf. Karl Barth: *The Doctrine of Reconciliation*, Scribners, 1956.

REFORMATION, PROTESTANT—the event and heritage of Martin Luther and John Calvin by which the church has been "*Re*formed according to the Covenant Word of God," xxiv, 101, 171 f., 194, 218, 220, 226

RELIGION—a basic category for understanding our human situation; symbolizes a person's being "bound back" (re-ligare) and, therefore, obligated to the Ground of his being; raises the question of security, destiny, devotion, faith, hope, love, et al., 56, 75
Cf. LIFE'S POLAR TENSIONS; EXISTENCE.

REMNANT, ROLE OF—the faithful few, in Israel and in the Church, who become the "servant people of God," 34 ff., 38, 41, 59, 62
Jesus as the Remnant of One, 41, 45, 64, 201

RENEWAL—newness of life; restoration of oneself, for freedom and to responsibility; the gift of God's own holy Spirit through the mediation of Jesus as redeemer and reconciler, 11, 16 ff., 19, 23 f., 25 f., 28, 33 ff., 37 ff., 44, 46, 49, 62, 64, 107-111, 112-117, 170, 183, 188, 191, 200, 208, 241
Cf. LIFE'S CENTER OF GRAVITY.

REPENTANCE—Cf. FORGIVENESS AND REPENTANCE.

RESURRECTION—Cf. CRUCIFIXION AND RESURRECTION OF JESUS.

RETREAT AND RETURN—the inner rhythm of the Christian life, in response to our Lord's own promise ("Come unto me!") and demand ("Go ye into all the world!"), 58 f., 116 f., 227

REVELATION (SELF-REVELATION) OF GOD—the Lord's communication of himself to his people, involving the mystery of "the hidden and the revealed"; the divine action in the divine-human encounter, 6 ff., 49 ff., 159 ff., 168, 189
Cf. COVENANT ENCOUNTER, DIVINE-HUMAN; WORD OF GOD; ACTS OF GOD, MIGHTY.
Cf. H. Richard Niebuhr: *The Meaning of Revelation*, Macmillan, 1941.

SACRAMENTAL PATTERN OF A LIFETIME—the church's way of announcing God's providential government over us and his identification with each individual through the whole of a lifetime, and continuously with the generations as they relate to each other, 163, 217-245
Cf. Chart, 222
Cf. MEANS OF GRACE.

SACRAMENTS OF HOLY COMMUNION AND BAPTISM—xxiii, 144, 217, 220 ff.
Roman Catholic view, 219
Reformation view, 6, 217-220
Cf. LORD'S SUPPER; BAPTISM.
Cf. D. M. Baillie: *The Theology of the Sacraments*, Scribners, 1957.

SATAN—symbol for the power which enslaves us to our own pretensions, 45, 95, 100 f., 113, 115, 119, 208, 240
Cf. EVIL, POWERS OF.

SCIENCE (MODERN) AND FAITH (BIBLICAL)—two different disciplines: one attempting to describe the world and its processes, the other attempting to uncover the meaning of our human existence; our actual conflict is not between science and faith, but between a modern science and an ancient science that some men of faith have adopted as superior; or again it is between biblical faith and some other faith, e.g., Baalism, nationalism, communism, scientism, 70, 70 fn.

SEVEN LAST WORDS—a collection of the words of Jesus, spoken from his cross, gathered from all four of the written Gospels, 102

SERVANT PEOPLE OF GOD—the church in Israel and the universal Church of Jesus Christ, respectively; those whom God has chosen for the task of mediating his righteous love in the deliverance of the nations of the world from their enslavement to poverty, ignorance, meaninglessness, tyranny, and war
Cf. SUFFERING SERVANT.

SIN—the distortion of "life's center of gravity"; putting some human *pretension* in the place of God, 19, 63, 80, 82, 85 ff., 89 ff., 95, 113 f., 129, 199 f., 239 f.
   as action: the rebellion against God's righteousness (disobedience) and the rejection of his love (infidelity), 16, 26 f., 35, 45, 62 f., 84, 94, 169, 174, 194; expresing itself in rivalry, 33; jealousy and enmity, 105
   as status: estrangement from the love of God and enslavement to the shadows of our own pretensions, 19, 29, 31, 45, 62 f., 69, 94 f., 97, 103, 194, 199 f.
   as to forms:
      pride—irresponsible acts of self-deification and arrogant injustice to others, 91 ff.
      sensuality—irresponsible acts of self-abdication and wanton self-destruction, 91 ff.
   results in misery and judgment, 27, 35, 52, 94 f., 104, 127, 173, 201
   Cf. EVIL, POWERS OF; GUILT; ATONEMENT.
   Cf. Reinhold Niebuhr: *The Nature and Destiny of Man*, Scribners, 1941.
   Cf. Paul Tillich: *Systematic Theology*, Vol. 2, University of Chicago, 1957.

SOCIAL ACTION—bringing the love and righteousness of God into the life of the world, revolutionizing the world's social structures and reconciling the world's people to each other and to their God, 60, 183, 206, 208 ff.
   Cf. CHURCHMANSHIP AND CITIZENSHIP.

SPIRIT OF GOD, THE HOLY SPIRIT—the healing power of God's love in action, xxv, 13, 60, 71, 79, 137 f., 142 f., 162, 167, 170, 194, 208 f., 219
   the Gift of the Holy Spirit:
      in revelation, 49, 161, 213
      given to the church, 64, 123 f., 119 f., 183
      channeled through the Body of Christ, 46
      in worship and holy communion, 227, 242
   Cf. F. W. Dillistone: *The Holy Spirit*, Westminster, 1947.

SPRINGS OF OUR HUMAN ACTION (FAITH VS. UNFAITH)—the
mysterious resources of Everyman's response-ability, 8, 66-149
Cf. COVENANT DRAMA, PLOT OF THE:
PROLOGUE: Anxiety
ACT I—Infidelity and Guilt
ACT II—Faith and Courage
ACT III—Gratitude and Concern
EPILOGUE: Hope
(Cf. separate references.)

STAGES ON LIFE'S WAY—a term borrowed from Sören Kierkegaard,
180 f., and used, in addition, to refer to the "pilgrimage of a lifetime," 222, 235 ff.
Cf. Lewis J. Sherrill: *The Struggle of the Soul*, Macmillan, 1951.

STATUS OF OUR LIFE IN COVENANT ENCOUNTER—a perspec-
tive upon the stages of the divine-human covenant drama which
focuses upon the question: "Where do I stand, now, in the purpose
of God?" 66-149
Cf. COVENANT DRAMA, PLOT OF THE:
PROLOGUE: Election
ACT I—Estrangement and Enslavement
ACT II—Atonement and Reconciliation
ACT III—Communion and Community
EPILOGUE: Destiny: Eternal Life
(Cf. separate references.)

STEWARDSHIP—Man's role as the responsible guardian of God's entire creation, both human and natural, 67, 77, 81, 176

SUFFERING SERVANT—the biblical figure to describe the covenant
people in terms of their God-given mission to the world; cf. Servant
People of God. Both the motivation and the power to carry on this
mission are rooted, however, in the people's paradoxical confession:
"Our God is a Servant-Lord!"
The Servant-Lord (God in Christ), 40 ff., 44 f., 54, 71, 136, 142, 200 f.
His Servant People (the Church), 17, 41 f., 54, 58 ff., 77, 96, 98, 122,
136, 180, 237, 240 f.
Cf. "The Servant Lord and His Servant People," theme of the 18th
General Council, World Alliance of Reformed Churches, Cam-
pinas, Brazil, 1959.
Cf. JESUS AS THE CHRIST; CHURCH.

TEMPTATION—the construction of human freedom as offering an
open choice between truth and untruth; the appeal of untruth, of
"pretension"; a man wanting what he does not need, 42, 81-87
Cf. FALL OF MAN; SIN.

271

TEN COMMANDMENTS—Cf. LAW OF GOD; TORAH, 173, 183.

THEOLOGY OF HISTORY *(HEILSGESCHICHTE)*—prophetic and apostolic interpretation of the life of Israel and of Jesus as the Christ, respectively, in terms of the covenant purpose of God. The German term means "salvation-history," that is, biblical history seen as the drama of man's redemption by God, xii, 9-65, 199 ff.
from the perspective of the cross, 175

Cf. COVENANT DRAMA, PLOT OF THE; COVENANT THEOLOGY.

TIMES—since events are the warp and woof of history, biblical theology constructs many of its basic categories in terms of "time," "times," and "timing."
the existential dimensions of our human life:
present involvement
past retrospection
future anticipation
22, 29, 33, 68 f., 136, 140
God as the Eternal "I am," 50, 136, 140-145
the middle of history, of life (B.C. and A.D.), 20, 22, 68, 204, 244
"now" and "now that," 114 f.
kairos vs. *chronos* (cf. separate references.)
timing and the time-span of covenant encounter in the church's life:
daily Bible study, the Lord's Day liturgy, the Christian Year, the pilgrimage of a lifetime, 163, 164-245

TORAH—the Jewish name for the Mosaic revelation; both "the Law" as contained in the Decalogue and the five books of "the Law"; fundamentally the Lord's Covenant of love and righteousness, 20 f.
Cf. LAW OF GOD.

TRANSFIGURATION—a vision of Jesus contrasted with Moses and Elijah, 50
Cf. RETREAT AND RETURN.

TRIUNITY OF GOD—the triune Name, Father, Son, and Holy Spirit, representing the mystery of God's personal life, is the most distinctive doctrine of the Christian faith. It arises out of the historical events and personal encounters of the biblical drama. Theologians have used a variety of analogies to express the meaning of the doctrine, 50, 52, 71 f., 79, 136 f., 139-143, 189, 235 f., 236
Cf. Claude Welch: *In This Name*, Scribners, 1952.

UNITED CHURCH OF CHRIST—
Curriculum of Christian education, xvii, 167, 175, 231
varieties of tradition, 219

UNITED NATIONS AND LEAGUE OF NATIONS, 130, 211

WANTS AND NEEDS—Cf. TEMPTATION, 81-87.

WONDER—more than curiosity; being awed by the mystery of God; the beginning of theology, 3, 6, 244 f.

WORD OF GOD, THE—God's eternal covenant with humankind and the Bible, 21, 160 f., 168, 179, 189 ff., 242
preaching, 163, 166, 191, 200
living, 49 f., 168, 197, 224
incarnate in Jesus, 97, 154, 196 f., 200
and sacrament, 217 f.

Cf. COVENANT TROTH, THE.

Cf. Karl Barth: *Doctrine of the Word of God*, Scribners, 1936.

WORLD COUNCIL OF CHURCHES—Cf. ECUMENICAL MOVEMENT, 211, 216.

WORSHIP—the ultimate religious act of man; the glorification of God, 56 f., 185-195

Cf. CELEBRATION; LITURGY FOR THE LORD'S DAY.

WRATH OF GOD—Cf. DEMONIC, 95.

Index of Names

Index of Biblical References

This list makes the foregoing book into a commentary on Bible verses which the reader may wish to use in private and public worship.